W9-ABI-818

LIBRARY
NATIONAL SCIENCE FOUNDATION

Open Innovation

Open Innovation

The New Imperative
for Creating and Profiting
from Technology

Henry W. Chesbrough

HARVARD BUSINESS SCHOOL PRESS

Boston, Massachusetts

Copyright 2003 Harvard Business School Publishing Corporation

All rights reserved

Printed in the United States of America

07 06 05 04 03   5 4 3 2 1

No part of this publication may be reproduced, stored in or introduced into a
retrieval system, or transmitted, in any form, or by any means (electronic,
mechanical, photocopying, recording, or otherwise), without the prior permission
of the publisher. Requests for permission should be directed to
permissions@hbsp.harvard.edu, or mailed to Permissions, Harvard Business
School Publishing, 60 Harvard Way, Boston, Massachusetts 02163.

Library of Congress Cataloging-in-Publication Data

Chesbrough, Henry William.
Open innovation : the new imperative for creating and
profiting from technology / Henry W. Chesbrough.
p. cm.
Includes index.
ISBN 1-57851-837-7
1. Technological innovations—Management. 2. Research,
Industrial—Management. 3. Diffusion of innovations.
4. High technology industries—Technological innovations—
United States—Case studies. I. Title.
HD45 .c469 2003
658.5'14—dc21

2002151060

The paper used in this publication meets the requirements of the
American National Standard for Permanence of Paper for Publications
and Documents in Libraries and Archives z39.48-1992.

For Katherine

Contents

p. 28
Bell Labs
GTE
DuPont

Foreword   ix

Acknowledgments   xiii

Introduction   xvii

1. **Xerox PARC   1**
   The Achievements and Limits of Closed Innovation   , then trust to open industry

2. **The Closed Innovation Paradigm   21**   - Xerox PARC

3. **The Open Innovation Paradigm   43**   - IBM

4. **The Business Model   63**
   Connecting Internal and External Innovation

5. **From Closed to Open Innovation   93**
   The Transformation of the IBM Corporation

6. **Open Innovation @ Intel   113**   bringing in external tech

7. **Creating New Ventures out of Internal Technologies   135**
   Lucent's New Ventures Group   Lucent moving out internal tech

8. **Business Models and Managing Intellectual Property   155**

9. **Making the Transition   177**
   Open Innovation Strategies and Tactics

Notes   197

Index   217

About the Author   227

Foreword

Innovating Innovation

A s a student of innovation for more than twenty years, I still find it amazing just how difficult innovation continues to be. But today we are faced with the extra problem that our ideas of innovation have gone stale. So we need to be innovative in the area of innovation itself, which is what this book will help us to do and what I mean by calling this foreword "Innovating Innovation." By *innovation* I mean something quite different from *invention*. To me, innovation means invention implemented and taken to market. And beyond innovation lies *disruptive innovation*, which actually changes social practices—the way we live, work, and learn. Really substantive innovation—the telephone, the copier, the automobile, the personal computer, or the Internet—is quite disruptive, drastically altering social practices.

Disruptive innovation presents some major challenges. First, although it may be relatively easy to predict the potential capabilities of a technological breakthrough in terms of the products it enables, it is nearly impossible to predict the way that these products or offerings will shape social practices. The surprising rise of e-mail is but one example. It is not technology per se that matters, but technology-in-use, and that is precisely what is so hard to predict ahead of time. Nevertheless, technological breakthroughs that do end up shaping our social practices can produce huge payoffs, both to the innovator and to society.[1]

A second major challenge is that a successful innovation often demands an innovative business model at least as much as it requires an innovative product offering. This is a hard lesson for research departments of large corporations to learn. It is also why so many great-sounding innovations in the research lab fail to see the light of day. In the lab, we have devised many ways to rapidly prototype an idea, explore its capabilities, and even test lead customers' reactions to it. But innovations that intrigue the customer don't necessarily support serious business models—as the dotcom boom and bust showed again and again—and even those that do may support a model that threatens to cannibalize the sponsoring corporation's existing business models. So, as one aspect of innovating innovation, we need to find ways to experiment not only with the product innovation itself, but also with novel business models. Rapid business model prototyping is therefore critically important to the future of technological innovation, and Henry Chesbrough makes it a centerpiece of the "open innovation" scheme of this book.

There are additional reasons to innovate innovation. Most prior models turned on the creativity within the firm; in today's world we are faced with two new realities. The first is that there are now powerful ways to reach beyond the conventional boundaries of the firm and tap the ideas of customers and users. Indeed, the networked world allows us essentially to bring customers into the lab as coproducers. We can tap not only the customers' explicit knowledge, but also their tacit knowledge made manifest as they start to use a prototype. Prototypes used by real customers who are at work on their own problems afford a kind of reflection in practice that helps to flush out serious flaws, misleading instructions, and missing functionality before the product is brought to market.

The second reality has to do with the fact that today most of the world's really smart people aren't members of any single team but are distributed all over the place in multiple institutions. Similarly, we are now looking for innovations in the interstices between different disciplines—for example, between bio- and nanotechnologies. Any new model of innovation must find ways to leverage the disparate knowledge assets of people who see the world quite differently and who use tools and methods foreign to those we're familiar with. Such people are likely to work both in different disciplines and in different institutions. Finding successful ways to work with them will lie at the heart of innovating innovation.

New technology offers us new tools to help in this meta-innovation. I have already mentioned the use of the Net to bring customers' practices (rather than just the customer's voice) into shaping a prototype. Even cars are first rendered in software before they are actually built, and as such they can be directly experienced (and, in some cases, driven) as a soft, highly malleable prototype and can evoke a customer's tacitly held opinions. With the power of today's computers to simulate massively complex and nonlinear systems coupled to phenomenal visualization techniques, the customer can be brought ever closer to the design process.

There is another set of tools that can deeply shape the practices of innovation, and, in particular, work on the business models that innovation also needs. These are financial tools that build bridges between the flexibilities of the venture world and the predictable financial constraints of a public company. These tools use real options theory for managing the cash flow decisions in an innovation process. Unlike the use of net present value (NPV) calculations, which inherently view the innovation process as static, compound real options honor its inherently dynamic nature. These options provide a way to fold into the decision processes two sources of learning, one involving learning by doing (what is learned about the technology while developing the product), the other involving learning while waiting (what is discovered from the market as the product is being developed). At each stage for potentially scaling or exiting the project, both sources of information come into play. Furthermore, an options approach moves us from viewing the pursuit of an innovation as making a bet to viewing it as buying a possibility for the future while still delaying substantial cash flow. Although this is a complex topic all its own, I mention it here because it provides a wide variety of tools for modeling many of the ideas of open innovation, such as capturing some of the better properties of the venture capital world, only now it can be done inside the corporation.

The open innovation model that Chesbrough describes shows the necessity of letting ideas both flow out of the corporation in order to find better sites for their monetization, and flow into the corporation as new offerings and new business models. Finding the right balance and mechanisms for this situation to take place is critical. If a rising corporate star brings forth a risky innovation that ends up failing, his or her career is apt to be damaged considerably more than that of the executive who squelches an innovation that could have been a winner. An open innovation model diminishes both the error of squelching a winner and that of backing a loser, and moves us closer to a world where protective moves and face-saving mechanisms no longer cause potentially great innovations to be shelved. Innovation is too important to let either corporate politics or outmoded assumptions carry the day. Let us be wary of the old, conservative, but still very powerful wisdom that can always find reasons or examples from the past to prove that any particular innovation is foolhardy.

Let us all, instead, engage in the vitally important work of innovating innovation. *Open Innovation* is a timely, carefully researched, and thoughtfully articulated effort toward that end.

—John Seely Brown
Director Emeritus,
Xerox Palo Alto Research Center
(PARC)

Acknowledgments

THIS BOOK results from a former Silicon Valley manager's reflections on his own experience in managing technology in industry and then considering the innovation process more generally from within academia. I hope that this book combines the practical with the theoretical, so that both managers and academics will find it to be of value.

Many of my colleagues at Harvard Business School have made substantial contributions to the work contained in this book. Foremost among them is Richard Rosenbloom. His many decades of careful, thoughtful scholarship have greatly increased my understanding of the innovation process. Dick has also worked closely with senior leaders at the Xerox Corporation, and his insight into that company's internal processes added immeasurably to my research on the spin-off companies that left the Xerox nest. Clayton Christensen and Dorothy Leonard have also taught me a great deal about the problems of innovation. Each read an early draft of the entire manuscript and offered useful criticism. Other scholars of innovation at Harvard who have added to the thoughts in this book include Mary Tripsas, Stefan Thomke, and Josh Lerner. The Harvard Division of Research provided generous financial support for this research. Edward Smith helped with many of the Xerox spin-off company field interviews, while Anthony Massaro and Clarissa Ceruti also provided helpful research support. I am also indebted to my editor at HBS Press, Jeff Kehoe, for his support and guidance through the manuscript's development and editing process.

Since this book highlights the importance of external sources of knowledge to the innovation process, it is no surprise that my own understanding has advanced because of the work and ideas of others outside my own academic institution. David Teece, David Mowery, and Bronwyn Hall all deepened my appreciation of the innovation process and the wealth of prior scholarship in the area. Richard Nelson, Steven

Klepper, and Keith Pavitt have provided timely criticism as the project moved forward. Others, including Brian Silverman, Fiona Murray, Kwanghui Lim, Annabelle Gawer, Andrea Prencipe, and Arvids Ziedonis, have helped me refine numerous points in this book.

A third critical source of information for this book has come from managers of companies struggling with the innovation process in their own firms. At Xerox, I have benefited tremendously from discussions with John Seely Brown, Mark Myers, Herve Gallaire, Mark Bernstein, Richard Bruce, Ramana Rao, William Spencer, and many other former Xerox employees who migrated into one of the thirty-five spin-off companies I studied. At IBM, I had useful exchanges with Nicholas D'Onofrio, Paul Horn, Philip Summers, John Wolpert, and John Patrick. At Intel, Leslie Vadasz, Sun-Lin Chou, Keith Larson, Howard High, David Tennenhouse, and the late Sandy Wilson generously shared their time with me. At Lucent, Andrew Garman, Tom Uhlman, Ralph Faison, and Stephen Socolof discussed their experiences with me. At Procter & Gamble, Larry Huston and Scott Cook outlined their new, externally focused innovation strategy. I hope that this book is worthy of these managers' time and candor.

Other thoughtful observers of the problems of industrial innovation shared their perspectives with me. They included Arati Prabhakar, Pat Windham, Jerry Sheehan, Nancy Confrey, U.S. Navy Captain Terry Pierce, and Cameron Peters. My close friends Ken Novak, Rich Mironov, and Rudy Ruggles patiently endured early articulations of concepts in the book.

The students in my classroom have been a vital part of my own process of reflection on industrial innovation. Although they do not yet have the years of experience that my managerial sources possess, they bring a fresh perspective that challenges the conventional wisdom that often accompanies deep experience. Their questions, arguments, and conclusions have helped me test and revise my own thinking about innovation.

I am also indebted to my parents, Richard and Joyce Chesbrough, for their unflagging moral support while I wrote this book. My daughters, Emily and Sarah, have helped me keep perspective during the writing process and were (usually) understanding about letting me finish it. My deepest gratitude, however, goes to my wife, Katherine. From the early beginnings of the field research, to the conception of the book itself in the cool air of the Sierra Nevadas, to the numerous revisions of the resulting manuscript, she has given unconditional support and insightful criticism throughout. This book is far better as a result of her commitment to its realization. With my deepest appreciation and love, I dedicate this book to her.

—*Henry Chesbrough*
henry@chesbrough.com

Introduction

M OST INNOVATIONS FAIL. And companies that don't innovate die. This is a book about the process of innovation, about how companies utilize and advance technologies to create new products and services. In today's world, where the only constant is change, the task of managing innovation is vital for companies of every size in every industry. Innovation is vital to sustain and advance companies' current businesses; it is critical to growing new businesses. It is also a very difficult process to manage.

Innovation in the Twenty-First Century:
A Tale of Two Models

To paraphrase Charles Dickens, for innovation in this new century, it is the best of times and the worst of times. Industrial technology is advancing our understanding of the natural world at an accelerating rate. In the oldest industry in the world, agriculture, companies are learning to use genetic and genomic technology to make crops more resistant to pests, droughts, and diseases, even as they produce more output per acre. In another ancient industry, retailing, the advances in computing and communications are bringing retailers into closer contact with their customers as well as their suppliers, enabling them to provide more variety with less inventory than ever before. The burgeoning services businesses all benefit from technologies that offer better communications with more capabilities at lower prices. The largest service industry, health care, is experiencing an explosion in our scientific understanding of the forces that create life, with the result being the prospect of longer, healthier lives for us all.

Yet in many ways, it is the worst of times for innovating companies. Many leading companies are having a terrible time sustaining their internal R&D investments. Take the premier industrial research laboratory of the twentieth century, Bell Labs. Not long ago, Bell Labs would have been a decisive strategic weapon in Lucent's battle with Cisco in the telecommunications equipment market.

Lucent, the telecommunications equipment company created in the breakup of AT&T, enjoyed significant momentum from its spin-off from AT&T in 1996, calling itself "the largest start-up in history." It also inherited the lion's share of Bell Laboratories from the old AT&T, which endowed Lucent with a wealth of research and technology to focus on the telecommunications equipment market. And over the next five years, Lucent enjoyed many victories in the market with its new products. Cisco nevertheless consistently managed to keep up with Lucent, and occasionally got to market ahead of it. Although Bell Labs technologies did create many new products and services for Lucent, Cisco also seemed to introduce many new products and services, despite its lack of anything like the deep research capabilities of Bell Labs.

Though they were direct competitors in a very technologically complex industry, Lucent and Cisco were not innovating in the same manner. Lucent devoted enormous resources to exploring the world of new materials and state-of-the-art components and systems, to come up with fundamental discoveries that could fuel future generations of products and services. Cisco, meanwhile, did practically no internal research of this type.

Instead, Cisco deployed a rather different weapon in the battle for innovation leadership. It scanned the world of start-up companies that were springing up all around it and that were commercializing new products and services. Some of these start-ups were founded by veterans of Lucent, AT&T, or Nortel. These people took the ideas they worked on at these companies and attempted to build companies around them. Sometimes, Cisco would invest in these start-ups. Other times, it simply partnered with them. And more than occasionally, it would later acquire them. In this way, Cisco kept up with the R&D output of perhaps the finest industrial research organization in the world, without doing much internal research of its own.

Lucent's experience with the limits of its research capability is not unique. IBM's research prowess in computing was of no avail against Intel and Microsoft in the personal computer business. Similarly, Nokia has catapulted itself ahead of Motorola, Siemens, and other industrial titans to the forefront of wireless telephony in just twenty years, building on its industrial experience from earlier decades in the low-tech industries of wood pulp and rubber boots. GE's labs are no longer the powerhouse they once were. Xerox has now formally separated from its famous Palo Alto Research Center. Hewlett-Packard's HP Labs have been broken up between HP and Agilent.

This leads to a number of paradoxes that confront all innovating companies in the early twenty-first century. While ideas abound, internal industrial research is less effective. While innovation is critical, the usual process of managing innovation doesn't seem to work anymore. While ideas and external capital are plentiful, companies struggle to find and finance internal growth opportunities. While industrial R&D spending is high, many worry that we are exhausting the "seed corn" of basic knowledge that will propel technology a generation from now.

Not long ago, internal R&D was viewed as a strategic asset and even a barrier to competitive entry in many industries. Only large companies with significant resources and long-term research programs could compete. Research-based companies like DuPont, Merck, IBM, GE, and AT&T did the most research in their respective industries. And they earned most of the profits as well. Rivals who sought to unseat these firms had to ante up their own resources and create their own labs, if they were to have any chance against these leaders.

These days, the former leading industrial enterprises are finding remarkably strong competition from many newer companies. These newcomers—Intel, Microsoft, Sun, Oracle, Cisco, Genentech, Amgen, Genzyme—conduct little or no basic research on their own. Although they have been very innovative, these companies have innovated with the research discoveries of others. And there is a legion of other, even newer companies waiting to supplant these firms if an opportunity should arise. These latter newcomers are also likely to rely on someone else's discoveries to ascend to leadership.

To make matters worse, some companies that made significant long-term investments in research found that some of the resulting output, however brilliant, wasn't useful to them. They found ways to gracefully exit from the further funding of these projects and moved on to more promising work. Then, to their amazement, some of those abandoned projects later turned into very valuable companies. This was the experience of the Xerox Corporation, for example, with its Palo Alto Research Center (PARC). Numerous valuable computer hardware and software innovations were developed at PARC, but few of them made any money for Xerox and its shareholders.

A Shift in Innovation Paradigms

What accounts for the apparent decline in the innovation capabilities of so many leading companies, at a time when so many promising ideas abound? My research suggests that the way we innovate new ideas and bring them to market is undergoing a fundamental change. In the words of the historian of science Thomas Kuhn, I believe that we are witnessing a "paradigm shift" in how companies commercialize industrial knowledge.[1] I call the old paradigm Closed Innovation. It is a view that says *successful innovation requires control*. Companies must generate their own ideas and then develop them, build them, market them, distribute them, service them, finance them, and support them on their own. This paradigm counsels firms to be strongly self-reliant, because one cannot be sure of the quality, availability, and capability of others' ideas: "If you want something done right, you've got to do it yourself."

The logic that informed Closed Innovation thinking was an internally focused logic. This logic wasn't necessarily written down in any single place, but it was tacitly held to be self-evident as the "right way" to innovate. Here are some of the implicit rules of Closed Innovation:

- We should hire the best and the brightest people, so that the smartest people in our industry work for us.

- In order to bring new products and services to the market, we must discover and develop them ourselves.

- If we discover it ourselves, we will get it to market first.

- The company that gets an innovation to market first will usually win.

- If we lead the industry in making investments in R&D, we will discover the best and the most ideas and will come to lead the market as well.

- We should control our intellectual property, so that our competitors don't profit from our ideas.

The logic of Closed Innovation created a virtuous circle (figure I-1). Companies invested in internal R&D, which led to many breakthrough discoveries. These discoveries enabled those companies to bring new products and services to market, to realize more sales and higher margins because of these products, and then to reinvest in more internal R&D, which led to further breakthroughs. And because the intellectual property (IP) that arises from this internal R&D is closely guarded, others could not exploit these ideas for their own profit.

For most of the twentieth century, this paradigm worked, and worked well. The German chemicals industry created the central research laboratory, which it used to identify and commercialize a tremendous variety of new products. Thomas Edison created a U.S. version of this laboratory, used it to develop and perfect a number of important breakthroughs, and founded General Electric's famed laboratory. Bell Laboratories discovered amazing physical phenomena and harnessed its discoveries to create the transistor, among its many important achievements. Moreover, the U.S. government created an ad hoc central research laboratory to conduct a crash project on nuclear fission, which led to the development of the atomic bomb.

Figure I-2 depicts this Closed Innovation paradigm for managing R&D. The heavy solid lines show the boundary of the firm. Ideas flow into the firm on the left and flow out to the market on the right. They are screened and filtered during the research process, and the surviving ideas are transferred into development and then taken to market.

In figure I-2, the linkage between research and development is tightly coupled and internally focused. Our extant theories of managing R&D are built on this conception. Examples of this thinking are the stage gate process, the chain link model, and the product development funnel or

(handwritten annotation) what good example for closed model

FIGURE I-1

The Virtuous Circle

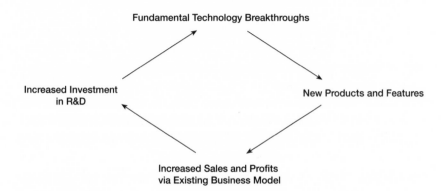

FIGURE I-2

The Closed Paradigm for Managing Industrial R&D

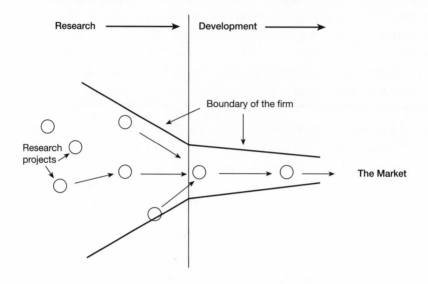

pipeline found in most texts on managing R&D.[2] Projects enter on the left at the beginning, and proceed within the firm until they are shipped to customers on the right of the figure. The process is designed to weed out *false positives*, projects that look initially appealing, but later turn out to be disappointing. The surviving projects, having survived a series of internal screens, hopefully have a greater chance of success in the market.

Erosion Factors That Undermined the Logic of Closed Innovation

In the last years of the twentieth century, though, several factors combined to erode the underpinnings of Closed Innovation. One factor was the growing mobility of highly experienced and skilled people. When people left a company after working there for many years, they took a good deal of that hard-won knowledge with them to their new employer. (The new employer, though, neglected to pay any compensation to the previous employer for that training.) A related erosion factor was the burgeoning amount of college and post-college training that many people obtained. The growing number of such people allowed knowledge to spill out of the knowledge silos of corporate central research labs to companies of all sizes in many industries. A further factor was the growing presence of private venture capital (VC), which specialized in creating new firms that commercialized external research and converting these firms into growing, valuable companies. Often, these highly capable start-up firms became formidable competitors for the large, established firms that had formerly financed most of the R&D in the industry—the very ideas these new companies fed off of as they competed for industry leadership. ③ *increased complexity/cost of R&D*

The logic of Closed Innovation was further challenged by the increasingly fast time to market for many products and services, making the shelf life of a particular technology ever shorter. Moreover, increasingly knowledgeable customers and suppliers further challenged the firm's ability to profit from their knowledge silos. And non-U.S. firms became more and more effective competitors as well. *tech capabilities elsewh*

When these erosion factors have impacted an industry, the assumptions and logic that once made Closed Innovation an effective approach no longer applied (figure I-3). When fundamental technology breakthroughs occurred, the scientists and engineers who made these breakthroughs were aware of an outside option that they formerly lacked. If the company that funded these discoveries didn't pursue them in a timely fashion, the scientists and engineers could pursue these breakthroughs on their own—in a new start-up firm. The start-up company would commercialize the breakthroughs. Most often, the company

FIGURE I-3

The Virtuous Circle Broken

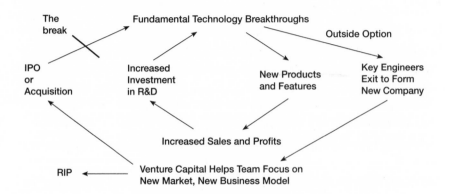

failed (shown in figure I-3 as Rest in Peace [RIP]). But if it became successful, it might achieve an initial public offering (IPO) or be acquired at an attractive price. The successful start-up would generally *not* reinvest in new fundamental discoveries. Like Cisco, it would instead look outside for another external technology to commercialize.

The presence of this outside path broke the virtuous circle. The company that originally funded the breakthrough did not profit from its investment in the R&D that led to the breakthrough. And the company that did profit from the breakthrough generally did not reinvest its proceeds to finance the next generation of discovery-oriented research. This severed link between research and development meant that there would not be another round of investment in basic research to fuel another round of advances.

In situations in which these erosion factors have taken root, Closed Innovation is no longer sustainable. For these situations, a new approach, which I call Open Innovation, is emerging in place of Closed Innovation. Open Innovation is a paradigm that assumes that firms can and should use external ideas as well as internal ideas, and internal and external paths to market, as the firms look to advance their technology. Open Innovation combines internal and external ideas into architectures and systems whose requirements are defined by a business model. The business model utilizes both external and internal ideas to create value, while defining internal mechanisms to claim some portion of that value. Open Innovation assumes that internal ideas can also be taken to market through external channels, outside the current businesses of the firm, to generate additional value. Figure I-4 illustrates this Open Innovation process.

In figure I-4, ideas can still originate from inside the firm's research process, but some of those ideas may seep out of the firm, either in the research stage or later in the development stage. A leading vehicle for this leakage is a start-up company, often staffed with some of the company's own personnel. Other leakage mechanisms include external licensing and departing employees. Ideas can also start outside the firm's own labs and can move inside. As figure I-4 shows, there are a great many potential ideas outside the firm. In figure I-2, the solid lines of the funnel represented the boundary of the firm. In figure I-4, the same lines are now dotted, reflecting the more porous boundary of the firm, the interface between what is done inside the firm and what is accessed from outside the firm.

FIGURE I-4

The Open Innovation Paradigm for Managing Industrial R&D

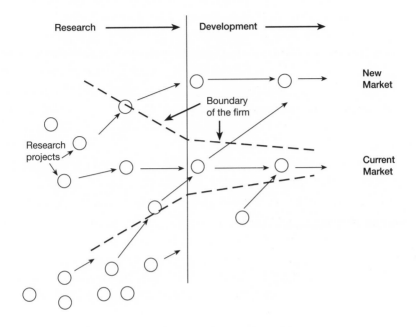

Although the Open Innovation process still weeds out false positives (now from external as well as internal sources), it also enables the recovery of false negatives, that is, projects that initially seem almost worthless, but turn out to be surprisingly valuable, as in the case of Xerox PARC noted earlier. Often these projects find value in a new market, rather than in the current market. Or they may be worthwhile if they can be combined with other projects. These opportunities were frequently overlooked by the earlier Closed Innovation process.

At root, the logic of Open Innovation is based on a landscape of abundant knowledge, which must be used readily if it is to provide value to the company that created it. The knowledge that a company uncovers in its research cannot be restricted to its internal pathways to market. Similarly, its internal pathways to market cannot necessarily be restricted to using the company's internal knowledge. This perspective suggests some very different organizing principles for research and for innovation.

Table I-1 shows some of the principles of this new paradigm and contrasts them with the earlier logic of the Closed Innovation approach.

Assessing the Prevalence of Open Innovation

The Closed Innovation paradigm has eroded in various industries. This book provides a number of detailed studies in industries such as those involving copiers, computers, disk drives, semiconductors, semiconductor equipment, communications equipment, pharmaceuticals, and biotechnology. These examples obviously all come from high-technology industries.

But don't be fooled—the concepts in this book are not specific to the high-tech portion of the overall economy. Every company has a technology, that is, a means to convert inputs into goods and services that the company sells. And no company can expect its technology to remain fixed for very long. It is far wiser to expect technology to change, sometimes in unpredictable ways, than it is to assume that things will remain in their current state for a prolonged period. Companies that don't innovate, die.

TABLE I-1

Contrasting Principles of Closed and Open Innovation

Closed Innovation Principles	Open Innovation Principles
The smart people in our field work for us.	Not all the smart people work for us. We need to work with smart people inside *and* outside our company.
To profit from R&D, we must discover it, develop it, and ship it ourselves.	External R&D can create significant value; internal R&D is needed to claim some portion of that value.
If we discover it ourselves, we will get it to market first.	We don't have to originate the research to profit from it.
The company that gets an innovation to market first will win.	Building a better business model is better than getting to market first.
If we create the most and the best ideas in the industry, we will win.	If we make the best use of internal and external ideas, we will win.
We should control our IP, so that our competitors don't profit from our ideas.	We should profit from others' use of our IP, and we should buy others' IP whenever it advances our own business model.

One example of the broad relevance of the Open Innovation approach comes from the decidedly non-high-tech consumer packaged goods industry. In 1999, Procter & Gamble decided to change its approach to innovation. The firm extended its internal R&D to the outside world through an initiative called Connect and Develop. This initiative emphasized the need for P&G to reach out to external parties for innovative ideas.[3] P&G has created a position entitled Director of External Innovation, and has set an internal goal of sourcing 50 percent of its innovations from outside the company in five years, up from an estimated 10 percent in 2002. The company's rationale is simple: Inside P&G are more than 8,600 scientists advancing the industrial knowledge that enables new P&G offerings; outside are 1.5 million. So why try to invent everything internally?[4] P&G also tries to move its own ideas outside as well. The ideas that P&G generates in its labs and that are not picked up by its internal businesses are available to other firms, even direct competitors, after three years.[5]

This is not to argue that all industries now operate in an Open Innovation regime. Some industries have not been severely impacted by the erosion factors noted previously, and they continue to operate in a Closed Innovation regime. Nuclear reactors and aircraft engines are two industries in which reliance on one's own ideas, and internal commercialization paths to market, appear to remain the dominant innovation mode. (The innovation process of designing and assembling aircraft using those engines, however, is undergoing important changes.)

Other industries have been in an Open Innovation mode for many years: The Hollywood film industry, for example, has innovated for decades through a network of partnerships and alliances between production studios, directors, talent agencies, actors, scriptwriters, specialized subcontractors (e.g., suppliers of special effects), and independent producers. Modern-day investment banking has been using external ideas for its innovations for many years as well. Newly minted Ph.D.s and even university finance professors develop new, exotic varieties of investment instruments, to hedge against risks that could not have been financed a generation ago.

These different industries can be located on a continuum, one end of which includes industries in which entirely Closed Innovation conditions prevail, the other end containing industries with fully Open Innovation conditions:[6]

Closed Innovation	*Open Innovation*
• Examples of industries: nuclear reactors, mainframe computers	• Examples of industries: PCs, movies
• Largely internal ideas	• Many external ideas
• Low labor mobility	• High labor mobility
• Little VC	• Active VC
• Few, weak start-ups	• Numerous start-ups
• Universities unimportant	• Universities important

Many industries are in transition between the two paradigms: Automotive, biotechnology, pharmaceuticals, health care, computers, software, communications, banking, insurance, consumer packaged goods, and even military weapons and communications systems are examples. It is within these transition areas that the book's concepts will be the most important. In these industries, many critically important innovations have emerged from what seemed like unlikely places. The locus of innovation in these industries is moving beyond the confines of the central R&D laboratories of the largest companies and is spreading to start-ups, to universities, and to other outsiders. If the locus of innovation is shifting in your business too, then this will be a valuable book for you.

If your industry appears to be largely buffered from the erosion factors that undermine the Closed Innovation approach, then you might expect little of value in this book. Before you close this book and place it back on the shelf, however, be sure you consider your industry carefully. Business history is full of prosperous, successful companies that were doing very well financially, even as the basis for their success was being cut out from underneath them. Some companies described in this book were also doing well for many years by adhering to the Closed Innovation model; fewer were able to detect and respond to the erosion factors they encountered before it was too late. Is it possible that your industry is also under pressure from one or more of these erosion factors and the effects just haven't materialized yet? If so, it would be wise to learn about the experience of other industries, to gain some insights about what you might do if those effects should happen to you.

Insights from the Book

When the innovation context shifts from Closed toward Open, the process of innovation must change as well. A number of insights that result from this new view of innovation will be presented in this book.

Chapter 1 presents the experience of the Xerox Corporation in dealing with a highly productive research laboratory, the Palo Alto Research Center. Xerox selected PARC technologies that fit its business model, and eschewed those that did not. These rejected technologies were later commercialized outside of Xerox's value chain, enabling instead different value chains across numerous companies. Some of the same technologies that Xerox rightly rejected as being of little value for its business model went on to become quite valuable indeed, albeit through the use of very different business models. Xerox's management of its PARC technologies illustrates in a nutshell the transition from Closed Innovation to Open Innovation.

Chapters 2 and 3 explore the Closed and Open Innovation models in more detail. This gives rise to a key insight: Useful knowledge has become widely diffused. A century ago, many leading industrial companies held knowledge monopolies; they led the industry and indeed the world in the critical discoveries that supported their industry. Today, these knowledge monopolies have been largely broken up, sometimes by government antitrust policy, but more often by the onslaught of new start-up companies, accompanied by the increasing quality and productivity of university research. The distribution of knowledge has spilled out well beyond the knowledge held by central research laboratories, with important pools of knowledge distributed among companies, customers, suppliers, universities, national labs, industry consortia, and start-up firms.

Chapter 3 also argues that companies don't take full advantage of this wealth of information. Companies often err by making too little use of others' ideas in their own businesses, causing wasteful duplication of innovative effort. This makes their internal R&D slower to achieve results, and less productive as well. Companies also often err by allowing too little use of their own ideas in others' businesses, forgoing additional profits from others' use of their ideas.

A related insight is that ideas that are not readily used can be lost. The erosion factors that undermine Closed Innovation also undermine companies' preferences to place ideas on the shelf until they can be used internally. Such mothballing of ideas is increasingly untenable: Ideas, and the people who create them, no longer can be warehoused until the companies' own businesses are ready to make use of them. Companies that do not use their ideas with alacrity risk losing them—and the people who thought of them—to outside organizations.

Chapter 4 presents a fourth insight: The value of an idea or a technology depends on its business model. There is no inherent value in a technology per se. The value is determined instead by the business model used to bring it to market. The same technology taken to market through two different business models will yield different amounts of value. An inferior technology with a better business model will often trump a better technology commercialized through an inferior business model. The business model defines what customer problems are being solved, and looks for external and internal ideas to solve them. It also specifies how some portion of that value will be claimed. This also has implications for managing intellectual property, as we will describe later.

Chapters 5 through 8 provide detailed illustrations of Open Innovation concepts in action at leading firms. Chapter 5 recounts the transformation in how IBM manages innovation. IBM was one of the paradigmatic practitioners of Closed Innovation for most of its existence. Yet today it has shed much of the mental baggage associated with that approach, to the point that IBM frequently uses others' technologies in its business and offers its technology for sale to others to use in their business.

Chapter 6 depicts the very different innovation model of the Intel Corporation. From its very inception, Intel eschewed many ideas of the Closed Innovation paradigm. In a very high-tech industry, Intel does relatively little internal research and has organized itself instead to leverage external technologies. It does this through careful monitoring of external academic research and through corporate VC investments in external start-up companies.

In contrast to Intel's approach to bringing external technology inside, chapter 7 describes Lucent's approach to taking internal technology outside. Lucent's New Ventures Group acts as an internal VC group within Bell Labs. Its presence influences the way that Lucent commercializes Bell Laboratories technologies—both the technologies that remain within Lucent and those that go to market through a newly formed venture.

Intel and Lucent illustrate another key concept for Open Innovation: The presence of VC changes the innovation process for everyone. The impact of VC extends well beyond the start-up companies it finances.

Venture capital ultimately influences the companies that lose people to start-ups or that buy from, sell to, compete with, or partner with them. Venture capital processes for adding value to the companies they finance are not well understood in technology circles, yet these processes are critical in the Open Innovation paradigm. Established companies at a minimum must learn to coexist with VC. Ideally, they should learn to exploit VC's ability to fund multiple organizational experiments to commercialize technologies, and treat those experiments as early market explorations for their own future growth.

Chapter 8 examines the management of intellectual property (IP) in the innovation process. This chapter highlights a final insight of Open Innovation: In a world of abundant knowledge, companies should be active buyers—and active sellers—of IP. Few companies take full commercial advantage of their own IP beyond using it in their own business. And every company can benefit from utilizing external IP in its business, rather than inventing it from scratch on its own. This requires an entirely different mind-set toward managing IP: Instead of managing your IP to exclude rivals, manage your IP to profit from others' use of it. And don't be afraid to profit from others' IP in your own business. Millennium Pharmaceuticals, IBM, and Intel illustrate the fascinating opportunities that exist in managing IP.

Chapter 9 explores how companies can make the transition to a more Open Innovation system. The chapter explains how a company can exploit the principles of Open Innovation. It examines how external technologies can fill the gaps in a company's current business. It also looks at how internal technologies can generate the seeds of a company's new business.

These chapters collectively call for a new vision of the innovation process. This vision eagerly seeks external knowledge and ideas, even as it nurtures internal ones. It utilizes valuable ideas from whatever source in advancing a company's own business, and it places the company's own ideas in other companies' businesses. By opening itself up to the world of knowledge that surrounds it, the twenty-first-century corporation can avoid the innovation paradox that plagues so many firms' R&D activities today. In so doing, the company can renew its current business and generate new business. For an innovative company in a world of abundant knowledge, today can be the best of times.

Open Innovation

I

Xerox PARC

The Achievements and Limits of Closed Innovation

T HE XEROX CORPORATION, the leading copier company, has a storied history of innovation. Much of that innovation arose from
Xerox's Palo Alto Research Center (PARC), which was aimed at a new
market for Xerox, the computer industry. While Xerox's problems with
capturing value from its investments in innovation at PARC are well
known, few know the whole story.

For Xerox's experience with PARC poses a challenging puzzle: How
could a company that possessed the resources and vision to launch a
brilliant research center—not to mention the patience to fund the center for more than thirty years, and the savvy to incorporate important
technologies from it—let so many good ideas get away? Did Xerox mis-
manage PARC? Did PARC pursue the wrong projects? Did it abandon
the wrong projects? Why did so many of PARC's computer industry innovations yield so little for Xerox and its shareholders?

The answers to these questions point both to the accomplishments
and the problems associated with the way that Xerox managed its research and technology. Xerox's approach was consistent with the best
practice of most leading industrial corporations in the twentieth century. A brief history of Xerox illustrates the many benefits of this approach and the increasing difficulties that it has recently encountered.

Xerox's Innovation Achievements

In 1970, the Xerox Corporation was riding high. It had grown from a
tiny company called Haloid in the 1950s into a *Fortune* 500 colossus.

With a dominant share of the booming office copier market, Xerox was growing fast and was very profitable. Its stock was a darling on Wall Street, one of the so-called Nifty Fifty.

To the company's credit, Xerox realized that this good fortune would not continue indefinitely. If the company wanted to ensure its future, it realized that it would need to make important investments to position itself for that future. In 1969, its chief executive, Peter Mc-Colough, commissioned Jacob Goldman, who was then the head of research at Xerox, to build a new laboratory within the corporate research organization. This new laboratory would provide the company with the technology necessary to realize McColough's vision of "the architecture of information." McColough's vision was that Xerox would transcend its current business of being the leading office copier company to become the leading office equipment supplier of information-intensive products.

Goldman eagerly accepted the assignment. He strongly felt that such investments were needed if Xerox were to avoid the fate of companies such as RCA. RCA had been a pioneer in consumer electronics, both in radio and later in television. The company had developed strong capabilities in vacuum tube technology to give its products the best quality at low cost. When William Shockley and his colleagues at Bell Laboratories produced the transistor, RCA responded by deepening its investments in vacuum tube technology. Although RCA did achieve further improvements, it failed to foresee the tremendous potential in solid-state electronic technology.[1] By the 1960s, RCA had lost all of its technology edge in the market and had become a hollow shell of its former greatness. In Goldman's view, only vigilant investment in leading-edge technologies could protect Xerox from a similar fate in its own business.[2]

The Creation of PARC

Goldman recruited Xerox scientist George Pake to lead this new research facility. Pake received his assignment at a fortuitous time, when government research spending on computer technology was declining. As a result, Pake and his staff were able to recruit many of the world's best researchers in the field. In 1970, Pake established the Palo Alto Research Center in Palo Alto, CA, to house this group.

PARC would turn out to be a true research success. It led the discovery of a variety of important innovations that today are a critical part of the personal computer and communications revolution. The graphical user interface originated at PARC. The bit-mapped screen, which replaced the green ASCII characters on terminals, was also born there. The Ethernet networking protocol was developed there, as were other, higher-speed networking protocols. The leading font rendering program, PostScript, descends directly from PARC. Later PARC projects included document management software, Web searching and indexing technologies, and online conferencing technologies.

PARC also made important research contributions in semiconductor diode lasers and in laser printing, developments that would prove highly important to Xerox's copier and printer businesses. But, with the benefit of hindsight, much of PARC's research and technology would create tremendous economic value for society, yet yield little value for its parent company.

PARC's inability to capture value from its technology for Xerox has been debated at length. Some accounts fault Xerox's corporate management in Stamford, CT, for failing to perceive the value of the technology being created at its West Coast laboratory. Other accounts fault the politics and infighting within the PARC facility, in addition to errors at corporate headquarters, for the problems in capturing value from PARC technology.[3]

These reasons seem unsatisfying. The Xerox Corporation had the vision to create and generously support PARC for more than thirty years. If the corporation were truly unaware of the value of the lab, it is hard to believe that this support should have continued for so long. And PARC scientists were not simply creating technology. They were building highly advanced systems that integrated many different types of hardware and that ran very complex software applications. Accomplishing this integration required cooperation and connection across a variety of scientific disciplines, which seems at odds with the notion of a research center riven by dysfunctional infighting.

These proffered accounts miss the root cause of PARC's problems. The research center was not mismanaged; rather, it was managed according to the best practices of the leading industrial research laboratories. Nor were PARC's leaders ignorant; they were intelligent, reasonable people who were up to date on good R&D management practice.

And PARC was not ineffective; indeed, it contributed much of the systems architecture and technology behind the personal computer and communications industries. Nor was the research center irrelevant to the rest of Xerox; the laser printers and advanced copiers sold by Xerox came directly out of PARC research breakthroughs.

We can learn a great deal by identifying the root cause of Xerox's problems with PARC, because it determines the lessons we learn from Xerox's experience. Some observers attribute Xerox's problems to corporate management's ignorance or to internal politicking. The implications are that the rest of us have little to learn from Xerox's experience. If, however, Xerox managed its R&D according to the best practices that were typical of most leading industrial organizations, then the lessons from Xerox's difficulties are vitally important for every innovating organization to understand. Understanding PARC's situation more deeply may illuminate a different way to manage innovation activities going forward.

The Root Cause of Xerox's "PARC Problem"

After carefully reviewing many projects within Xerox and interviewing nearly one hundred current and former managers, I have concluded that Xerox's problems with PARC arose from the way Xerox managed its innovation process. Xerox managed PARC through a Closed Innovation paradigm: The corporation sought to discover new breakthroughs; develop them into products; build the products in its factories; and distribute, finance, and service those products—all within the four walls of the company. This paradigm was hardly unique to Xerox; it was used to manage all the leading industrial R&D facilities operating in the U.S. economy after World War II.

The greatest technological achievements that emerged from PARC, by contrast, could only take root—and create real economic value—when pursued in a far different context, a context of Open Innovation. Most of these achievements were realized only when key PARC researchers left Xerox and went to other, smaller companies or went out on their own to start up new companies. These companies could not afford to pursue the model of deep vertical integration that Xerox followed. Instead, they had to define a business model to commercialize their own technologies. They had to create systems and architectures that enabled their products to work with other companies' products to build a system. Those start-ups that achieved commercial success did so by applying their technology quite differently from how the researchers had originally envisioned when they left Xerox.

Some of the technologies took root through the departure of key employees to Apple, where the Macintosh computer embodied many of the user-interface design concepts created at PARC. Other technologies were commercialized at Microsoft. For example, the Bravo word processor was the precursor to Microsoft Word. Despite their present-day size, both Apple and Microsoft were themselves very young companies when they absorbed some of PARC's technologies, and neither had any internal research capability at the time.[4]

The majority of technologies that left PARC, however, did so via newly formed, independent start-up companies, which were staffed by departing PARC researchers and funded by venture capitalists.[5] Table 1-1 shows twenty-four of these PARC "spin-off companies" that were created to commercialize one of Xerox's technologies from 1979 through 1998. As one would expect, many of these companies soon withered and died. Some companies, though, managed to prosper. Ten went public, and a few (such as 3Com, Adobe, and Documentum) were still operating as independent companies in 2002.

Table 1-1 also debunks another myth that has grown up around Xerox's management of its spin-off technologies. Most of these technologies did not "leak" out of Xerox through inadvertence and neglect on the part of Xerox's research managers. Instead, Xerox gave its explicit permission for most of these technologies to leave—via a nonexclusive technology license from Xerox—and Xerox maintained an equity stake in many of them in return for that license.

If Xerox didn't fumble these spin-offs, then why did it allow them to leave? Although the specific answer varies with every spin-off company, the general answer is that Xerox saw little further potential for each technology within Xerox. Continuing to develop each technology was expensive and took money away from other new initiatives that might be more important to Xerox. When Xerox's research managers judged that a research project had little more to contribute to Xerox's fundamental knowledge or to its businesses, they cut off further funding of the research. In many cases, the researchers chose to work on new research projects with greater discovery potential or value to Xerox. Sometimes, though, the researchers wanted to continue with the project. Xerox chose to allow these researchers to gracefully exit the company and take the project with them.[6]

TABLE 1-1

Xerox PARC Spin-Off Companies from 1979 to 1998

Company Name	Did Xerox Grant a License to Spin Off?	Spin-Off Date	Disposition Event	Disposition Date	Technology Description	Original CEO or General Manager
3Com	Y	6/79	IPO	3/84	Hardware, network	Robert Metcalfe
VLSI	N	8/79	IPO	3/83	Other	Jack Balletto
GRiD	N	12/79	Acquired	7/88	Hardware, software	John Ellenby
Aurora	Y	2/80	Chapter 11	12/88	Hardware, software	Richard Shoup
Optimem	Y	6/80	Sold off	6/91	Hardware	George Sollman
Metaphor	N	10/82	Sold off	10/91	Hardware, software, network	Don Massaro
Komag	Y	6/83	IPO	3/87	Hardware, other	Tu Chen, Steve Johnson
SDLI	Y	6/83	IPO	3/95	Other	Donald R. Scifres
Adobe	N	11/83	IPO	8/86	Software	John E. Warnock
Microlytics	Y	3/85	Chapter 11	11/96	Software, other	Michael Weiner
SynOptics	Y	10/85	IPO	10/88	Network	Andy Ludwick
StepperVision	Y	4/87	Licensed	10/88	Hardware, software	Worth Ludwick

Company Name	Did Xerox Grant a License to Spin Off?	Spin-Off Date	Disposition Event	Disposition Date	Technology Description	Original CEO or General Manager
ParcPlace	Y	3/88	IPO	2/94	Software	Adele Goldberg
AWPI	Y	6/89	Bought back	1/91	Hardware, software	Tony Domit
Documentum	Y	1/90	IPO	1/96	Software	Howard Shoa
Semaphore	Y	10/90	Acquired	4/98	Hardware, software, other	Charles Hart
Document Sciences	Y	10/91	IPO	9/96	Software	Tony Domit
LiveWorks	Y	8/92	Shut down	7/97	Network	Richard Bruce
CTI	N	5/94	Going concern		Software, other	Henry Sang
X ColorgrafX	Y	10/94	Going concern		Printer	Barry Lathan
DpiX	Y	3/96	Sold off	7/99	Diode, other	Malcolm Thompson
PlaceWare	Y	11/96	Going concern		Software	Richard Bruce
Inxight	Y	12/96	Going concern		Software	Mohan Trikha
Uppercase	Y	1/98	Going concern		Hardware, software	Frank Halasz

Although some of these departing technologies later became highly valuable, they did not start out as clear winners. The success of some of these departing spin-offs was largely unforeseen—and unforeseeable. When they left, these spin-offs were far more like ugly ducklings than elegant swans. The projects underwent significant development—and even transformation—on their journey to market after leaving Xerox. If they had stayed inside Xerox, this transformation would never have occurred and the value of these spin-offs likely never would have materialized. Their success arose more from their response to subsequent external events than it did from the initial promise of the technology or the people. The path of this transformation is illustrated in the evolution of SynOptics, a successful, though lesser known, Xerox PARC spin-off company.

The Transformation of SynOptics

SynOptics technology grew within PARC with the goal of making a fast version of Ethernet work over optical cables in the mid-1980s. The project continued the Ethernet research that Robert Metcalfe had commercialized out of PARC with his 3Com start-up five years earlier. But commercializing this technology required other technologies that were many years away from being widely available, such as optical cables for computer networks, to be installed at customers' locations. In order to use SynOptics technology, the customers would have to install networks with entirely new wiring to connect the computers, printers, and other devices—making the cost of installing and using the technology very expensive. Xerox decided that this was one technology it needn't pursue any further internally—it was too far ahead of customers' needs in the mainstream computer market.

Andy Ludwick and Ronald Schmidt decided to take this technology outside to see if they could make it into a company. They could afford to be patient for optical cabling media to become established in the market, and they thought that they could distribute their products through value-added distributors who were selling and installing optical gear. It might take a while and it might initially be expensive for customers to buy complete, optically wired networks, but once the market did get going, they would be well positioned to participate in the growth that would follow. A graceful exit from Xerox ensued, with Ludwick and Schmidt taking the technology outside, and Xerox retaining a 15 percent equity share of the company.

Once out on their own, though, Ludwick and Schmidt soon realized that they had an even more valuable opportunity: The software and protocols they were writing to drive Ethernet packets over optical cables could actually be applied to copper-wire networks. Their efforts therefore could make Ethernet run faster over copper-wire networks as well. (The acceleration of Ethernet transmission speeds enabled by SynOptics was only true initially for the particular topology of wiring known as IBM's token ring, though it would soon migrate to other types of local area networks.) Instead of continuing to pursue the technically challenging aspects of making high-speed Ethernet work on a new transmission medium (optical cables), the company chose to emphasize the more technically mundane approach of using its technology on copper-wire networks that were already installed and operating.

This insight changed the company's commercial prospects dramatically. Instead of selling its products into future networks that had yet to be installed, SynOptics could upgrade the speed and performance of thousands of networks already up and running. Customers could spend a small fraction of the costs of buying new optically wired networks, and get transmission speeds five or ten times faster on the networks they had already paid for. This was a compelling value proposition.

SynOptics did very well in commercializing this approach. It went public in October 1988, just three years after it was founded. A small development project that started within PARC on a shoestring budget soon became a billion-dollar company. It later merged with an East Coast firm, Wellfleet, to create Bay Networks. (Later, Bay was acquired by Nortel.)

It is too glib and simplistic to attribute the eventual success of SynOptics to the early lab work at Xerox. The source of the value realized by SynOptics wasn't simply embodied in the early software and hardware created inside PARC and let go by Xerox. It was the creative *recombination* of that technology, using a different type of cabling and joined to a different type of network, that yielded such a boost in value. Instead of helping Xerox systems products run faster in the distant future, SynOptics learned how to make IBM and other networks run faster *today*. Instead of focusing on entirely new networks, SynOptics added value to already installed networks. This happened only after the company left the cozy confines of the PARC lab within Xerox, which prompted SynOptics to conceptualize an alternative way to apply its technology.

Of course, many projects that left PARC never amounted to any-thing. For these projects, the search for an alternative approach to building value came to naught. But those companies that did prosper managed to do quite well for themselves and their shareholders. Their technologies helped fuel the personal computer revolution and also contributed to the complementary industry of computer networking and communications. Figure 1-1 shows the market value of these com-panies once they went public.[7] For comparison, Xerox's own market value is included as well. As shown, Xerox's own stock did very well in the 1990s and fell a great deal in 2000 and 2001. Xerox's spin-off com-panies, however, did even better in the 1990s, overtaking Xerox in 1995 and again in 1999. Though they too fell sharply in 2000 and 2001 as a result of the collapse in technology stock prices, the market value of these spin-off companies at the end of 2001 collectively exceeded that of their parent company, Xerox, by a factor of two.

FIGURE 1-1

The Market Value of Xerox PARC Spin-Offs, in Relation to Xerox

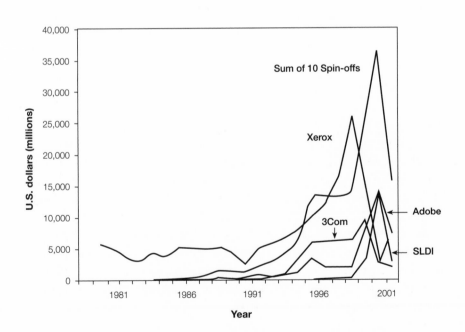

The financial success of the Xerox spin-offs seems astonishing in retrospect and was certainly unexpected by the research and technology managers within Xerox. Yet, as demonstrated by SynOptics, these technologies did not look particularly important to Xerox, or promising in their own right, when they first left the company. Like the technological innovations at SynOptics, the other spin-off technologies changed greatly only after they left the internal lab within Xerox. Taken together, the spin-off companies collectively deconstructed Xerox's vertically integrated value chain for its copiers and printers into individual component technologies. They then engineered these technologies into system architectures that established horizontal businesses for these technologies, primarily in the personal computing and communications industries. In these industries, the technologies could be linked to many other companies' technologies, instead of just those found inside Xerox copiers and printers.

These new opportunities were hard to foresee from within the confines of the corporate laboratory, despite the considerable resources of the Xerox Corporation, which dwarfed the resources of these spin-offs. Something in the process that these fledgling companies followed led them to a more powerful, more useful way to commercialize their technology and enabled them to address new, growing markets. It is in this process, this journey of a technology to a new market, where the root cause of Xerox's problem lies. Although Xerox's capabilities and vision enabled it to surmount many technical uncertainties for its current business, its innovation processes were poorly suited to dealing with the combination of technical and market uncertainties for a potential new business.

Managing Both Technical and Market Uncertainty

As the example of SynOptics illustrates, the successful commercialization of a new technology involves the management of both technical and market uncertainty. The capability and performance of the fledgling technology involved is not yet well understood, nor are its relationships with other parts of a system well characterized. This technical uncertainty is compounded by market uncertainty, when early-stage technology projects also address an uncertain market. How a technology might be used by customers, and what benefits it might provide them, are also not well understood.[8]

The application of a new technology is better understood when it addresses a current market with a known set of customers. While the technology itself may remain technically very daunting, its use and its benefits are largely defined by the experience these customers had in this market with the earlier versions of the technology. Xerox had little apparent difficulty dealing with even high degrees of technical uncertainty when, for example, the fruits of its projects could be directly applied to its copier and printer markets. The company managed to convert its entire technology base from a mechanical one in its early years, to an electromechanical base in its high-growth years, to a fully electronic and digital platform in the 1990s. It pioneered the use of semiconductor-based laser diodes in its high-end copier and printer businesses as well. In so doing, Xerox successfully avoided the technical obsolescence that sunk RCA in an earlier period.

Where the challenge frustrated Xerox was where the company had to apply its promising technologies *outside* its current markets and customers. Here, the technical uncertainty that the company had to contend with was joined to a new market uncertainty: which customers and which uses of its technology would be the most valuable.

Coping with market uncertainty greatly complicates the already difficult challenge of managing technical uncertainty, because resolving the technical uncertainty depends on which market the technology is intended to serve. Choosing where to focus your technology, and for which application to optimize that technology, effectively means choosing a market. The technology that eventually became SynOptics was originally created inside PARC to make Xerox copiers run faster. Such a task is entirely different from running external networks like IBM's token ring network, which connects IBM and compatible personal computers to Hewlett-Packard printers and other compatible components. Until someone knows the most valuable uses of a technology and the best markets to target, he or she does not know where to focus the technology development activity.

When commercializing a new technology requires the resolution of both technical *and* market uncertainty, you cannot anticipate the best path forward from the very beginning. You simply don't know all the possibilities in advance. Not only is the future unknown, it is *unknowable*. No amount of planning and research can reveal the facts, because they simply don't exist yet. Instead, you must make an initial product to learn what some customers like and dislike about it. Then you must adapt your plans in response to the feedback as you go along, and make adjustments as more information becomes available. In these circumstances, it is also a good idea to try to use that technology in more than one possible market and in more than one configuration. The varied approaches increase your chances of finding a highly valued use for the technology. The history of innovation is full of examples in which the eventual best use of a new product or technology was far different from the initial intended purpose of the idea.[9]

This market experimentation is something that large companies typically find hard to do. While companies have well-developed processes for testing new technologies in a variety of ways in their current business, they usually lack processes for trying out early technologies in a variety of different markets that might become a new business. Companies also regard such experimentation as a waste of money, since many of the early trials will be unsuccessful and will have to be discontinued.[10] This perception of inefficiency misses the point, because it falsely presumes that one can know in advance where to apply a technology. Because you do not—and cannot—know the best way forward, it is better to try a number of experiments, instead of relying on a single effort.[11]

In summary, then, the best way to develop new technologies in new markets is to follow a few important guidelines: First, seek to explore a variety of possibilities, for which you should seek rapid feedback at as low a cost as practicable. Second, search for tests that are highly faithful to the eventual market, so that early success with the test is highly correlated with later market success. Finally, instead of detailed, thorough, and careful planning, you should instigate some initial probes and then react quickly to the new information that these probes reveal.

Playing Chess, Playing Poker

The development of nascent technologies in new markets is very different from the advancement of technologies in current markets. One process is wholly unlike the other; it is like the difference between playing chess and playing poker. This contrast was first described to me by former IBM research director James McGroddy:

> When you're targeting your technology to your current business, it's like a chess game. You know the pieces, you know what they can and cannot do. You know what your competition is going to do, and you

know what your customer needs from you in order to win the game. You can think out many moves in advance, and in fact, you have to, if you're going to win.

In a new market, you have to plan your technology entirely differently. You're not playing chess anymore; now you're playing poker. You don't know all the information in advance. Instead, you have to decide whether to spend additional money to stay in the game to see the next card.[12]

McGroddy's analogy provides a valuable insight into Xerox's management of its PARC technology. Xerox's innovation processes were good for playing chess, but were poorly suited for playing poker.

Research projects within PARC usually started through the initiative of an individual researcher, who was fascinated with some new technical possibility. This individual enthusiasm was regarded as critical to the innovation process, because the personal initiative infused passion and commitment into the project. Many internal researchers were celebrated for their initial inspiration and subsequent persistence in pursuing their vision of a future technological opportunity. This was the first test that every research project had to pass.

The second test facing a project was whether any other researchers in the lab became interested in joining the project. Instead of managers dictating that researchers would have to join a project, an informal bottom-up process prevailed, wherein individual researchers decided where they wanted to work next. This informal policy allocated researchers to projects of the greatest interest to them and signaled to Xerox which projects were viewed as "hot" within the lab.

Not all projects passed this test. Xerox managers would then have to intervene, to terminate further work on the initial project and to steer researchers onto other projects. Because the spirit and creativity of researchers was so critical to this process, the termination of further funding had to be done gently. John Seely Brown, who managed PARC for most of the 1990s, told me, "I never, ever killed a research project. But I often met with researchers to suggest that there may be an even better, more exciting, more important research opportunity that needed their talents."[13]

Once a small group had formed to push a technology initiative further, the project began to require more resources to continue its progress. At this point in the project, the research management of

Xerox began to apply more formal tests. At one level, the managers assessed the technical potential of the project: the technical challenge facing the team, the quality of the team, the progress realized so far, and the potential for continued progress. At another level, they had to make judgments about the project's economic value to the company. To do this, they sought to engage with Xerox's business units to gather their sense of the project's potential value.

Xerox's businesses were focused on growing their revenues and profits within the general reprographics market—chiefly copiers, printers, and associated supplies. Eager to obtain technologies for their current businesses, they often invited their leading customer accounts to visit Xerox's labs to preview technologies under development. These visits were a powerful sales tool, helping to persuade customers that Xerox had a commitment to serving them in the future, as well as the present.

Customers, in turn, provided feedback to Xerox managers about which technologies seemed most promising from their perspective. This feedback became important input for the annual budgeting process, where resources were allocated to technology projects and where businesses committed to transfer technologies from the lab into their own P&L. These businesses would have to forecast the revenues expected from the incorporation of the new technology, either through new versions of their offerings, improved prices for their offerings, or reduced costs of providing their offerings. Naturally, these forecasts tended to reflect the response of the current market and current customers and tended to discount the possible response of other markets and customers.[14]

As projects got bigger and consumed more resources, they experienced more intensive review from within the company. Projects that were nearing commercialization might be reviewed all the way up to the CEO when multimillion-dollar investments were involved. These internal reviews took time, but ensured that the many ramifications of big decisions—such as the financial impact of the project, the project's impact on the quality of the company's products, the distribution of the project, and the international implications of the project—were considered throughout the company.

Figure 1-2 illustrates how ideas progressed within Xerox through this review process. Each dashed vertical line indicates a review point, where research projects were evaluated. As projects moved from left to right, they used more resources and became fewer in number. They also got closer to the market and received more customer exposure. At the right side of this process, projects were directed to Xerox's business groups (BGs), incubated as a new enterprise (NE), or were licensed out or spun out.[15]

This process was an effective way to play chess. The tests gave clear feedback on each project and did not incur high costs. (Tests such as customer visits actually helped sell products, reducing the tests' effective cost even more.) The fidelity of the tests was high; projects that customers liked tended to do very well later on in the market. The process created a number of useful projects for the Xerox BGs.

This process was poorly suited, however, to playing poker outside its current businesses. This path directed projects to either the new enterprise or to license/spin-out paths, as shown in figure 1-2. Here, the process for assessing the market opportunity and potential economic value of the project broke down.

Customers often did not know what to make of a new technology they were seeing at PARC. They might be intrigued by its technical dimension, but have no sense of how to make use of it. Xerox's own sales force similarly might struggle to find a value proposition for a fledgling

FIGURE 1-2

Xerox's Innovation Process, Circa 1996

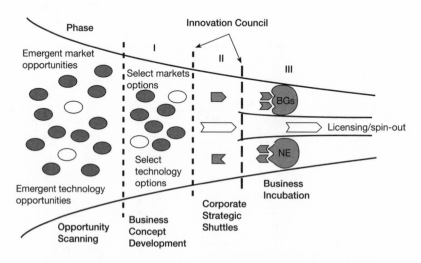

Source: H. Chesbrough, "PlaceWare: Issues in Structuring a Xerox Technology Spinout," Case no 9-699-001. Boston: Harvard Business School, 1999. Copyright © 1999 by the President and Fellows of Harvard College. Reprinted with Permission.

technology.[16] As a result, PARC had to develop ad hoc ways of testing market potential and customer requirements, using consultants, external research, and its own intuition. But these ways did not share the attributes of good experiments. They were not quick to yield results, the results were often unclear, and what results were obtained had little relationship to being successful in the market. Not surprisingly, these projects did not fare well in the annual budgeting process, when they had to compete with other projects that had passed much clearer tests for application within Xerox's businesses. Eventually, many projects were cut off from further internal funding, which led to the departure of technologies that became the spin-off companies shown in table 1-1.

PARC Technologies Meet Silicon Valley Venture Capital

The departure of spin-off companies from Xerox is only half of the story, because it omits the journey of these projects once they departed from Xerox. Almost all the companies listed in table 1-1 funded their additional development through a very different process from the one that supported the projects within Xerox. These technologies were further funded by external venture capital (VC). PARC, after all, was located in Palo Alto, in the middle of Silicon Valley, and its most salient technologies exited PARC just as the VC industry was accelerating its size, presence, and scope in the Valley.

Venture capital was a cottage industry through the 1970s, but it was becoming a powerful institutional force by the mid-1980s in Silicon Valley. And this force wasn't simply another source of money for promising ideas. Rather, it was a new process for creating new companies to commercialize new discoveries. This process contrasts sharply with the way that Xerox and most other large companies internally evaluated their research projects, as other studies suggest.[17]

In many respects, the VC process is inferior to the one that large companies use to review their technology projects. Fewer inputs are fed into the process. The VC company conducts less analysis on the project, and the technical review is more shallow. Far fewer people are involved: Customer input is usually less extensive, and few other senior managers review the project. Overall, the VC process for reviewing technology projects is not a good way to play chess.

But the VC process has attributes that make it good for playing poker. If it looks like the hand is a winning hand, this realization triggers additional investment in a short period, with a single level of review, by the board of directors of the venture. If the hand appears to be a losing hand, this triggers quick reconsideration and might result in folding the hand (i.e., shutting down the venture). Again, the board's decision to shut down the venture is final, with no further review by another part of the organization. The process of setting and then meeting milestones forces accountability for existing commitments and facilitates adaptation to new information. Decisions get made fast, and actions follow quickly.

The quality of the tests is better too, in terms of searching for opportunities with novel technologies in nascent markets. The young ventures are estimating market and customer needs with real products being sold to real companies, instead of relying on market research conducted by larger companies, in which possible customers are asked their opinions about possible offerings. Although the technical depth of the project is shallow, this weakness is managed through the creative use of available technologies to link to and build on others' technology and by quick adjustment to new information.

The technologies that left Xerox and became valuable spin-off companies all went through this second process. Their subsequent success owes less to the fundamental talent of the departing researchers or the inherent quality of their work and more to the virtues of the external VC process that converted vague and ambiguous research ideas into powerful, valuable technologies. This process was far more effective than the process used within Xerox to explore technologies outside of Xerox's traditional markets.[18]

This, then, is the lesson of PARC's experience. PARC's successes *and* its failures derive from the same root cause: Xerox's approach to managing its research output outside its own business. PARC's successes illustrate the strengths of what I call Closed Innovation, or an internal paradigm of industrial R&D, in which playing chess is critical to success in extending the current businesses. In Closed Innovation, Xerox applied useful, valid tests. PARC's failures, on the other hand, show the limits of the Closed Innovation model. To identify and exploit new markets, success requires poker-playing skills. Under these circumstances, Xerox lacked effective tests and the requisite ability to adapt quickly to new information.

On the other hand, VC's tests and adaptability are better suited to pursuing nascent businesses. Venture capital processes—the same ones needed for playing poker—are in fact a new and different way to innovate. Venture capitalists expect that most new ideas and knowledge will emerge from outside a company. They understand that a company's people can and will leave if there are insufficient opportunities to grow and apply their talents within the firm. The rapid obsolescence of internal ideas is expected in VC firms, which seek ways to exploit new ideas more quickly and more widely. Venture capital often involves a new way of thinking about technology, about intellectual property, and about the choice of business model for a company.

In a world of rapid change leading to new potential markets, innovating companies will need to learn how to play poker as well as chess. These companies cannot capture the potential value latent in their ideas unless they change the way they think about taking them to market. No company can afford to rely entirely on its own ideas anymore, and no company can restrict the use of its innovations to a single path to market. All companies will need to improve their ability to experiment with new technologies in new markets. As companies develop their poker-playing skills, they will view venture capitalists, start-ups, and spin-offs in a new light. Instead of regarding them as problems that complicate their chess game, they will instead view the newcomers as experiments that might lead to new sources of technology and growth.

Companies that fail to learn these skills may suffer Xerox's fate: a proud and capable inventor of promising discoveries, which struggles mightily to capture the benefits of its vision for its owners. Xerox was playing chess with its technologies, whereas Silicon Valley was playing poker with them. And Xerox's shareholders didn't get to cash in the chips generated by the latter approach to innovation.

2

The Closed
Innovation Paradigm

T HE CLOSED INNOVATION PARADIGM and its associated mind-set toward organizing industrial R&D has led to many important achievements and many commercial successes. It is the mental model that Xerox's management used to run its PARC research facility. Indeed, it is the model used by most major U.S. corporations to run their labs for most of the twentieth century.

The past success of the Closed Innovation paradigm accounts for its persistence in the face of the changing landscape of knowledge. It is an approach that is fundamentally inwardly focused, which, as we shall see, fit well with the knowledge environment of the early twentieth century. However, the paradigm is increasingly at odds with the knowledge landscape at the beginning of the twenty-first century.

How to Access Useful Knowledge:
A Thought Experiment

Let's begin with a thought experiment. Suppose that you are running a successful, growing company at the beginning of the twentieth century. Your products are selling well, and you have become a leading firm in your industry. Realizing that this fortunate situation will not last forever, you determine that the best way to ensure continued leadership in the industry is to create new and improved products to sell to the market in the future.[1] What is the best way for you to pursue the creation of these new products and services? Where is the useful knowledge you need, and how can you incorporate it into your business?

You might begin by assessing what the state of knowledge is for your industry outside your own firm. The state of external scientific knowledge had expanded enormously during the nineteenth century. By the early 1900s, we had learned about microbes, X-rays, the atom, electricity, and relativity. We had also learned about a more systematic way to conduct scientific research. As Alfred North Whitehead once remarked, the greatest invention of the nineteenth century was the method of invention.

Notwithstanding the scientific breakthroughs realized in the nineteenth century, for most industries around 1900, you would likely conclude that there wasn't that much external knowledge to build on to advance your industry. Although science was entering an era of enormous ferment (this is the period of Einstein, Bohr, Roentgen, Maxwell, Curie, Pasteur, and Planck), much of the science was just beginning to be understood, and its eventual commercial uses were far from apparent.

Moreover, the norms of science at that time suggested that any practical use from this science would come without much help from the scientists themselves. Emulating the norms of "pure" science held in German universities, U.S. scientists regarded the pursuit of practical knowledge as "prostituted science." Consider the bitter protest of Henry Rowland, who lamented the fame of "tinkerers" like Edison relative to men of science such as himself. Addressing the American Academy for the Advancement of Science in 1883, he proclaimed, "The proper course of one in my position is to consider what must be done to create a science of physics in this country, rather than to call telegraphs, electric lights, and such conveniences, by the name of science. . . . When the average tone of the [scientific] society is low, when the highest honors are given to the mediocre, when third-class men are held up as examples, and when trifling inventions are magnified into scientific discoveries, then the influence of such societies is prejudicial."[2]

At this time, many highly respected leaders in science argued that scientists had no place applying their talents and training to commercial problems. To do so, they believed, would imperil the value and quality of science itself. They looked on people like Thomas Edison as scientists of lesser ability, who had compromised themselves and corrupted the process of scientific discovery in so doing.

Unsurprisingly, the people who were trained as scientists in this period were mastering the tremendous intellectual breakthroughs in understanding the physical world, but were largely uninterested in applying those insights to practical problems. There was a large void between the science embodied in university classroom lectures and the beneficial use of those insights in commercial practice. Although the knowledge being created within universities seemed to hold great promise, your growing enterprise could not rely on this knowledge being put to use in your industry on its own. Moreover, universities lacked the financial resources to underwrite and conduct significant experiments themselves.

Nor could you expect the government to be of much assistance. The overall size of government in the economy was much smaller during this period in history than it is today. And the government did not play much of a role in the research system then. It did pursue a few initiatives, such as the creation of a patent system, and provided limited funding for particular inquiries in weights and measures and in military materials such as improved gunpowders. In the United States, the government also provided some creative funding of land-grant universities for agricultural studies. And the government's antitrust actions did break up the largest monopolies. But overall, the government played a very limited role in organizing or funding science.

If universities and government were not leading the commercial application of science, what was driving these technical advances? Industry was the primary source of research funding for the commercial use of science, and industry R&D laboratories were the primary locus of this industrial research.

Weighing the costs and benefits of these challenges, you would likely conclude that pursuing the discovery and commercial development of scientific knowledge within your own firm was the only choice you could really make. You could not wait indefinitely for the external scientific community to become interested in practical applications of science. Nor could you wait for other companies to start operations to provide critical pieces of the end product you were producing. After careful consideration, you decide to create your own internal R&D organization.

As you began to enact your choice, you learned that you would have to involve your organization on a wide range of topics, from the basic materials science underlying your products, to their many applications, to the industrial processes that fabricate them, to the means of utilizing them. Your laboratory must therefore reach far down into basic materials and reach all the way up to final products. You must attract highly trained people out of the universities and offer them lifelong employment as scientists and engineers in your company. You must create an internal environment of intellectual ferment and a research community that stimulates creative thinking and excellence in conducting research.

You might look around at other leading companies and see what they were doing to advance their knowledge. You would find that industrialists in leading industries of that time—chemicals and petroleum, for example—had reached the same conclusion you did: to pursue innovation through an internal R&D organization. German chemicals firms were systematically expanding their product offerings through increasingly advanced investigations of the properties of the materials they were using to create new dyestuffs.[3] Petroleum companies were rapidly improving their yields in refining crude oil through their understanding of the properties of that oil. In the process, they were innovating additional new products out of this raw material as well.

Historian Alfred Chandler has documented the choices of many leading industrial enterprises during this period.[4] Among his important discoveries was the role of companies' internal R&D functions in creating economies of scale in their business. These R&D facilities were so successful in extracting more efficiency out of increased understanding that they created natural monopolies in many leading industries, or economies of scale. These labs also spawned the discovery of new properties in materials. The resultant new possibilities in products led to the creation of new business opportunities, or economies of scope.

The institution of the central research lab and internal product development was thus a critical element of the rise of the modern industrial corporation. Centrally organized research and development were central to companies' strategies and were regarded as critical business investments. R&D functions were a salient feature in the knowledge landscape of the economy, relatively insulated from the universities and small enterprises, relatively unconnected to the government, and largely self-contained.

One could therefore regard the knowledge landscape in the early twentieth century as a series of fortified castles located in an otherwise impoverished landscape. Within the castle walls of each company's central R&D organization were deep repositories of understanding based on thorough, detailed investigations of a wide range of phenomena.[5] Each castle was relatively self-sufficient, receiving occasional visits from outsiders, and its inhabitants ventured out occasionally into the surrounding landscape to visit universities or scientific expositions. But most of the action occurred within the castle walls, and those outside the castle could only marvel at the wonders produced from within.

Shifts in the Knowledge Landscape

One important change in this knowledge landscape was the unique relationship between the public university system and corporations that developed in the United States in the first half of the twentieth century. Unlike the higher education system in European nations, the U.S. system was highly decentralized, even among public universities. State schools were funded by state governments and thus responded to local commercial needs to a greater extent than did their peers across the Atlantic. Industries such as mining, farming, and engineering profited greatly from the focus on science and technology in the public university system. Private universities were neither accountable to a national authority nor responsible even to a state authority and were thus free to pursue their own science and technology agendas.

The earlier snobbery of Henry Rowland, imported from Germany's own attitudes toward the commercialization of science, began to be leavened by the obvious utility of that commercialization. Out of industrial R&D, tinkerers like Edison were creating blockbuster products that led to enormous commercial advantage, as Chandler's work has shown. As a result of the decentralized, local funding and focus of higher education, the rise in the number and quality of U.S. universities expanded the pool of qualified engineers and scientists from which corporations could staff their own in-house industrial research labs.

Two developments exemplify the functioning of this decentralized system. First, the federal government established a land-grant program for state universities that focused on science and technology after the Civil War. Today's "Big Ten" universities largely grew out of these land grants. Most important, these schools were start-ups, unconstrained by any history and not locked into a prior approach to their mission. They were quick to embrace the engineering disciplines as worthy of study, unlike the established universities such as Harvard and Yale, which initially adopted an attitude toward this practical application of science that was similar to Rowland's.

Second, the federal government established funding for agricultural extension initiatives with the Morrill Act of 1862 and successive acts in 1887 and 1906.[6] This legislation created a network of government-funded, locally based research offices, to disseminate new ideas in agriculture (some of which came out of these Big Ten schools!). This system increased the productivity of U.S. farms dramatically, with innovations such as hybrid seeds, crop rotation, and pest control.

Together, these research initiatives solidified the nascent links between the federal government, higher education, and industry. And these links would be strengthened substantially by the advent of World War II.

World War II:
Mobilizing Scientific Knowledge in U.S. Society

World War II production efforts were a catalyst for a new emphasis on efficiency, production, and innovation in U.S. industry. President Franklin D. Roosevelt sensed that the wartime system that had successfully created the atomic bomb and the first computer could be applied to peacetime innovations as well: "New frontiers of the mind are before us, and if they are pioneered with the same vision, boldness, and drive with which we have waged this war, we can create a fuller and more fruitful employment and a fuller and more fruitful life."[7] Near the end of the war, on November 17, 1944, with the preceding statement, Roosevelt commissioned Vannevar Bush, the director of the Office of Scientific Research and Development (which had overseen the military research programs during the war) to study the ways in which the United States could capitalize on its military and scientific advances in peacetime. Roosevelt asked Bush how the government could translate military sciences into civilian improvements, increase the number of trained U.S. scientists, and aid research activities in the public and private sector. Bush's resulting report, entitled *Science: The Endless Frontier*, became the cornerstone of U.S. postwar policy toward science and technology.

Paramount to Bush was the need for an increase in the federal funding of basic research at the university level. Although the United States had made considerable strides in applied R&D (evidenced by technologies such as the airplane, the radio, and radar), these innovations had been dependent on basic research imported from Europe. Even the atomic bomb had depended critically on the knowledge of scientists who had been trained in Europe. This dependence could no longer continue, Bush argued: "[A] nation which depends on others for its new basic scientific knowledge will be slow in its industrial progress and weak in its competitive position in world trade, regardless of its mechanical skill."[8]

To address this deficiency, Bush proposed the formation of a National Research Foundation, which would be responsible for coordinating

Japan, China now

efforts between the branches of government, the universities, the military, and industry. Government would distribute funding directly to universities to increase basic research initiatives; these developments would benefit both industry and the military. In turn, commerce and the military would then be able to focus primarily on applied technology.

While Bush's central coordination mechanism was resisted, the decentralized approach he advocated to using federal monies to stimulate more R&D in the universities and in industry was adopted. Table 2-1 shows both the rapid increase in government funding for R&D, and the different players in the R&D system. This system characterized the U.S. innovation system for the next forty years. Note that the amount of funding for R&D from the government exceeded that of industry for most of the postwar period until 1985. Since then, industry has provided the majority of funding for R&D.

TABLE 2-1

Sources of Funding for U.S. R&D by Sector (1992 Dollars in Millions)

Year	Government	Industry	Universities, Colleges	Other Nonprofit	Total
1930	248	1,195	210	59	1,712
1940	614	2,077	280	94	3,063
1955	17,977	12,902	453	318	31,650
1960	39,185	20,281	666	538	60,670
1970	53,559	26,944	1,099	894	82,498
1975	49,534	34,543	1,544	1,122	86,743
1980	43,070	37,084	1,810	1,273	83,237
1985	48,022	50,133	2,175	1,469	101,799
1991	63,035	95,030	3,505	3,372	164,942
1995	59,375	102,994	3,816	3,679	169,864
1998	59,083	125,469	4,342	3,717	192,611

Sources: Years 1930 and 1940: Vannevar Bush, *Science: The Endless Frontier* (Washington, DC: U.S. Government Printing Office, 1945); years 1955–1985: Richard Nelson, ed., *National Innovation Systems* (Oxford: Oxford University Press, 1993); and years 1991–1998: National Science Foundation, *National Patterns of R&D Resources* (Washington, DC: National Science Foundation, March 1999).

For this coordination to succeed, Bush recognized that the quality and the quantity of scientific personnel had to be dramatically increased. To remedy this situation, the Seventy-Eighth Congress passed Public Law 346. This law, "commonly known as the GI Bill of Rights, provides for the education of veterans of this war under certain conditions, at the expense of the Federal Government."[9] In addition, soldiers with scientific talent were eligible for new scholarships that would encourage them to pursue advanced degrees in the sciences. The GI Bill extended the federal government's role of funding academic research to funding the tuition of deserving students.

This expanded charter and increased funding enormously expanded the role of universities in the U.S. innovation system. The processes that Bush's office used during wartime led to the successful deployment of radar, the atomic bomb, timed fuses, and cryptography. These same processes now deeply influenced his proposed peacetime model of innovation. Indeed, the virtue of Bush's model wasn't simply that more money was being spent; rather, it was *how* the money was spent. Bush's vision of an "endless frontier" elevated academic science to become an equal partner with government and industry in the mission to apply science to military and societal needs. Government would fund basic scientific research, but most of that research would *not* be conducted by government labs; instead it would be housed at leading academic universities, governed by norms of scientific inquiry and publication. This arrangement greatly expanded the pool of knowledge available to society and to industry, particularly through the rising tide of college graduates and post-college graduates.

This expanded but decentralized pool of knowledge inspired industrial firms to increase the amount of resources they devoted to their own R&D. This led to the expansion of many corporate labs that had been formed before the war, such as Bell Laboratories and General Electric's and DuPont's labs. It also led to the formation of new labs, such as the T. J. Watson Laboratories at IBM, the Sarnoff Labs at RCA, and later on, HP Labs and Xerox PARC.

Some enormous commercial scientific achievements were realized as a result of these in-house industrial laboratories. Bell Labs scientists who were exploring the source of background static in microwave satellite transmissions found that the source of this static was rooted in a previously unknown phenomenon. They eventually received the Nobel Prize for the discovery of dark matter in the universe. Scientists at IBM received another Nobel Prize for their discovery of superconductivity.

DuPont discovered and innovated a number of new chemical fibers and new materials. A rapidly growing young company, Xerox, exploited the discovery of using electrostatic charges to fix toner onto paper and catapulted itself into the *Fortune* 500 through its successful commercialization of xerography.

Companies that made the investments leading to these discoveries manifestly benefited from them. With a legal monopoly in telecommunications, AT&T could introduce new products that embodied applications of its science out of Bell Labs without fear of misappropriation. IBM had a near monopoly in its mainframe computer business. The company mastered the art of staging the introduction of new technological advances in ways that maximized its own profits and maximized the problems of its competitors who attempted to follow IBM's lead. Xerox similarly held a commanding share of its market with the most advanced copiers, able to copy the highest volumes and to perform the most elaborate feeding, sorting, and binding functions. These and many other successes caused companies to pursue strategies of significant investment in basic research, organized through central research laboratories.

The result was a golden age for internal R&D. Corporate R&D organizations were working at the cutting edge of scientific research. Inside their four walls, they featured the best equipment, staffed by the best people and focused on long-term R&D programs that were funded at significant levels. There seemed to be strong economies of scale in R&D as well: The largest companies in the industry were able to fund the most research and generally enjoyed the most advanced technologies as a result. These companies' lead in research and technology helped them achieve the largest profits of all the firms in the industry. And this commitment to internal R&D was viewed as a barrier to entry for their competitors: Any company that wanted to enter the industry would have to make similarly large, long-term investments in order to compete. One had to think ahead many moves to win this game of chess.

X The logic underlying this approach to innovation was one of closed, centralized, internal R&D. At its root, the logic implies a need for deep vertical integration. In other words, in order to do anything, one must do everything internally, from tools and materials, to product design and manufacturing, to sales, service, and support. Outside the fortified central R&D castles, the knowledge landscape was assumed to be rather barren. Consequently, the firm should rely on itself—and not feeble outside suppliers—for its critical technologies.

This was when the term *not invented here* was first coined. The term originally had a negative meaning. If a technology was not produced inside a company (i.e., not invented here), the company could not be sure of the quality, performance, and availability of the particular technology. IBM, for example, began making its own heads and media in its disk-drive business in the 1960s, because it could not get these critical components made to its requirements from outside suppliers on a timely basis. It developed the basic components, assembled them into subsystems, designed systems out of these components, manufactured the systems at its own factories, distributed and serviced the systems themselves, and even handled the financing of the systems.[10]

Similarly, Xerox needed to make its own toner, its own copier, its own light lens, and its own feeding and sorting subsystems in order to deliver high-volume, high-quality xerography to its customers. Because Xerox was pushing mechanical and electrical systems further than anyone else in its applications, there was no available supplier base with which to work. During the early years, Xerox found that it even needed to make its own *paper*, to get the optimal paper characteristics that would feed well through its copier systems. The golden age of R&D was an age of deep vertical integration, born of necessity (since there were few capable external alternatives) and of virtue (since it was easy to capture value from one's R&D when one controlled the entire value chain of business activities, thanks to dominant positions in one's product markets).

Figure 2-1 shows this Closed Innovation paradigm for managing R&D. The solid lines show the boundary of each firm, A and B. Ideas flow into each firm, on the left, and flow out to the market on the right. They are screened and filtered during the research process, and the surviving ones are transferred into development and then taken to market.

Figure 2-1 also shows the knowledge landscape that arose from the pattern of deep, vertically integrated R&D organizations such as firm A and firm B, and the impoverished landscape that surrounded them. Although there were many ideas, few of them were available outside the walls of these firms.

These concepts implicitly assume that all these activities are conducted within the firm. There is no other path for ideas to come into the firm, nor is there any other path for products and services to leave the firm. This tight coupling also assumes no leakage out of the system. Provided that the company keeps a flow of new ideas into its R&D pipeline, it will turn many of these ideas into new products and capture

FIGURE 2-1

The Knowledge Landscape in Closed Innovation

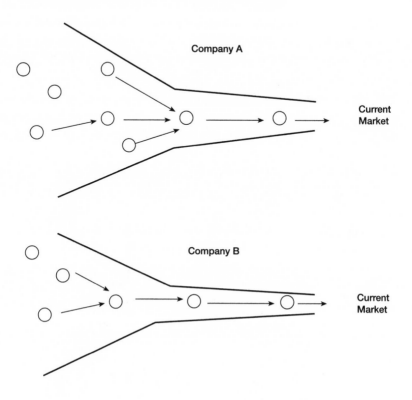

the value from these ideas. This flow will allow the company to reinvest in further research, which in turn will lead to future profitable products. Thus, the company's R&D system is sustainable over time.

The Tension Between Research and Development

This is not to say that this period of industrial innovation had no problems. One tension was the different incentives of research and of development in responding to a particular technology project. Research is fundamentally about the exploration of new frontiers, punctuated by occasional flashes of insight that lead to exciting new discoveries. These discoveries cannot be predicted in advance; nor can they be scheduled to arrive at particular dates. Nor do the people recruited into research organizations regard schedules as particularly valuable structures to aid in their discoveries. Most corporate researchers are highly trained scientists and engineers, often with Ph.D.'s in their fields. Companies recruit these individuals by offering them attractive salaries, significant discretion over the choice of projects they work on, and considerable freedom to publish their results. These researchers' skills are highly specialized to narrow domains of scientific inquiry, which makes them hard to retrain if and when business conditions changed.

These highly trained professionals are able to monitor significant research developments in their professional communities and then apply them to the company's business. They typically work on projects that have a long way to go before the results are ready to go to market. Indeed, most research organizations do not actually take their ideas all the way to market. Instead, companies restrict their research function to the discovery and early exploration of ideas, and then hand over the task of developing these into products to the development organization.

The research function is almost always structured as a cost center. Its financial goal each year is to stay within budget. Over time, the manager of the research function wants to kick out the mature, established research projects, in which most of the conceptual learning has already taken place. The manager also wants to move out the older researchers gracefully, to make room for young research talent. This turnover allows the manager to start new projects and infuses new ideas and energy into the research organization. This process of renewal makes the labs more attractive as a place to work for aspiring researchers.

Development, by contrast, takes the output of research as an input into its own process. This function is led by engineers, who are trained to solve problems within certain constraints, such as time and budget. It produces products and services that embody the research ideas so that they may be sold into the market. Such development involves a more predictable time horizon than that of the research process. Development managers seek to identify, characterize, and then minimize risks in creating new products and services. In contrast to the "blue sky" environment of research, development is fundamentally about making and hitting schedule targets and budgets, to convert discoveries into new products and services.

The development function is usually part of a business unit, which is structured as a profit center, with its own profit-and-loss (P&L) statement. Managers of development want to incorporate new inputs from research when they are as well characterized and understood as possible.

In this way, the managers can use the new research inputs with little further expense. Inputs that are not well understood require further development before they can be used in new products. This further development work is costly and hurts the business's P&L. Worse, poorly understood inputs pose a greater risk that the development group will miss the product introduction schedule. Since the development organization must integrate the new research inputs with many other technologies, the interactions of the new technology with the rest of the system make it extremely difficult to execute complex programs.[11]

The conflicting objectives of research and development create a budgetary disconnect between the two. The research cost center wants to get moving on to a new idea, whereas the development profit center wants more work done on the current research idea before taking over its further funding:

Research Organization	*Development Organization*
• Cost center	• Profit center
• Discovery: Why?	• Execution: How?
• Hard to predict	• Hit targets
• Hard to schedule	• Hit schedules
• Create possibilities	• Minimize risk
• Identify problems and how to think about them	• Solve problems within constraints

One way that many companies ended up managing this disconnect was to create a buffer that separated the two processes, so that development was not tightly coupled to research. This buffer effectively placed research ideas "on the shelf" until the development organization was ready to work on them. The research center would essentially say, "We're done with this," while the development people would reply, "We don't think it's ready yet." Thus, projects would stop receiving funding from research, while development would defer funding their further development. The projects would sit in the buffer, on the shelf, waiting for the organization to make use of them. Many organizations found that they had numerous research discoveries piled up on the shelf in this fashion.

This characterized the innovation system of many leading U.S. companies during the postwar golden age. Large companies invested in large central research labs and enjoyed significant downstream market positions that allowed them to capture a significant portion of the value they created from the technology in their labs. The companies were able to control the output of their knowledge and create value-added products with their technology. They could reinvest these returns in more research and create a virtuous cycle. This research output was managed as a knowledge bank, in which ideas were kept on the shelf until a downstream business was ready and willing to use them.

In certain industries, the golden age continues, and this internally focused approach to R&D remains well suited to managing innovation. In these industries, the protection of intellectual property is very tight, or regulatory restrictions are very high, or both; start-ups seldom arise; and VC makes little investment. The firms have the ability to store their technologies on the shelf until they are ready to take their discoveries to market, without fear of significant leakage of that technology out of the company and into a start-up or another rival company.[12]

In many other industries, though, the logic underlying the Closed Innovation paradigm has become fundamentally obsolete. Several factors have eroded this paradigm.

Erosion Factor 1:
The Increasing Availability and Mobility of Skilled Workers

One erosion factor that has led to the demise of the Closed Innovation paradigm is the increasing availability and mobility of skilled workers. This factor has many causes. Among them was the explosion in college graduates and postgraduate students fostered by the GI Bill and other programs to stimulate the expansion of higher education. The supply of well-trained, knowledgeable people expanded tremendously during the postwar period. The growth of this population represented a large increase in the "raw material" able to produce useful knowledge.

Other trends in the labor market increased the mobility of these highly trained workers, diffusing the knowledge that they possessed from the fortified towers of internal R&D organizations to suppliers, customers, partners, universities, start-ups, consultants, and other third parties. With information more widespread, new companies could access useful knowledge that previously they could not. One company could profit from the training and experience of another company by hiring away some of the latter company's workers, or through hiring consultants who used to work at another company, without paying any compensation in return.

This mobility of well-trained workers created something of an auction market for highly qualified talent. Talented engineers could "surf" from company to company, selling their talents to the highest bidder. A fluid labor market permitted even start-up firms to pioneer the commercialization of promising new technological opportunities. For individual entrepreneurs, this fluid market created a powerful attraction to exit the larger firm for the opportunity to earn a significant reward. It also created strong reasons for individuals to invest in their own education, to learn as much as they could so that they might increase their value in the auction market for talent.

A particularly dramatic example of this "learning by hiring away" came in the hard-disk-drive industry. IBM for many years was the dominant innovator in the industry, earning the lion's share of the industry's profits, performing most of the long-term research driving the technology, and obtaining the majority of the patents in the industry.

Despite the company's dominance, the mobility of disk-drive engineers caused IBM's leadership to erode over time. An engineer named Al Shugart left IBM to go to Memorex, where he helped Memorex improve its hard-disk drives that plugged into IBM mainframe computers. Then he left Memorex to start a company called Shugart Associates, pursuing a new kind of hard-disk drive, the 8-inch disk drive, intended for minicomputers and workstations. Eventually, when he fell out with the financial backers of Shugart, he left to start another new company, called Seagate, which made still smaller 5¼-inch drives for personal computers.

With each job change he made, Shugart took a substantial number of people with him to the new company. Each of Shugart's new start-up companies was thus able to hit the ground running, with highly experienced personnel that were trained on someone else's money. Nor is Shugart unique in this approach. Of the ninety-nine U.S.-based start-up companies that entered the disk-drive industry, twenty-one had former IBM employees on their founding teams.[13] Figure 2-2 shows a partial genealogy of hard-disk-drive firms from 1973 through 1996. It shows the diaspora of companies with former IBM personnel in their top management teams at the time they were founded. The shaded companies were still in operation in December 1996. Most of the offspring, though, have gone out of business. In 2002, IBM itself sold its hard-disk-drive business to Hitachi, culminating almost fifty years of innovation in magnetic storage.

U.S. immigration policy also played an important role in the availability of skilled professionals, drawing in talented graduate students from other countries. Though viewed as a "brain drain" by the home countries of these graduate students, the students' migration was a "brain gain" for many U.S. firms and industries. A 1998 study by the National Science Foundation found that over 50 percent of the postdoctoral students at MIT and Stanford University were not U.S. citizens and that more than 30 percent of computer professionals in Silicon Valley were born outside the United States.[14] Again, the U.S. firms paid no compensation to the home countries that educated these people, who then moved to the United States.[15]

The influx of highly talented foreigners and the high mobility of other skilled workers has been wonderful for the U.S. economy. U.S. firms get some of the best and the brightest people working on problems whose solutions create real economic value. But there are real

FIGURE 2-2

IBM and Its Offspring Hard-Disk-Drive Companies, December 1996

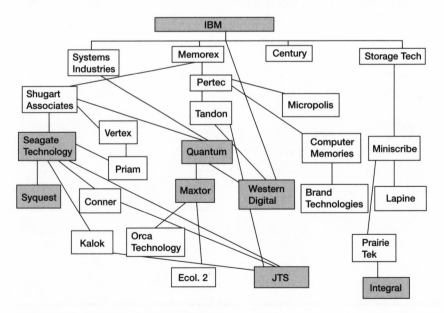

☐ Still making hard-disk-drives as of December 1996.

problems created by high-mobility labor markets for the firms with leading-edge R&D investments built up during the golden age of internal R&D. Rival firms can access their extensive experience and capabilities at a fraction of their true cost by simply hiring away "the best and the brightest." This creates a hazard for the previous employer, which jeopardizes that firm's ability to continue to invest in R&D.

Erosion Factor 2: The Venture Capital Market

Prior to 1980, little VC was available in the United States. Although there were start-up companies that arose from people who migrated out of large firms, these new enterprises had to struggle to find capital. The ability of companies to attract other talented staff to the new venture was also impaired by a lack of adequate capital to justify the risk of leaving a well-capitalized company for an unknown start-up company. While large companies with extensive investments in R&D weren't thrilled to see some of their employees leave, they weren't particularly concerned about how these departing employees would affect their own future business prospects.

FIGURE 2-3

Total Investment in U.S. Venture Capital, 1980–2001

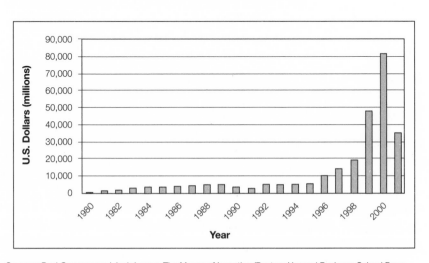

Sources: Paul Gompers and Josh Lerner, *The Money of Invention* (Boston: Harvard Business School Press, 2001), 72–73; and *Venture Economics for 2001*, <http:www.ventureeconomics.com/vee/news_ve/2002VEpress/VEpress02_04_02.htm>.

As others have discussed, there has been an enormous expansion of VC since 1980.[16] About $700 million in VC was invested in the United States in 1980, and the figure rose to more than $80 billion in 2000 (figure 2-3). Although the figure dropped to more than $36 billion in 2001, it still is an enormous amount, even when compared to the dollars invested just three years earlier.

This large and growing pool of VC created real hazards for the companies that made significant commitments to internal R&D. The knowledge that they created inside their own knowledge silos and stored in their buffers between research and development was now at much greater risk. Individual personnel from their labs could be lured away by attractive risk/reward compensation packages to join new start-up firms. This attraction was exacerbated by the booming stock market during the same period. The large firms could offer world-class equipment, tremendous freedom to choose one's research initiatives, and a stimulating intellectual environment. They could not, however, hope to match the stock-option packages of these new start-up firms.

Erosion Factor 3:
External Options for Ideas Sitting on the Shelf

The earlier tensions between the incentives of the research group and those of the development group gave rise to a buffer inventory of ideas sitting on the shelf. The tensions between these functions are not new, but now there is an important difference. As a result of the combination of erosion factors 1 and 2 (mobility and availability of workers, and VC) there exists a second, outside path to market for many of these ideas. If left on their own to wait until a development group works on them, these ideas might instead go outside on their own (shown as the dotted line in figure 2-4).

As product life cycles shorten and as external options grow, it becomes increasingly important for companies to increase the metabolic rate at which they process knowledge. Customers won't wait indefinitely for better products, and competitors won't make them wait for those products. If a company's internal development organization is not ready to use a new research result, it cannot blithely assume that the result will always remain on the shelf, available whenever the development group chooses to work with it. Disillusioned employees, possibly financed by VC, have other ways of commercializing their ideas. And

FIGURE 2-4

The Outside Option for Ideas on the Shelf

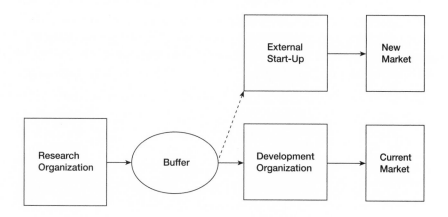

there may be new markets to explore with these ideas, which the established company may be poorly suited to address.

Erosion Factor 4:
The Increasing Capability of External Suppliers

(handwritten annotation: ~ specialized eng firms (SEFs) in Africa worked for tech)

When companies like IBM wanted to increase the performance of their early mass-storage systems, they found that they could not rely on external suppliers to supply components of sufficient technical capability in sufficient volume with high quality. More generally, companies seeking to create new products and services in the middle of the twentieth century found that the surrounding environment lacked the requisite knowledge, production experience, and financial capital to serve as reliable partners in building the materials, components, and systems needed to serve the market.

Thanks to the confluence of many of the factors already noted, such as the expansion of universities and university enrollments, the availability of well-trained workers to companies of all sizes, and the increased presence of VC, the external supply base is much more extensively developed in most industries today than it was after World War II. These suppliers' offerings are now often of equal or superior quality to what a company can achieve internally.

The presence of capable external suppliers is a double-edged sword for large companies with extensive internal R&D investments. On the one hand, it supports the ability to apply these R&D investments in a wide variety of areas in less time than it would take if the company had to perform every function in the value chain on its own. The large companies can thus move faster and cover more potential market opportunities. On the other hand, these external suppliers are available to all comers, which places pressure on companies that have built up substantial inventories of R&D projects currently sitting on the shelf. These external suppliers let other companies move faster and serve a wider range of markets as well. This could enable the unused buffer inventory of ideas and technologies lying on the shelf between research and development to move out of the firm into the market, with or without the participation of the company that funded the original R&D.

The Erosion of the Closed Innovation Paradigm

These erosion factors have loosened the linkage between research and development in the Closed Innovation paradigm. Ideas can no longer be inventoried on the shelf, because they will leak out to the broader environment over time. A company that fails to utilize its technology may later see variants of those ideas exploited by other firms.

At the same time, these erosion factors collectively create a rich variety of possible research inputs available outside the firm. These external results could be brought into the firm and turned into new products and services. What previously was a fundamentally closed, internal environment (where the firm had to create ideas in order to use them) has transformed into an open environment (where the firm can create ideas for external and internal use, and the firm can access ideas from the outside as well as from within).

More subtly, these erosion factors have rearranged the landscape of knowledge. The distribution of knowledge has shifted away from the tall towers of central R&D facilities, toward variegated pools of knowledge distributed across the landscape. Companies can find vital knowledge in customers, suppliers, universities, national labs, consortia, consultants, and even start-up firms. Companies must structure themselves to leverage these distributed pools, instead of ignoring them in the pursuit of their internal R&D agendas. Increasingly, companies cannot expect to warehouse their technologies until their own businesses make use of them. If a company does not use its ideas with alacrity, it may lose those ideas to outside organizations.

This shift in the knowledge landscape is disturbing to people familiar with the earlier paradigm. Isn't it problematic for ideas to start in the firm, but then leak outside? If the firm invests in research, but the results leak out to other firms, which free-ride on the investing firm's efforts, how can the original firm continue to invest in research going forward? Where will the vital discoveries and breakthroughs come from? Seen from the perspective of the Closed Innovation paradigm, these are valid, even urgent questions. Seen from the perspective of a broader knowledge landscape, though, they put the emphasis on the wrong issues and distract firms from how they might profit from a different knowledge landscape. How firms can benefit from a different innovation model will be the focus of chapter 3.

3

The Open
Innovation Paradigm

I N THIS CHAPTER, we will explore an emerging paradigm that is re-
placing the earlier paradigm of Closed Innovation. This new approach is based on a different knowledge landscape, with a different
logic about the sources and uses of ideas. Open Innovation means that
valuable ideas can come from inside or outside the company and can go
to market from inside or outside the company as well. This approach
places external ideas and external paths to market on the same level of
importance as that reserved for internal ideas and paths to market during the Closed Innovation era.

Figure 3-1 depicts the knowledge landscape that results from the
flow of internal and external ideas into and out of firms A and B. Ideas
abound in this environment, not only within each firm, but also outside
the firms. These ideas are available to be used, and often the people who
created them are similarly available for hire. The availability and quality
of these external ideas change the logic that led to the formation of the
centralized R&D silos of the Closed Innovation paradigm.

How to Access Useful Knowledge:
The Thought Experiment One Hundred Years Later

Let's return to the thought experiment of chapter 2. What if you had become a leading company in your industry in 2000, rather than in 1900?
How would you go about creating a mechanism to generate useful
knowledge, to continue to advance the technologies that support your
growing business? Would you choose to create an internal, central
R&D organization that was responsible for investigating all the important areas of science behind the technology you plan to use?

FIGURE 3-1

The Knowledge Landscape in the Open Innovation Paradigm

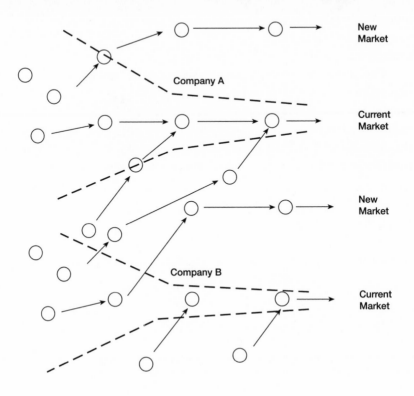

The knowledge landscape in which you operate makes a big difference in how you would answer that question. Today, there is an abundance of knowledge in virtually every field around you. The proliferation of public scientific databases and online journals and articles, combined with low-cost Internet access and high transmission rates, can give you access to a wealth of knowledge that was far more expensive and time-consuming to reach as recently as the early 1990s.

The universities are full of professors with deep expertise. Better yet, these professors are surrounded by graduate students, who apprentice themselves to these professors. While the science that they do is excellent, many professors and their graduate students are clearly eager to apply that science to business problems. The norms of science and engineering have changed as well: There aren't many Henry Rowlands in university science departments anymore.

As government funding for basic scientific research declines in real terms in most scientific fields, faculty have even learned to seek out industry support for their research. Their search has helped them become more astute about the needs and problems of industry. Their future research agendas are coming to reflect important problems being confronted in industry.[1]

This abundance of knowledge is not limited to just the top handful of universities. Literally dozens of universities boast world-class research capabilities in at least a few areas (though only the top universities can maintain scientific excellence across a broad range of areas). Moreover, the demonstrable success of U.S. higher education has led to the imitation of that model in many other areas of the world. Whether it is the top technology institutes in India, the Hong Kong University of Science and Technology, the National University of Singapore, or the Technion in Israel, the quality of scientific knowledge has spread well beyond the shores of the United States to reach much of the developed world. In the world of the Internet, leading scholars from around the world contribute new papers to online archives, creating a global community of scholars.

The End of the Knowledge Monopolies

The rise of excellence in university scientific research and the increasingly diffuse distribution of that research means that the knowledge monopolies built by the centralized R&D organizations of the twentieth century have ended. Knowledge is far more widely distributed today, when compared to, say, the 1970s. And this far greater diffusion of knowledge changes the viability and desirability of a Closed Innovation approach to accessing and taking new ideas to market.

Another example of the greater distribution of knowledge in the knowledge landscape is the change in the distribution of patent awards. Patents are one outcome of a knowledge generation process, and thanks to the U.S. Patent and Trademark Office (USPTO), there are good data available on who receives U.S. patents. Table 3-1 shows which firms were the top twenty patent recipients of U.S. patents during the 1990s. Of the 153,492 patents issued by the USPTO in 1999, these top twenty companies received 17,842 patents in that year, only 11.6 percent of all awarded patents. On a related issue, the number of patents held by individuals and small firms has risen from about 5 percent in 1970 to more than 20 percent in 1992.[2]

TABLE 3-1

List of Top Twenty Organizations Holding U.S. Patents (ranked by cumulative patents held)

Company	NUMBER OF PATENTS						
	Pre-1986	1986	1990	1995	1999	Total
1. International Business Machines	9,078	598	609	1,383	2,756	26,342
2. General Electric Company	14,763	714	787	758	699	25,868
3. Hitachi, Ltd.	5,957	731	908	910	1,008	19,055
4. Canon Kabushiki Kaisha	3,067	523	870	1,087	1,795	18,784
5. Toshiba Corporation	3,598	694	893	969	1,200	16,881
6. Eastman Kodak Company	5,780	229	721	772	992	16,032
7. AT&T Corp.	9,213	437	430	638	278	14,837
8. U.S. Philips Corporation	6,519	503	637	504	735	14,575
9. E. I. du Pont de Nemours and Co.	7,560	329	481	441	338	13,735
10. Motorola, Inc.	3,244	334	394	1,012	1,192	13,682
11. Mitsubishi Denki Kabushiki Kaisha	1,619	360	868	973	1,054	13,408
12. Siemens Aktiengesellschaft	6,388	410	508	419	722	13,324

NUMBER OF PATENTS

Company	Pre-1986	1986	1990	1995	1999	Total
13. NEC Corporation	1,601	234	437	1,005	1,842	12,464
14. Bayer Aktiengesellschaft	6,541	389	499	327	341	12,189
15. Westinghouse Electric Corp.	7,896	398	436	170	11	11,970
16. Matsushita Electric Industrial Co., Ltd.	3,193	224	343	854	1,052	11,782
17. U.S. Navy	7,820	216	265	330	348	11,691
18. General Motors Corporation	6,781	294	379	282	275	11,660
19. Xerox Corporation	5,106	219	252	551	665	11,638
20. Fuji Photo Film Co., Ltd.	3,092	448	768	504	539	11,401
Total patents awarded, top 20 firms					17,842	
Total patents awarded, all firms					153,492	

Source: U.S. Patent and Trademark Office, "Technology Assessment and Forecast Report, August 1999," in *All Technologies Report January 1, 1963 to June 1, 1999* (Washington, DC: USPTO, 1999), B1–B2.

Of the 153,492 patents granted in the United States in 1999 (against 270,000 applications), foreign companies and individuals held 45 percent. Japanese individuals and firms held 20 percent of all 1999 U.S. patents issued, making them the largest single foreign owner, and Japanese firms were in eight of the twelve top spots for new U.S. patents granted to companies in 1998, receiving 10,438 that year. Worldwide, the Japanese Patent Office had the highest ratio of domestic to foreign applications, 90 percent, while both the United States and Japan had high ratios when compared with European systems (Germany had 45 percent and Britain 29 percent).

A second indicator of increased knowledge diffusion is how many U.S. patents non-U.S. companies now hold. As table 3-1 shows, 45 percent of these patents were held by companies headquartered outside the United States. Some of these foreign companies are now among the top twenty recipients of U.S. patents. This is a second indication of knowledge diffusion, a diffusion beyond the borders of the United States.

A third indicator of this diffusion is reflected in U.S. government statistics of R&D by size of enterprise within the United States. From 1981 through 1999, the share of industrial R&D has increased greatly for companies with less than one thousand employees (table 3-2). Although large-company R&D remains an important source of R&D spending, its share of overall industrial R&D spending has fallen to 41 percent. As of 1999, the majority of R&D spending in the United States is now done by companies with less than twenty-five thousand employees—a marked change since 1981, when the largest companies did more than 70 percent of industrial R&D spending. And most of this shift occurred in the last ten years depicted on the table, between 1989 and 1999. There seem to be fewer economies of scale in R&D these days.[3]

A fourth indicator of knowledge diffusion is the rise in college graduates and post-college graduates in the United States. This rise reflects the social investment in human capital, which creates the raw material to discover and develop ideas. The abundance of well-educated workers

TABLE 3-2

Percentage of U.S. Industrial R&D by Size of Enterprise

Company Size	1981	1989	1999
< 1,000 employees	4.4	9.2	22.5
1,000 – 4,999	6.1	7.6	13.6
5,000 – 9,999	5.8	5.5	9.0
10,000 – 24,999	13.1	10.0	13.6
25,000 +	70.7	67.7	41.3

Sources: National Science Foundation, Science Resource Studies, "Survey of Industrial Research Development, 1991" (Washington: National Science Foundation) and National Science Foundation, Science Resource Studies, "Research and Development in Industry: 1999," <http:www.nsf.gov/sbe/srs/nsf02312/pdf/secta.pdf> (accessed 9 October 2002).

is a great success of U.S. public policy after World War II, though one reads little about this triumph.

There is an international dimension to this diffusion of human capital as well. At Stanford University and the Massachusetts Institute of Technology, for example, more than half of the postdoctoral scientists and engineers come from outside the United States.[4]

These diffusion forces seem likely to persist. Within the United States, the pattern of high labor mobility is unlikely to return to the earlier pattern of long-term or "lifetime" employment.[5] Pension systems in the United States are increasingly portable, meaning that they travel with the worker, rather than with the job, further promoting mobility. Although VC has retreated from the heady days of the dot-com bubble, it remains a reality that will not go away, thus enabling start-up companies to exploit the diffusion of knowledge.[6]

Knowing all this, what mechanisms would you create to access this abundance of knowledge? Would these mechanisms bear any resemblance to the central R&D lab of chapter 2?

The answer is no. The central R&D lab is based on a logic of deep vertical integration, through which a single company conducts every aspect of a business internally. But this do-it-all-yourself approach only makes sense in a world of scarce external knowledge. If instead, a leading firm wishes to advance its technology in a world of abundant knowledge and competence, it will find a great deal of value on the outside. Expertise is readily available for hire and need not require extensive internal training or the inducement of lifelong employment. One can also choose ideas from a diverse menu of discoveries at a variety of universities. A wealth of capable suppliers applying their own impressive expertise across numerous businesses is another resource ready to be tapped to harness and develop these ideas. Venture capital start-ups are developing useful technology, which was sitting on the shelf of another company, or is coming out of a university.

The logic underlying the innovation process is now completely reversed. Even the expression *not invented here* (NIH), described in chapter 2 as outside technology of which a company must be wary, today has an entirely different meaning. Today NIH means that companies need not reinvent the wheel, since they can rely on external sources to do the job effectively. Indeed, internal sources may deliver wheels at lower volume and higher cost, relative to what a world-class outside vendor, serving a worldwide market, can provide. In an abundant knowledge landscape, one can now do a great deal by focusing in a particular area, without having to do everything.

If you were trying to develop mechanisms to access useful knowledge today, you would start by surveying the surrounding knowledge landscape. You would like to use as much of the surrounding knowledge as possible and fund the creation of as little new knowledge as necessary to get the knowledge you need on a timely basis. In addition to the specialized knowledge your researchers developed to enact a strategy of deep vertical integration, your researchers will also need to scan and understand a wide range of science and technology. Then they must use this understanding to envision how to integrate promising discoveries into new systems and architectures.

What would you do to access external knowledge? At the simplest level, you might employ university professors for a summer to work alongside your own people. An even cheaper idea would be to hire some graduate students of a professor to work with you. If you wanted to carry this further, you could even choose to fund external research at a nearby university. Although you could not expect to own the results of this research, you could expect to gain early access to any promising results, and perhaps get a head start on applying those results to your industry.

If you funded a number of projects, you could expect to get proposals from researchers looking for funds. This is a low-cost way to scan the opportunity horizon in the scientific and engineering fields in which you are interested. Before you spend any money, you get to review a variety of research proposals from scholars who know a great deal about the state of the art in that area.

You might scout the activities of young start-up companies working in areas of interest to you. You could learn about their efforts in a number of ways, ranging from occasional business development discussions, to strategic alliances, to giving money to interested venture capitalists to invest in areas of value for you, to investing directly yourself in promising start-up companies.

As we will explore in chapter 6, some companies such as Intel have actually conducted our thought experiment. Intel is a rather young company, founded in 1968. Despite its impressive size, it only began a truly formal advanced R&D strategy back in 1989. The company relied almost entirely on external research up to then. Today, although Intel has created an internal research capability to some degree, it plans its research efforts by assessing what is available from the outside before charting its own course inside. Intel has a very well thought-out program of funding university research projects, spending more than $100 million a year. The company also follows closely the activities of start-ups in the computer and communications industries, through a variety of means that range from informal alliances to corporate VC investment.

In the life sciences, another scientifically intensive industry, several even younger companies such as Millennium and Genzyme are thinking hard about their own innovation strategies. Yet, as chapter 8 will show, their solutions for managing innovation also depart significantly from the traditional paradigm of R&D. Even large, successful firms such as IBM and Merck, which prospered in the Closed Innovation regime, are broadening their approach to research. They are moving beyond their internal programs, toward building access mechanisms to tap into the wealth of external knowledge around them.

Toward a New Logic of Innovation

Some longtime observers note these trends and throw up their hands in despair. The research game is over, they bemoan. Where will the seed corn that fuels the next generation of discovery come from? is another concern often voiced. Even more measured published work has concluded that industrial research is "at the end of an era."[7]

The traditional paradigm that companies used to manage industrial R&D is indeed over in most industries. But that does not mean that internal R&D itself has become obsolete. What we need is a new logic of innovation to replace the logic of the earlier period. Companies must structure themselves to leverage this distributed landscape of knowledge, instead of ignoring it in the pursuit of their own internal research agendas. Companies increasingly cannot expect to warehouse their technologies, waiting until their own businesses make use of them.

The new logic will exploit this diffusion of knowledge, rather than ignore it. The new logic turns the old assumptions on their head. Instead of making money by hoarding technology for your own use, you make money by leveraging multiple paths to market for your technology. Instead of restricting the research function exclusively to inventing new knowledge, good research practice also includes accessing and integrating external knowledge. Instead of managing intellectual property (IP) as a way to exclude anyone else from using your technology, you manage IP to advance your own business model and to profit from your rivals' use. Your own R&D strategy should benefit from external start-up companies' abilities to initiate multiple organizational experiments to commercialize technologies. You might even occasionally help fund a young start-up to explore an area of potential future interest.

This is not to say that firms should discontinue all internal research activity (see box 3-1). Nevertheless, whatever research is done internally should take into account the wealth of activity outside the firm. Nor does the new logic maintain that all outputs will henceforth fit with the company's current business. Some research outputs will not be well utilized by the firm's own businesses. However, these underutilized outputs will not last long on the shelf and should be managed accordingly. The projects that sat on the shelf between the research groups and the development groups were part of "the cost of doing business" in the old paradigm. They become revenue opportunities and potential new business platforms in the new paradigm.

The factors that promote knowledge diffusion create new opportunities. Knowledge diffusion rewards focused execution: You need not invent the most new knowledge or the best new knowledge to win. Instead, you win by making the best use of internal and external knowledge in a timely way, creatively combining that knowledge in new and different ways to create new products or services.

The New Role of Research:
Beyond Knowledge Generation to Connection

Open Innovation thinking changes the role of the research function. It expands the role of internal researchers to include not just knowledge generation, but also knowledge brokering. Previously, researchers simply added to the knowledge sitting in the silos. Today, they are also charged with moving knowledge into and out of the silos. In this new role, knowledge located from outside may be just as useful as knowledge created from within—and it should be similarly rewarded.

The additional role of identifying and accessing external knowledge, in addition to generating internal knowledge, changes the career paths of researchers inside R&D firms. While deep understanding remains valuable, its utility is multiplied when linked to and built on the investigations and achievements of others. With this Open Innovation approach to knowledge, research managers must evaluate researchers' performance in different ways. Managers may apply different paths of

Box 3-1 **The New Rationale for Internal R&D**

In a bountiful knowledge landscape, a company organizes its internal R&D for the following reasons:

- To identify, understand, select from, and connect to the wealth of available external knowledge

- To fill in the missing pieces of knowledge not being externally developed

- To integrate internal and external knowledge to form more complex combinations of knowledge, to create new systems and architectures

- To generate additional revenues and profits from selling research outputs to other firms for use in their own systems

The company will also need technologies that its internal research organization will not create. Research takes a long time to deliver useful outcomes, and company strategies change at a far faster rate than the rhythm of basic research. In the new paradigm, the company's businesses cannot (and should not) wait for the internal technologies to arrive; instead, they should access what they need, as soon as they need it—either from inside the company's own research labs or from the knowledge created in someone else's lab.

promotion and may give their researchers rotational assignments in areas that interact with external participants outside the company, such as business development.

One example of this new role comes from Merck, perhaps the leading pharmaceutical firm in the world in terms of doing its own research. Merck is well known for its commitment to significant internal scientific research and is proud of the research discoveries that its scientists have made in the twentieth century. But its 2000 annual report noted that "Merck accounts for about 1 percent of the biomedical research in the world. To tap into the remaining 99 percent, we must actively reach out to universities, research institutions and companies worldwide to bring the best of technology and potential products into Merck. The cascade of knowledge flowing from biotechnology and the unraveling of the human genome—to name only two recent developments—is far too complex for any one company to handle alone."[8]

Toward that end, Merck has now charged its internal scientists with a new task: to create a virtual lab in their research area. This means that Merck scientists don't just create excellent science in their own lab; rather, they identify and build connections to excellent science in other labs, wherever these labs may be. In the words of Merck's head of R&D, "Every senior scientist here running a project should think of herself or himself as being in charge of all the research in that field. Not just the 30 people working in our lab but the 3,000 people, say, in the world working in that field."[9]

This is a case where the messenger is as important as the message. Few would dispute that Merck is among the most scientifically capable pharmaceutical firms in the world. When a firm with Merck's reputation for the excellence of its own science determines that it needs to connect deeply with the external knowledge base to be successful, other firms would do well to follow Merck's lead.

A New Perspective Toward Venture Capital

Venture capital is a reality that will not go away. Although VC returns were terrible in 2001 and 2002 and the amount of VC funding has dropped by more than 70 percent from its peak in 2000, the amount of money available for investment remains at levels that were considered historic highs as recently as 1998.[10] The recent drop has wrung out some of the excesses in the VC industry and weeded out many of the marginal participants. But the leading firms have billions of dollars of capital under management and are making new investments in a number of promising areas.

Open Innovation companies accept that VC, and the myriad start-up firms it funds, will be an enduring part of the landscape for innovation. Companies caught in the Closed Innovation paradigm view the venture capitalists as pirates and parasites—people to be punished if possible and avoided if not. But Open Innovation companies have gotten beyond the negative consequences of venture capital. They have come to understand that there are some markedly positive benefits from having a vibrant VC community around them.

The same VC groups that threaten to extract key personnel and technology from within also constitute a seedbed of new organizations experimenting with new combinations of technologies. The groups often apply new technological combinations to nascent markets that are being neglected by the large companies. These start-ups function as a series of small laboratories that can guide the technological strategies and the market directions of large firms. Open Innovation firms regard companies financed by VCs as pilot fish for potential market opportunities, because these start-up firms are selling real products to real customers, who pay with real money. These pilot fish provide the most valid, most useful market research on future technologies and future market opportunities that money can buy.

These novel combinations provide learning opportunities for established companies to monitor, and potentially leverage, if and when they prove valuable. As evidence of the viability of these "lessons" emerges, Open Innovation firms may actually change their own technology strategies as a result. They learn faster and adapt their own strategies more rapidly, as a result of coexisting with an environment filled with venture capitalists and their start-up firms. Dismissing these groups as pirates and parasites forfeits important learning opportunities from observing the portfolio companies that they fund.

Some Open Innovation companies carry this logic even further. They may choose to foster the creation of useful start-up firms, investing in some of these experiments early on or partnering and allying with them later.[11] Occasionally, they may even acquire a few of the most promising start-ups. Open Innovation companies regard the VC community, and the start-ups the community funds, as mutualistic participants in a complex ecosystem of firms that create, recombine, compete, imitate, and interact with each other.[12]

Other Open Innovation firms actually utilize VC internally to catalyze their own innovation process. Chapter 7 shows how Lucent invests corporate VC to create new technology companies out of its underutilized technology within Bell Labs. The creation of these spin-offs affects Lucent's internal R&D in at least three important ways:

- It provides an outside path to market for technologies that might otherwise sit on the shelf within the labs. This brings in additional money to Lucent, creates additional options for its research staff, and frees up resources to hire new researchers.

- It forces technology to move faster out of the lab. Whenever the NVG identifies a candidate technology for spin-off, this starts a clock within the company's businesses. If the company doesn't commit to use that technology itself, then the NVG gets the opportunity to spin it off into a new venture. This creates a forcing function to pull technologies out of the lab at a faster rate.

• Lucent's NVG ventures provide an experimental setting for the observation of Bell Labs' technologies in different uses in different markets. As a result, Lucent acquires valuable feedback not available if the technology had stayed bottled up in the lab. By getting the technology out to the market sooner, Lucent learns more quickly about customer needs, trends, and new opportunities.

Customers also have important information that can be vital to open innovation. The most advanced, most demanding customers often push your products and services to the extreme. In doing so, they themselves attempt to create new combinations with your offerings as part of the building blocks. In a real sense, they are innovators themselves, what Eric von Hippel calls lead users.[13] These experiments may again yield new knowledge. People may use your technology in ways you never expected. In the process, customers' experiments often yield new features or requirements for what you build yourself. If you respond to these required changes, then a new round of learning can begin.

This process of innovation and discovery seeks out these iterative loops of learning. Before, companies chose to wait until the technology was "ready" to ship to customers. The mind-set was "We know what they want, and they'll wait until we say it's ready." Open Innovation companies invite the customer into the innovation process as a partner and coproducer. Here, the mind-set shifts to "Here are some of our thoughts, and here's a product that features them. What can you usefully do with it? What can we do to help you do something even more useful?"

Open Innovation and Managing Intellectual Property (IP)

Many companies relegate licensing decisions and patent protection to their legal department. To the extent that IP is part of a company's technology strategy, it is usually managed so as to preserve the design freedom of the company's internal staff. Open Innovation companies regard IP as an integral part of technology strategy and insist on managing it at a strategic level within the company. Not only are these companies interested in selling IP; they are motivated and informed buyers of IP as well.

These firms accept that rarely can a company exclusively control an important technology for an extended period. The forces that diffuse knowledge are so many and so strong, that the wiser course is to plan your technology strategy under the assumption that it will be rapidly diffused and imitated.

In a world of powerful forces that rapidly disseminates useful knowledge, the mind-set toward IP changes greatly. One implication of Open Innovation is that companies must increase the "metabolic rate" at which they access, digest, and utilize knowledge. Companies cannot treat their knowledge as static; they must treat it as fundamentally dynamic. A company cannot inventory technology advances on the shelf, for the day when they may prove valuable. Open Innovation companies use licensing extensively to create and extend markets for their technology. And the faster the technology gets out of the lab, the sooner the researchers will learn new ways to apply, leverage, and integrate that technology into new offerings.

But doesn't this run the risk of cannibalizing your own business? This fear is based on a false premise: If you don't make your products obsolete, no one else will either. While this premise may be true on occasion, it will more often be false in a world of widely distributed knowledge and competence. Competitors often find ways of inventing around a firm's IP, which allows them to enter the market very quickly, even when the firm seeks to exclude rivals from using its ideas.

The costs for moving too late are much greater than they are for moving too soon. If you err on the side of premature cannibalization, you lose some potential profit you might have been able to eke out otherwise. If you err on the side of delay, the costs are deeper and longer lasting. You lose market share among your customers and must now confront stronger competitors, who now receive additional resources from your former customers.

There is also a subtle, internal cost. Think of your researchers who worked hard to bring the technology through many difficult hurdles and got it ready to go to market. They then watch as someone on the business side squanders their efforts by holding it off the market so that current sales and margins will be maximized. How motivated will these researchers be for the next big push? Will they be willing to provide the ammunition for recapturing the terrain lost to companies that didn't delay the deployment of their new technology? If you were one of these researchers, wouldn't you be tempted to move to a company that would make active use of your ideas as soon as you had them available? Most researchers are thrilled to see their ideas in action and to learn from the use that others make of them.

Internal Competition:
Increasing the Metabolism of Knowledge

As described in chapter 2, there was a mismatch between the incentives of a laboratory, operating as a cost center, and the incentives of a development group, operating as a profit center. Open Innovation companies try to overcome this mismatch by providing additional channels to market for the technology and enabling business units to source knowledge from places beyond the internal laboratory.

Subjecting the internal path to market (i.e., the business unit expecting to receive the technology) to some competition from other paths to market is an excellent way to increase one's metabolism of new knowledge. Just because your research team comes up with a better mousetrap does not mean that your sales team is the best way to sell that mousetrap. Your sales team may be distracted by selling earlier successful innovations you have made, while some other organization may be hungry to exploit your discovery in some new and interesting way.

Most companies refuse to countenance licensing to an outside company or refuse to take equity in a new start-up to pursue the technology, because of the risk of internal competition that would result. Open Innovation companies think that a little competition may not be a bad thing. They also know that their internal marketing and sales group may pay more attention and move faster toward adopting a new technology if an external group starts having success with the technology.[14]

Setting and Advancing the Architecture with Internal R&D

The Open Innovation paradigm is not simply an approach that relies on external technologies for innovation. There remains a critical role for internal R&D in this approach: the definition of an architecture to organize the many parts of a new system. An architecture, a hierarchy of connections between disparate functions within a system, joins the technologies into a useful system. In any early stage of a technology's evolution, there are many possible ways that the different component technologies might relate with one another. The greater the number of components, the greater the number of possible interconnections between them.

Utilizing internal R&D allows the firm to create a new architecture when the many possible connections within a system are not known.

Early in the life of a promising new technology, its characteristics and capabilities may be only poorly understood. The complexities of the new approach create many ambiguities about how best to incorporate it into systems. At this stage, it is difficult to specify interconnections between the new technology and the larger system.[15] There are many possible ways to partition the system to reduce its overall complexity, and there may be no obvious best way to proceed.

Complete reliance on external technologies to determine these interconnections in such uncertain, complex circumstances is doomed to failure, since the companies making these technologies will all differ on the best way to utilize their technology. In fact, each component maker will want its technology to serve as the critical technology in the system, to enable its maker to obtain more profits and more control over the system. They may even hold up the development of the overall system, to ensure their control over a key part of the system. Moving the resolution of this interconnection problem within the firm allows the firm to bypass the possible holdup tactics by outside companies who perceive that they have obtained control over a key part of the system, due to how the relationships among its parts are defined.

In order to coordinate the complexities and resolve the ambiguities, firms must develop deep expertise in many areas—systems-level expertise—to understand how a technology really works. In so doing, they assess what aspects of the new technology have what consequences for the larger system. The activities in one functional area influence the work of another functional area, so that there is intensive information exchange both within a function and between functions. As these influences become clearer over time, companies are able to partition tasks to resolve the earlier ambiguity they faced.

The resulting interdependencies between the parts of the system are shown in figure 3-2. In this figure, components A, B, and C constitute the system, and they all interrelate. Changing one component requires changes in all the other parts of the system, because the relationships between the parts are not clearly understood.

Developing this understanding of the relationships between the parts of a system and the system as a whole is a critical role for a company's innovation system. Technically, researchers need to experiment with many varying parameters of the technology to map out how changes in one part of the system affect the response of other parts of the system. In figure 3-2, if someone changes component A in the

FIGURE 3-2

An Interdependent Architecture

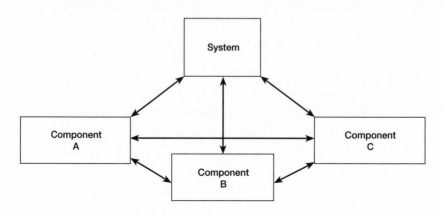

highly simplified system shown, components B and C must also change. In real systems of thousands of constituent parts, the possible interactions between the components in the system could number in the millions. Mapping out the interactions and then creating architectures to bind these interactions, without having to worry about which parts are advantaged in the struggle for profits and control, are best done through an internal R&D process.

The use of architectures to reduce interdependencies and limit complexity is only one element of the value added by internal R&D. Companies' architectures also have powerful implications for how the value chain and surrounding ecosystem will be structured. A valuable architecture not only reduces and resolves technical interdependencies, but also creates opportunities for others to contribute their expertise to the system being built. A good architecture does this even as it reserves opportunities for the firm to carve out a piece of the chain for itself to profit from the research that led to the creation of the new technology. Even very good technologies will flounder if they do not connect effectively to outside complementary technologies, while seemingly inferior ones may overtake them if they are better connected. The need for effective connections requires firms to collaborate with others in their ecosystem, as well as to compete with them.[16]

Over time, as the technology matures, interdependencies become clearer and more manageable. Companies can specify what they want,

FIGURE 3-3

A Modular Architecture

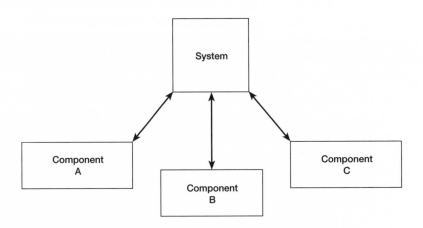

they can verify what they get, and they can add or drop vendors to reward or punish compliance. Intermediate markets can now emerge at the interfaces in the architecture, and specialist firms can enter to serve one layer within the architecture. The earlier vertical character of technological competition in the immature phase of the technology, in which internal R&D was critical to sort out the complexities, gives way to a more horizontal phase of technological competition, in which external technologies compete within the partitions of an established architecture.[17]

Figure 3-3 shows the system with the component interdependencies now well understood. In this system, components A, B, or C could change without causing any change in the other components. Firms can now compete to produce the best component A, without having to worry about the potential impact of their better product on other parts of the system. This modular mode enables companies to assemble systems more easily, since they can "plug and play" components whose interface characteristics are now well understood. In a well-established architecture, hundreds and even thousands of firms can innovate better component technologies without worrying about the possible impact of their improvements on other parts of the system.

Open Innovation firms must be adept enough to shift their approach when this transition to a modular architecture arises. Deeply vertical integration, which was vital to sorting out the intricacies of the immature technology in the earlier phase, now becomes a millstone around a company's neck. Companies must open themselves horizontally by participating in the intermediate markets within the architecture. This may involve externally buying some parts that save money, reduce development time, or provide desired features to the system. It may involve offering components externally to companies that compete at the systems level.

Crafting an Architecture for the Business

Crafting connections between technologies inside a system is necessary to manage the tremendous complexity of modern-day products and services. As challenging as that is, it is only a portion of the task of the innovating firm. It is at least as important to identify how the firm is going to create and capture value from its innovation activities. In chapter 4, we will explore the business model as a construct that creates an architecture for the business through a blend of internal and external activities. As we will see, the activities of external firms can help create significant value for a firm and its customers, while the firm's own activities are central to retaining a portion of that value for itself.

4

The Business Model

Connecting Internal and External Innovation

Not everything we start ends up fitting with our businesses
later on. Many of the ideas we work on here involve a paradigm
shift in order to deliver value. So sometimes we must work particularly hard to find the "architecture of the revenues" . . .
Here at Xerox, there has been a growing appreciation for the
struggle to create a value proposition for our research output,
and for the fact that this struggle is as valuable as inventing the
technology itself.

—*John Seely Brown*

IN CHAPTER 3, I argued that Open Innovation companies needed to
combine internal research with external ideas and then needed to deploy those ideas both within their own business and also through other
companies' businesses. The key for these firms is to figure out what necessary missing pieces should be internally supplied and how to integrate
both internal and external pieces together into systems and architectures.

The business model is a useful framework to link these technical decisions to economic outcomes. Although the term *business model* is usually applied in the context of entrepreneurial firms, it also has value in
understanding how companies of all sizes can convert technological potential into economic value. Firms can create and capture value from
their new technology in three basic ways: through incorporating the
technology in their current businesses, through licensing the technology

to other firms, or through launching new ventures that exploit the technology in new business arenas.

One critical aspect of this process is that technology by itself has no single objective value. The economic value of a technology remains latent until it is commercialized in some way, and the same technology commercialized in two different ways will yield different returns. In some instances, an innovation can successfully employ a business model already familiar to the firm. Other times, another company will have a business model that can make use of the technology via licensing, and "hires" the technology that it will in turn commercialize.

In still other cases, though, a possible new technology may have no obvious business model. Here, technology managers must expand their perspectives to find an appropriate business model or "the architecture of the revenue," to capture value from that technology. If the managers fail to do so, these technologies will yield less value to the firm than they might have yielded otherwise. If others outside the firm uncover a better business model, they may realize more value than would the firm that originally discovered the technology. Put differently, a mediocre technology pursued within a great business model may be more valuable that a great technology in a mediocre business model.

The term business model is often used, but not often clearly defined. My colleague Richard Rosenbloom and I have developed a specific and useful working definition.[1]

The functions of a business model are as follows:

1. To articulate the *value proposition*, that is, the value created for users by the offering based on the technology

2. To identify a *market segment*, that is, the users to whom the technology is useful and the purpose for which it will be used

3. To define the structure of the firm's *value chain*, which is required to create and distribute the offering, and to determine the complementary assets needed to support the firm's position in this chain

4. To specify the revenue generation mechanism(s) for the firm, and estimate the *cost structure* and *target margins* of producing the offering, given the value proposition and value chain structure chosen

5. To describe the position of the firm within the *value network* linking suppliers and customers, including identification of potential complementary firms and competitors

6. To formulate the *competitive strategy* by which the innovating firm will gain and hold advantage over rivals

Value Proposition

The process begins with articulating a value proposition latent in the new technology. This requires a preliminary definition of what the product offering will be and in what form a customer may use it. A useful way to think about a value proposition is from the intended customer's point of view: What customer problem are you solving? And how big a problem is that to the customer?

It is helpful to distinguish between small problems and large problems, through the metaphor of comparing vitamins with pain relievers. We all know that vitamins are good for us and that we should take them. Most of us, though, do not take vitamins on a regular basis, and whatever benefits vitamins provide do not seem to be greatly missed in the short term. People therefore pay relatively little for vitamins. In contrast, people know when they need a pain reliever. And they know that they need it now, not later. They can also tell quite readily whether the reliever is working. People will be willing to pay a great deal more for a pain reliever than they pay for a vitamin. In this context, the pain reliever provides a much stronger value proposition than does a vitamin— because the need is felt more acutely, the benefit is greater and is perceived much more quickly.

In other cases, a seemingly modest technology advance can provide a powerful value proposition. When Japanese companies such as Canon and Ricoh began making small, desktop-sized copiers in 1976, Xerox sneered at their technology. And well it might, for the small, cheap machines could not make very many copies per minute. Moreover, the machines couldn't feed multiple sheets automatically, collate copies, or expand or reduce the size of the copy image. What Xerox missed, though, was the very different value proposition that these smaller machines offered: Instead of going to a copy center to make your copies, you could have one in your own personal office—a real convenience.[2]

Market Segment

Of course, defining the value proposition depends on which customer
you target, which is the second attribute of the business model definition. The business model must target a group of customers, or a market
segment, to whom the proposition will be appealing and from whom resources will be received. A customer can value a technology according
to its ability to reduce the cost of a solution to an existing problem or its
ability to create new possibilities and solutions. What's more, different
prospective customers may desire different latent attributes of the technology. Xerox's large corporate customers did not see much value in the
first-generation copiers of Canon, Ricoh, and other Japanese entrants,
although individuals and small businesses saw a great deal of value.

Firms need to define a set of customers so that they can decide what
technological attributes to target in development. In any market of reasonable size, there will likely be many technical alternatives, target markets, and prospective competitors for developers to consider. Targeting
a specific market with a clear value proposition informs choices of what
must be done—and what can be omitted—in the technical domain. This
targeting gives scientists and engineers signals for where they should
focus their activities. With this focus, firms can resolve the many trade-
offs that arise in the course of development (e.g., cost versus performance, or weight versus power). Until you know who your customers are
and what they value in your offering, you don't know what you must provide and what you can afford *not* to do. If a company fails to focus its project sufficiently, it risks burdening the resulting offering with too many
features of dubious benefit: resulting in vitamins, not pain relievers.

Value Chain

Only now are we ready for the third attribute, the position of the firm
within the value chain, which is the attribute that most people associate
with the business model. Knowing the intended market, the intended
value proposition, and the intended specification of the offering, you
can construct the value chain that will deliver these elements. The
value chain must achieve two goals: It must create value throughout the
chain (delivering that value to the customer at the end of the chain),

production & distribution

and it must allow the firm to claim some sufficient portion of value from the chain to justify its participation. The value chain coordinates the many activities needed to create and deliver the pain reliever to the intended customer.

Note that creating value is necessary, but not sufficient, for a firm to profit from its value chain. Once the firm has identified the value chain needed to deliver its offering, it must then address how it will appropriate some portion of that value for itself. As Michael Porter has powerfully demonstrated, the ability to claim value will depend on the balance of forces between the firm, its customers, its suppliers, and its competitors.[3] Other research has shown that claiming value also depends on the availability of complementary goods and services, which increase the value of a company's own offerings. And within the firm, the presence of complementary assets such as manufacturing, distribution, and brand helps the firm keep some of the value it creates.[4]

Cost Structure and Target Margins

Now we are ready to define the *architecture of the revenues*—how a customer will pay, how much to charge, and how the value created will be apportioned between customers, the firm itself, and its suppliers. There are many options here, including outright sale, renting, charging by the transaction, advertising and subscription models, licensing, and even giving away the product and selling the after-sale support and services. A company also can employ more than one payment mechanism, as newspapers do when they charge readers for circulation and advertisers for ad placements.

Once you know the general specifications of the offering and the general contours of the value chain, you can then develop an understanding of its likely cost structure. This preliminary sense of price and cost yields the target margins. Target margins provide the justification for the real and financial assets required to realize the value proposition. The margins and assets together establish the threshold for financial scalability of the technology into a viable business: In order for the business to attract sufficient capital for growth, it must offer investors the credible prospect of an attractive return on the assets required to create and expand the model.

Value Network

Creating and appropriating value also involves third parties outside the immediate value chain. Taken together, these outside parties form a value network.[5] The value network created around a given business shapes the role that suppliers, customers, and third parties play in influencing the value captured from the commercialization of an innovation. Besides increasing the supply of complementary goods on the supply side, the value network can increase the network effects among consumers on the demand side. Building strong connections to a value network can leverage the value of a technology. Failure to construct such a value network can diminish a technology's potential value, particularly if that technology competes with a rival technology that does enjoy a strong value network.

Competitive Strategy

We are now ready for the final function of the business model: how the firm formulates its competitive strategy for its chosen market. Porter's early 1980s research in this area emphasized the need to compete on cost, on differentiation, or on a niche basis. More recent work has examined the underpinnings of what allows a company to sustain a profitable position in the market. Key factors for sustaining competitive success include the ability to gain differential access to key resources, the creation of internal processes that are valuable to customers and difficult for competitors to imitate, and the past experience and future momentum of the firm in the market.[6]

The Cognitive Implications of the Business Model

As the explanation just noted reveals, there is a lot to consider when constructing a business model. And it is this very complexity that leads to a very important, less-often-discussed aspect of a business model: its cognitive implications.

As noted in chapter 1, a company often must pursue innovation opportunities in an environment of high technical and market uncertainty. It is extremely difficult for managers to understand the myriad possible choices that they must make to connect new technologies to new markets. And the world of technical choices differs greatly from the world of economic and social choices. Because each domain is rich and complex in its own right, companies usually have specialized personnel to focus within each domain. But defining the business model requires managers to link the physical domain of technical inputs (capacity, speeds, functions, etc.) to an economic domain of outputs (value to consumers, price, warranties, support, distribution channels, etc.) in the face of great technical and market uncertainty. In truth, no one person fully understands the totality of the task the organization is performing. This is the most important role of a business model: to create a heuristic, a simplified cognitive map, from the technical domain of inputs to the social domain of outputs, as depicted in figure 4-1.

As figure 4-1 shows, the business model serves as an intermediate construct that links the technical and economic domains. While technical managers may not understand the benefit to consumers from increasing the capability and performance of their technology, they may be able to comprehend how their decisions will impact a defined value proposition to a chosen group of customers. And marketing managers will not know the preferences of their customers on many technical topics, but will have a good idea of how specific improvements in the value proposition can be converted into higher prices, greater market shares, and greater profits. In figure 4-1, the firm's realization of economic value from its technology depends on its choice of business model, rather than from some inherent characteristic of the technology itself.

FIGURE 4-1

The Business Model as a Cognitive Map Across Domains

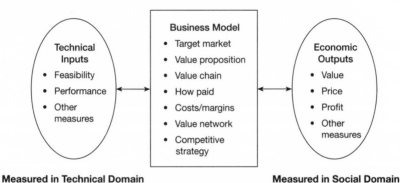

Measured in Technical Domain　　　　　　　　**Measured in Social Domain**

Constructing a business model requires managers to deal with significant complexity and ambiguity. We know from earlier research that managers cannot—and do not—exhaustively evaluate every alternative when they confront such situations. Instead, they apply cognitive filters to reduce this complexity to manageable levels.[7] Managers include information that fits with the logic of their current business model and filter out information at variance with that model. Such selection is helpful and even necessary to make sense of the tremendous amount of information that comes in each day. But in the process of using these filters, biases creep into managers' decisions, precisely because they screen out information that conflicts with their current business model. This bias can lead to a cognitive trap, in which the firm misses a better business model because it conflicts with the firm's current model.

This process is closely related to another concept, the dominant logic of a firm.[8] The dominant logic is the prevailing wisdom within the company about how the world works and how the firm competes in this world to make money. It is easily seen in the orientation materials that many firms give to new employees. This logic helps to reduce ambiguity and make sense of complex choices faced by firms, and helps new employees learn how the firm operates. As the term implies, the logic dominates alternative forms of logic that take a different view of the world. People within firms do not reevaluate their logical approach every time new information comes in. To the contrary, they search for ways to apply the dominant logic to interpret the new data. The shared assumptions behind the dominant logic will also help disseminate the meaning of the new information to others.

Although dominant logic is useful and beneficial in coordinating the actions of employees in a variety of situations, it comes at a cost. The choice of business model constrains other choices, removing certain possibilities from serious consideration. Over time, the business becomes more entrenched in its current model and is not able to recognize the information that may point the way to a different and perhaps better model. This is the potential trap.

For newly formed start-up companies, the six attributes above provide a perspective on the business model that must be forged at the launch of the enterprise. Start-ups must create an internal logic to make sense out of the chaos they experience. They must then strive to convey that logic throughout the firm, so that the firm can grow beyond a small number of people at a single location.

For established companies, though, the business model does not emerge from a clean sheet of paper. Instead, the model that will be applied to a new opportunity will bear a strong resemblance to the established business model already in use. And the more successful the current business model has been over time, the stronger its influence over how to commercialize the new opportunity that arises. This means that the future commercial development of a firm's technology will depend on the firm's prior history and experience. And the more successful the firm has been with its business model, the more wedded to the model it will be as new opportunities arise. We will see this effect quite clearly in the experience of the Xerox Corporation.

The Xerox Model 914 Copier: A Technology Looking for a Business Model

The original Xerox copier, the Model 914, provides a great illustration of the value of a business model and how hard it can be for successful companies to identify a good one. The story started in the mid-1950s when Joe Wilson, then the president of the Haloid Corporation, met Chester Carlson, who had developed a fascinating new technology. Carlson had figured out how to use an electrostatic charge to fix a powdered toner onto a piece of paper, a technology he called *xerography*. From an original image, Carlson's technology could produce a copy that was crude, but seemed to promise greater clarity, without the messiness of earlier copying methods.

At that time, copies were made for business use either by "wet" photographic methods or by dry thermal processes. Each method yielded low-quality images that did not age well. Prevailing business models for each process involved charging for the equipment at a modest markup over cost, and charging separately for supplies and consumables, usually at a much higher markup over cost—a "razor-and-razor-blade" business model. Both copier technologies required special paper and supplies, creating an aftermarket revenue stream for vendors. Typical office machines sold for $300. The average machine in use produced fifteen to twenty copies per day, and 90 percent of these machines were used for fewer than one hundred copies per month.

What would be the best economic use of the promising capabilities inherent in the technology of xerography? Wilson saw the potential for tremendous revenues from this new technology in office copying. As

Carlson and Wilson pursued the technology, they developed a proto-type machine that used xerography to make copies. In contrast to the prevailing technologies of the day, this technology produced dry copies of high quality without requiring thermal paper. However, Wilson estimated that the manufacturing cost of the machine would be about $2,000. And he estimated that its variable costs per copy were roughly on a par with earlier methods.

This created a problem for commercialization of the technology. The manufacturing costs of the machine were much higher than prevailing copy technologies, while its supplies costs were about the same as these rival technologies. How could this new technology penetrate the market, given these economics? The "razor" was much, much more expensive, and the "blade" was no cheaper. How could customers be induced to pay the much greater up-front costs of the new, higher-quality technology?

Since they knew that they would need significant resources to overcome these barriers, Wilson and Haloid sought to find a strong marketing partner for the 914. They approached some of the leading companies of the day with their technology, offering to provide the technology in return for the partner's providing the manufacturing and marketing. They were rebuffed by Kodak, General Electric, and IBM. Before making its decision, IBM commissioned a careful and highly professional market analysis by Arthur D. Little and Co. (ADL), a respected consulting firm. Happily, Richard Rosenbloom later came into possession of a copy of the ADL report to IBM, written in 1959. From that report, we can reconstruct much of IBM's evaluation of the 914.

Arthur D. Little could not conceive a successful business model for the xerographic technology, in part because ADL could not identify a salient value proposition: Although xerographic technology was good at many things, it was not excellent at any particular thing. And "better quality at much higher cost" didn't seem to be a winning value proposition. As they reported: "[Because] the Model 914 . . . has considerable versatility, it has been extremely difficult to identify particular applications for which it is unusually well suited in comparison with other available equipment. . . . [P]erhaps the very lack of a specific purpose or purposes is the Model 914's greatest single weakness."[9]

Arthur D. Little analysts essentially assumed the 914 would be offered within the razor-and-razor-blade business model, the dominant logic then extant in the office copy machine industry. This model charged customers the full price of the initial equipment and charged them again for supplies as needed. The analysts doubted that customers would invest thousands of dollars to acquire a copier (which was only used to make a few hundred copies a month in those days): "Although it may be admirably suited for a few specialized copying applications, the Model 914 has no future in the office-copying-equipment market."[10] Although this conclusion may seem quite myopic today, recall that Kodak and GE independently had come to a similar conclusion. None of these three leading companies saw much economic value in xerography.

Wilson sensed that they were wrong. On September 26, 1959, Haloid brought the 914 to market by itself, surmounting the obstacles of its high equipment cost by using a different business model. Instead of selling the equipment, Haloid offered customers a *lease*. A customer needed only to pay $95 per month to lease the machine, promising to pay four cents per copy beyond the first two thousand copies they made with the machine each month. Haloid (soon to be renamed Xerox) would provide all the required service and support, and the lease could be canceled on only fifteen days' notice.

This leasing proposal surmounted the razor-and-razor-blade problem and provided an attractive value proposition for customers. The new business model imposed most of the risk on the tiny Haloid Corporation: Customers were only committed to the monthly lease payment and paid no more unless the quality and convenience of the 914 led them to make more than two thousand copies per month.[11] Only if the 914 were to lead to greatly increased volumes of copying would this business model pay off for Haloid. The model essentially acknowledged that the ADL analysis was right, but was incomplete. Wilson bet that there was greater potential value in xerography than ADL had judged, but that a different business model would be required to unlock that value.

It proved to be a smart bet. Once the 914 was installed on customers' premises, the appeal of the machine was intense; users averaged two thousand copies per *day* (not per month), because of the high image quality and the convenience (no more smudged fingerprints from the wet copying processes, and no more yellowed, curled-up thermal paper). This tremendous surge in usage meant that most machines were generating incremental, per-copy revenues to Haloid by the second day of the monthly lease. This business model generated revenues far beyond even Wilson's most optimistic expectations, powering compound revenue growth at an astonishing 41 percent rate for a dozen years. As a result, the little $30 million Haloid Corporation turned into a global enterprise (renamed Xerox) with $2.5 billion in revenues by 1972. Thus, the same technology that IBM, ADL, Kodak, and GE had rejected as a niche opportunity created a multibillion-dollar enterprise—through the use of a different business model.

The Cognitive Effects of Xerox's Business Model

This enormous success had lasting effects on Xerox. The huge success of the 914's business model—which generated more revenues when more copies were made—established the dominant logic for Xerox's later copier business. Xerox's business model motivated the company to develop ever-faster machines that could handle very high copy volumes, with maximum machine uptime and availability. This resulted in a strong cognitive bias within Xerox, because the model discouraged development of low-speed copiers. As a later Xerox CEO observed: "[O]ur profits came from how many copies were made on those machines. If a copier was slow in generating copies, that was money plucked out of our pocket."[12]

Meanwhile, Xerox's monopoly of plain-paper copying technology ended abruptly. An antitrust action brought by the Federal Trade Commission forced the company to accept a consent decree requiring it to license its patents on a compulsory basis and to offer its machines for sale as well as on lease. Kodak and IBM entered the high end of the market, with their own high-volume, high-speed copiers, using business models very similar to Xerox's own. More challenging to Xerox, though, was the entry of a host of Japanese manufacturers at the low end of the market. They employed different pricing strategies, product configurations, and distribution channels to target a different market segment; in other words, they entered with a different business model.

Xerox's business model as of the early 1980s is summarized in table 4-1 according to the business model attributes just described. It targeted its products and sales efforts to major corporate customers and government organizations. Its value proposition was "high quality copies in high volume, at a low monthly lease rate." Xerox organized its value chain to deliver completely configured copier systems, sold through its own direct sales organization, and comprehensive maintenance services, provided by its own technicians. The company priced its products and services so that it made some money on its equipment, but made the bulk of its profits from sales of services and supplies (e.g., toner and paper).

This business model did not require partnerships with third-party organizations; indeed, Xerox chose to provide the many elements of its business model itself. Xerox conducted its own research, as we saw in chapter 1. It performed all the required product development activities to launch and support new products. Xerox manufactured its products internally. It distributed all of its products through its own channels of distribution. The company provided its own financing to customers, and its own service and support. Xerox even made its own paper, to provide the optimal feeding characteristics for its machines, though in this respect, Xerox had to be sure to operate with paper from other companies as well.

TABLE 4-1

Xerox's Business Model in Comparison with Japanese Low-End Copiers' Model

	Xerox	Japanese Copiers
Identified Market Segment	Corporate and government market	Individual and small business markets
Value Proposition	High-quality copies at a low monthly lease rate	Low cost of machine, greater affordability of copiers
Elements of Value Chain	Developed entire copier system, including supplies; sold through a direct sales force	Internal machine and cartridge; outsourced distribution, service, support, and financing
Defined Cost and Margins	Modest profit on equipment, high profit on supplies, or per "click"	Modest "box cost" for copier, higher margins on cartridges—a "razor and razor blade" model
Positioned in Value Network	First mover in dry-copy process; did not require or pursue partners	Recruit third-party office equipment dealers to expand to national coverage; user-serviceable cartridge
Formulated Competitive Strategy	Competed on technology, product quality, product capability	Compete on lowest box cost, convenient dealer locations, machine quality/self-service

Meanwhile, the Japanese entrants identified an Achilles' heel in Xerox's model. Xerox's model performed well when applied to the largest corporations, which needed high volumes of high-quality copy output. It did not fit as well, though, with the needs of small businesses and individuals. These groups did not need such high volumes of copying, were much more sensitive to the price of the copier, and were willing to compromise on the quality of the image to save money.

The Japanese entrants attacked this segment of the copier market with a different business model (the right-hand column of table 4-1).[13] They designed a product that could be serviced without a trained company technician. They accomplished this by making the most frequently failing parts of the copier into a replaceable cartridge. Doing so allowed the companies to reapply the earlier razor-and-razor-blade model, because the copier machines could be priced at a more modest gross margin, while the replacement cartridges could be priced with very high gross margins. They then created an indirect distribution channel of dealers and distributors to sell this equipment and to provide servicing and financing as required. An indirect distribution channel saved the Japanese companies the cost of creating a direct sales force. It also enabled them to build a nationwide distribution capability very rapidly and allowed potential customers the convenience of walking into a local storefront to try out the new machines before purchasing.

The Japanese entry proved to be a daunting challenge to Xerox. Xerox's engineers could design far more elaborate and impressive copiers, but responding to this challenge required them to abandon the dominant logic of the hugely successful company they had created. It meant that engineers who had previously excelled in moving paper faster through complex mechanical equipment now had to create much simpler products, at much lower costs. The sales department had to determine how to manage an indirect sales force alongside a direct sales force and spent countless hours arguing over whether and when a customer should be served through direct versus indirect channels. And marketing had to decide how to promote the Xerox brand at the low end of the market (which earned lower gross margins per machine) while still maintaining the high-end, high-margin sales that had catapulted Xerox to prominence. It took a decade for Xerox to cope with the threat of the Japanese entry into the home-office and small-business market. In 2001, under pressure across its copier businesses, Xerox abandoned this part of the market, deciding that it wasn't worth its effort and resources.

The effects of Xerox's business model and the dominant logic inherent within it would cast a second shadow as well, a shadow over the commercialization of new technologies in new business areas for the firm.[14] In 1968, Peter McColough, who had led the sales and marketing effort of the 914, was appointed chief executive of Xerox. As the rapid rate of growth of copier revenues began to slow at the end of the 1960s, McColough knew that Xerox would need to expand its business into new areas to maintain its historic rate of growth. He set a new direction toward the architecture of information. Yet even as McColough articulated this vision for Xerox's future, its management of that future would be constrained by the logic of its successful business model from its past.

Commercializing PARC Technologies

McColough's first steps toward realizing this vision were to enter the computer business in 1969 through the billion-dollar acquisition of Scientific Data Systems (SDS). This was an astounding sum to pay for an acquisition in 1969, and it would prove later to be a disastrous move. As we saw in chapter 1, Xerox established the Palo Alto Research Center (PARC) in 1970 to lead the way technologically into the computer industry and to feed new technologies into the SDS unit. Sadly, SDS soon collapsed and was shut down in 1975.

Despite SDS's failure, the research community within PARC flourished during the 1970s, with generous budgets and few restraints on its freedom to explore new boundaries. The first commercial payoff from PARC technology emerged in 1977, as Xerox entered the electronic printing business with a high-speed laser printer. Xerox's high-speed copier business model worked beautifully with the new printer technology. Laser printing enabled Xerox to make copiers that copied even faster, with even higher image quality. These technologies created a new, large, and profitable business for Xerox. The company's business model was able to quickly convert these powerful new technologies into additional sales and enhanced gross margins.

The same year, Xerox took the first steps toward building a major line of business intended to serve the office of the future. An Office Products Division, newly established in Dallas, marketed a stand-alone electronic word processor in 1977, but took this product primarily to Xerox's current customers and served them through Xerox's current marketing channels. In 1979, Xerox offered the first "office system," which used Ethernet technology to link word processors and printers. In 1981, the Star workstation was introduced as the centerpiece of an integrated system for office automation. Xerox did not offer these technologies as individual pieces; rather, they were offered exclusively as an integrated system.[15]

The latter move set a pattern for the business model that Xerox used to evaluate PARC's innovations in computing. Xerox applied PARC technologies to create complete computing systems, which constituted a value chain of proprietary technologies, with no option to use third-party equipment or software. Xerox initially offered the Star workstation for purchase at $16,995; the requisite network facilities and shared printer raised the total cost for a three-user system to more than $100,000. These systems were then sold primarily to *Fortune* 1,000 companies through a direct sales force and supported by a field service organization.[16] Xerox took this revolutionary technology to market via the business model that had worked so well for its copiers.

It is instructive to compare Xerox's business model with that employed by IBM when it first marketed a new, microprocessor-based personal computer (PC) (table 4-2). The target market was different for the two companies. Xerox restricted its Star office systems to its customer base of large corporations and government departments. Although IBM also sold its PCs to this market, it crafted a strategy to take its PCs well beyond these traditional customers to individuals and small businesses as well. It created a very successful Charlie Chaplin–esque advertising campaign to position these machines for the individual. IBM offered a version of its PC for $2,995 and created a retail distribution channel of over two thousand outlets through Sears, ComputerLand, and Businessland to reach individuals and small businesses. As we now know, IBM also created a technical architecture that outsourced the microprocessor and operating-system portions of the value chain—to Intel and Microsoft, respectively. The decision would change the course of the computer industry, and not to IBM's long-term advantage.[17] The point here, though, is that IBM did not constrain its entry into the PC industry by slavishly extending its own hugely successful business model in its mainframe business. By contrast, Xerox's commercialization of its PARC technologies never escaped the confines of its copier business model and associated business logic.

Although Xerox had some incredible technologies in its Star networked office systems, these superior computing technologies were no

TABLE 4-2

Xerox Star Workstation Business Model versus IBM PC Business Model, Around 1981

	Xerox Star	IBM PC
Identified Market Segment	Corporate and government market	Corporate, government, individual, and small business markets
Value Proposition	Leading edge performance; high-quality documents onscreen and in print; ability to share and send documents; state-of-the-art	Personal computing made affordable, from the best-known name in the industry; ability to run third-party hardware and software; ability to buy from local retailer
Elements of Value Chain	Developed entire Star system, from basic chips through manufacturing, distribution, service, financing, and support	Internal design and manufacture of PC systems; external sourcing for microprocessor, operating system, and third-party application software and hardware; direct and indirect distribution
Defined Cost and Profit Margins	Modest volumes, high unit gross profit margins	High volumes, moderate gross profit margins
Positioned in Value Network	In order to do anything, we must do everything	Recruit third-party dealers and hardware and software developers; outsource microprocessor and operating system; allow vendors to sell to "compatibles" manufacturers
Formulated Competitive Strategy	Win on engineering, state-of-the-art functionality and performance	Win on leading market share, control of PC architecture; ability to enlist thousands of independent developers to extend capabilities of PC

match for the vastly superior business model of the IBM PC. For example, the Star had a wonderful word processor; beautiful, laser-quality output; and an electronic mail capability far better than those available on the IBM PC. But the IBM open systems architecture enabled third parties to develop hardware and software products that greatly enhanced the value of IBM's systems. For example, the Xerox Star never developed a capable spreadsheet package, whereas IBM's PC sales were boosted tremendously by Lotus 1-2-3. Similarly, the IBM PC could run Ashton-Tate's dBase program, but the Star had no such database offering.

What's more, the IBM PC's own hardware capabilities were often en-hanced by the addition of third-party hardware. This additional hardware greatly assisted the PC in performing useful tasks and in running some third-party software. For example, companies like Hercules extended the graphics abilities of the PC, so that it could display Lotus 1-2-3 graphs. Intel and others, like AST and Quadram, marketed boards that expanded working memory. Plus Development, a company I was involved with from its beginnings, even created an add-on board with a built-in hard-disk-drive that could easily increase the hard-disk storage on a PC. The Hayes modem, 3Com's Ethernet board, and IRMA's 3270 emulation board enabled the PC to connect to a variety of other computers. The Star sys-tem, on the other hand, could only connect to another Star system.

The differences in the value chain extended to distribution as well. The Star was only available through Xerox's sales force, whereas the IBM PC could be obtained at more than two thousand retail stores around the United States, as well as from IBM's own sales force. This retail distribution channel was also available to companies who wanted to sell "IBM-compatible" hardware and software products. There was, however, no easy way for third-party developers to reach Xerox's work-station customers.

As the PARC scientists watched this competition, they sensed that Xerox could do more with the technologies they were creating than to simply commercialize them with the Xerox Star offering. They ques-tioned the pace at which Xerox was pursuing the commercialization of their inventions, or disagreed with the company's commitment to pro-prietary standards and "systems" marketing.

Some of the researchers eventually chose to leave Xerox to pursue commercial versions of their ideas. Instead of applying the Xerox sys-tems model for computing, though, they chose to start new companies to exploit individual component technologies, in a different, more open ar-chitecture of computing. The departure of some of these employees cre-ated a situation in which, during the 1980s and 1990s, several new PARC technologies were being exploited simultaneously by Xerox within its in-tegrated systems (usually in Xerox copiers and printers) and by inde-pendent entrepreneurial spin-off companies as stand-alone innovations.

This natural experiment afforded an unusual opportunity to com-pare commercialization practices in a setting where similar technologies were taken to market with sharply different business models. These models provide a comparison between a Closed Innovation paradigm (within Xerox) and an Open Innovation paradigm (the spin-off companies). Chapter 1 discussed some aspects of this co-evolution, with the example of SynOptics. Here, we will examine three other spin-offs and compare them explicitly with Xerox's business model.

3Com

3Com Corporation was the first of several highly successful spin-off companies based on technologies created at Xerox PARC. Robert Metcalfe was a young computer scientist at Xerox PARC when he invented the Ethernet local area network (LAN) technology.[18] Used within PARC as early as 1975, this technology connected different parts of Xerox's computers and its copiers. Sensing the latent opportunity of Ethernet and impatient with Xerox's indecision about commercializing PARC's pioneering technologies, Metcalfe left PARC in January 1979. He formed 3Com Corporation ("computers, communication, compatibility") in June of that year.

While pursuing his vision for 3Com, Metcalfe had to find ways to support himself. He was soon engaged as a networking consultant to Digital Equipment Corporation (DEC) by Gordon Bell, then the leading technical figure at DEC. In 1980, with Bell's encouragement, Metcalfe successfully persuaded Xerox to grant him a nonexclusive license to the Ethernet technology, on which Xerox held four strong patents, for the sum of $1,000.

Xerox's agreement to this proposal reflected a strategic choice rather than an oversight. Xerox was a large user of DEC computers and was eager to promote a technology to link Xerox printers and workstations to DEC minicomputers. DEC's help would be vital to accomplishing that.[19] By licensing the Ethernet technology, Xerox could promote its Star systems products. Spurred by Metcalfe's efforts, Digital, Intel, and Xerox formed an alliance (DIX) to define a standard for Ethernet LAN communication and to promote its widespread adoption as an "open standard" by the computer industry.[20] By comparison, the IBM PC would not be announced until August 1981.

Armed with the DIX alliance, 3Com began to seek venture capital in October 1980 in order to begin developing hardware products. In the absence of established markets for either PCs or workstations, the business plan for 3Com was necessarily vague. The search nonetheless paid off in February 1981, with first-round funding of $1 million from VC investors who looked beyond the formal plan and were attracted by Metcalfe's vision and charisma, as well as his team's strong technical talents.

Metcalfe's venture was hardly an instant success. 3Com's first products connected DEC minicomputers to Ethernet LANs, using Intel chips. This was a market in which a company sold primarily to scientists and engineers who used Unix operating systems and who did much of their own programming. Distribution was accomplished through direct sales or value-added resellers. Ungermann-Bass was the leader in this market, with 3Com lagging behind, partly because of 3Com's much smaller direct sales force.

3Com realized much greater success in the IBM PC marketplace, selling its Ethernet adapter cards to be installed inside IBM-compatible PCs in corporate networks running Novell's operating system. The core value proposition became the ability to share files and laser printers (which in those days were very expensive) via an Ethernet network protocol that was compatible with the nascent IBM PC standard. Later, Ethernet would also enable companies to use e-mail within their LANs, and still later, Ethernet helped networks connect to the Internet.

Once the PC business began to boom and 3Com had shifted away from its initial focus on workstations, 3Com began to take off as well. 3Com stock was first sold to the public in 1984, and the company was still operating as an independent company in 2002, with a market value at the end of 2001 equal to one-third of Xerox's market value.

Did Xerox make a mistake by licensing Ethernet for a mere $1,000? As this account shows, the latent economic potential of Ethernet was far from obvious at the time that Xerox decided to grant the license. In fact, Xerox was advancing its own strategy for its Star networked systems by agreeing to the license, in order to connect its equipment more effectively with DEC minicomputers.

Ethernet's value arose because the technology was commercialized in a new business model outside of Xerox workstations, DEC minicomputers, and the Unix operating system. The key ingredients of that model stood in sharp contrast to the business model of Xerox, which exploited unique proprietary technologies and sold them through a direct sales system to its leading office equipment customers (table 4-3). The latent value in the Ethernet technology did not materialize until the technology was targeted at a different market, which offered a different value proposition, utilized an open-technology platform populated by many third parties, and was sold through a new set of distribution channels. It seems reasonable to infer that a business model similar to 3Com's would not have evolved had the technology remained within Xerox. And Xerox could not have anticipated the value latent within the technology, unless it had conceived of a radically different way to take that technology to market.

TABLE 4-3

Summary Evaluation of Xerox and Selected Spin-Offs on Key Business Model Attributes

	Xerox	3Com	Adobe	Metaphor
Identified Market Segment	Corporate and government market	Corporate PC market	PC, MAC, and laser printer market	Knowledge workers in corporations
Value Proposition	High-quality copies at a low monthly lease rate	Establishes file and printer sharing between IBM PCs	Enables output of richer document types	Enables nontechnical queries of corporate databases
Elements of Value Chain	Developed entire copier system, including supplies, sold through a direct sales force	Focused on Ethernet protocol and add-on boards	Focused on supplying fonts to laser printer manufacturers and software firms	Developed and sold entire systems, from hardware to software to distribution
Defined Cost and Margins	Modest profit on equipment, high profit on supplies, or per "click"	High volume, low unit cost	Very high fixed cost, very low variable cost	High fixed costs, high margin, low unit volume
Positioned in Value Network	First mover in dry-copy process; did not require or pursue partners	Set the IEEE 802 standard; utilized PC distribution channel	Defined the PostScript standard for scalable fonts	No third parties or complementors utilized
Formulated Competitive Strategy	Competed on technical product quality, product capability	Compete on standard, new channels	Strong network externalities, high switching costs	Compete on superior technology, usability

Adobe

The spin-off of Adobe from Xerox followed a path similar to that taken by 3Com. Adobe's founders, Charles Geschke and John Warnock, left PARC in 1983 to commercialize a page-description language that became their first product, PostScript. PostScript allows printers to use digital fonts to reproduce a wide variety of characters generated from a PC.

The technology embodied in PostScript came from Interpress, a page-description software project developed while Warnock and Geschke were at Xerox PARC. (The project had drawn on earlier work they had done at Evans and Sutherland—this would later complicate Xerox's ability to control the ideas exclusively for itself.) Interpress was an internal, proprietary protocol used to print fonts generated from Xerox workstations on Xerox printers. This was an effective usage of the technology, because it linked tightly with Xerox's own business model and gave Xerox's products a competitive edge over other systems. But the potential value of the technology was limited to that of an important proprietary component in a larger Xerox system.

While at PARC, Warnock and Geschke had argued repeatedly with Robert Adams, then the head of Xerox's printing division, over whether to make Interpress into an open standard. Adams had strongly resisted, contending that he couldn't see how Xerox would make any money if the company "gave away" the font technology and weakened one of the most distinctive features of Xerox's own systems. After debating this inside Xerox for more than a year, they agreed to disagree, and Warnock and Geschke left PARC. As Geschke remembered it, "Certainly, within Xerox, none of this was going to happen. They wanted to have an industry standard, but they wanted to control everything at the same time."[21]

Arguably, Adams was at least partly right: It may well have been that Xerox's business model could never have benefited from making the technology an open standard. The business model that eventually realized significant economic value for Adobe differed substantially—both from Xerox's business model *and* from Warnock and Geschke's original intentions when they left. Indeed, Adobe's initial business model had contained many elements that were similar to the model then dominant at Xerox, but subsequent events persuaded the founders to change it. As Geschke recalled,

Our original business plan was different. We were going to supply a turnkey systems solution including hardware, printers, software, etc. With this in hand, we were then going to build a turnkey publishing system. It turns out other people were trying to do this at the same time—there would have been a lot of competition if we had gone this route. . . .

In many respects Steve Jobs and Gordon Bell (my teacher in graduate school) were key ingredients in getting things going the way they did. Gordon said, "don't do the whole system," and Steve came to us and said, "we don't want your hardware, just sell us the software." We said, "No!" Later Steve came back and said, "OK, then just license it to me." That's how the business plan formed. It wasn't there in the beginning."[22]

Selling and supporting a turnkey publishing system, complete with its own hardware and software, would have required a direct sales force and a field service network very much like the one Xerox managed in its copier business. In Geschke's view, such a system would have taken a long time to be developed and would have encountered a lot of competition. The font technology on its own might not have been that valuable in this configuration, since it was merely a component in a larger system—as Ethernet originally was inside of Xerox.

Instead, selling font libraries to original equipment manufacturers (OEMs) allowed the font technology to capture significant value by leveraging the efforts of computer OEMs like Apple and IBM and printer OEMs like Canon and Hewlett-Packard (HP) to create a new value network around desktop publishing. Adobe occupied a single important piece of this value chain, focusing on supplying the digital font libraries to laser printer and software manufacturers. As the manufacturers of PCs, printers, and software made faster and more powerful products, Adobe's position became increasingly valuable.

This very different approach to commercializing its technology also made Adobe a valuable company. Adobe Systems went on to become a public company in 1987 and continued to operate as an independent company in 2002. At the end of 2001, its market value was approximately equal to that of Xerox.

As with 3Com, the business model that eventually created significant economic value out of PostScript for Adobe differed greatly from the Xerox business model. Had Adobe persisted with its initial intentions, which had strong similarities to Xerox's model, that latent value might never have materialized.

Metaphor: A Xerox Spin-Off with a Xerox Business Model

3Com and Adobe created value from Xerox technologies only after they transformed their business models substantially from the one that Xerox usually employed. In contrast, the founders of Metaphor commercialized some promising user interface and database query concepts developed at Xerox PARC through a business model quite similar to the one at Xerox. Metaphor is thus an important contrasting case of how effective Xerox would have been if it had pursued its technologies further through its own business model.

Metaphor was created by David Liddle and Donald Massaro in 1982. It developed a series of technologies that allowed nontechnical users to create sophisticated queries of large databases. This enabled a new group of users to mine corporate data for a variety of new purposes, such as market research, pricing analyses, or analyzing trade-offs between possible new product features. Before, users would have to rely on corporate programmers to write report generators to extract data from a mainframe to get the data they needed. Because the programmers had many projects to perform for mainframe users, these requests typically landed in a large queue. Users were frustrated by the long lead time it took to get the requisite mainframe data they needed to do their jobs, and the technical programming required to generate the data was too arcane for them to access the data directly. Metaphor's technology let knowledge workers utilize a point-and-click graphical user interface to construct their own database queries directly to the corporate databank. The ability to extract useful corporate data directly was a potentially powerful value proposition. The technology would allow users to bypass the report-generation programming queue, would create faster access to data, and would empower the users with the ability to experiment with new combinations of data. It was one of the first true client-server applications, employing the graphical user interface technology out of PARC to construct previously arcane and complex database queries in an intuitive fashion.

Metaphor's ambitious technical approach was accompanied by a business model that would have been familiar to Xerox. This included the development of a proprietary software product and the sale of that software bundled in with proprietary hardware as a turnkey solution for the customers. Metaphor intended to reach customers through its own direct sales force. As with Xerox's business model, Metaphor had a strong systems approach to commercializing its technology and a similar approach toward proprietary technology. Essentially, it built an internal value chain and eschewed an external value network. Liddle defended this approach as the only viable means at the time to implement the company's product strategy: "The problem wasn't one of a business model. When we started Metaphor, standards weren't available and the only choice was to do the entire system—that's the way every body did it then. It's not like today. What's more, this kind of product couldn't be sold at a retail level. The only way to sell it was with a knowledgeable sales force. . . . There was no packaged software at the time; we had to make our own equipment."[23]

While Liddle's defense seems plausible, many aspects of Metaphor's circumstances appear to be similar to those facing Adobe. In 1983, when Warnock and Geschke left PARC (a year after Liddle and Massaro left), there were no standards for fonts or for generating computer characters mathematically on laser printers, either. Nor was there an obvious way to distribute such a product. And, as noted previously, Adobe's initial plans were to develop the entire system as well. Its value network had to be constructed *de novo*. Warnock and Geschke believe that, in hindsight, they would not have succeeded had they continued with their initial business plan. They were also aware of Metaphor's situation and felt that Metaphor employed this approach as a direct result of their experience in Xerox. In the words of John Warnock, "Metaphor took the Xerox business model with them."[24]

This probably was a mistake. Despite its innovative technology and its potentially powerful value proposition, Metaphor was not one of the great commercial successes spun out of PARC. The company did manage to survive from 1982 until its sale to IBM in 1991, but its financial performance was meager, and it burned through a great deal of venture capital. Although the amount that IBM paid in 1991 was confidential, it did not reach the amount of capital cumulatively invested in the company. While there are undoubtedly many explanations for Metaphor's performance, its failure to explore alternatives to the Xerox business model stands as one plausible explanation—particularly in comparison with the value network that Adobe erected for its font technology.

Metaphor's lack of success does not seem to reflect the limitations of its technology; rather, its disappointing fate lay in its inability to find the model that would unlock the latent value embedded in that technology.

Implications of the Business Model for Open Innovation

Chapter 3 argued that firms that wish to employ an Open Innovation approach need an architecture to integrate internal and external technologies and to fill in the missing pieces. The analysis in this chapter shows that this architecture extends far beyond the traditional boundaries of technical management to encompass marketing, sales, support, and even finance. The customer segment chosen and the value proposition offered have important ramifications for the particular attributes of a technology being developed. The value chain that is constructed around the offering determines the value being created and the ability of the firm to claim a portion of that value for the firm. The resulting margin structure casts a long shadow over future initiatives, which are judged in part on whether they can continue or enhance these margins.

These issues imply that R&D managers must play an important role in the development and execution of the business model. As John Seely Brown noted in the introduction to this chapter, these managers must regard "the architecture of the revenues" as a vital element of capturing value from technology. These issues also imply that R&D managers cannot abdicate their part of the responsibility for crafting an effective business model. Just as the business model itself must span the technical and economic domains, so must technical and business managers themselves reach outside their areas of responsibility to work toward an effective model.

Technology managers need to include experiments in alternative business models. This is as important as the experiments they conduct inside their labs to evaluate technical risks. While it is certainly valid to consider making all the elements of the value chain to deliver a new innovation internally, it is equally valid to explore the possibilities of focusing on one or more pieces of that chain, and possibly utilizing external elements for the rest of the chain. This will also require technology managers to create processes to explore the social domain far more thoroughly, from customers to third parties, and the surrounding elements of the value network. It is vital for business managers to create mechanisms to expose technologies to external companies and to imbue technology developers with greater understanding and empathy for the social context in which their ideas will ultimately be applied.

Venture Capital:
A Benchmark for Business Model Innovation

This expanded role for technology managers might seem to be a hopelessly ambitious task. In fact, though, the search for a viable business model happens quite regularly at many early-stage companies in the commercialization process funded by venture capitalists. Venture capitalists necessarily invest to commercialize technology in environments of significant technical and market uncertainty. Their portfolio companies also deploy business models that implicitly map between the technical and social domains. Indeed, the very term business model is commonplace in that community.[25] Many venture capitalists even conceive of their investment decisions as investments in business models. Instead of operating under a dominant logic from a successful corporation's business model, though, venture capitalists give active consideration to a variety of possible models and work with their portfolio companies to adopt one that seems to fit well in a particular venture.

Once invested in a venture, venture capitalists do not necessarily stick with the initial business model of that venture. They force a change in the venture's business model when it becomes obvious that the assumed model is not working. They then provide strong incentives to motivate entrepreneurs to run the risks involved in developing a new business model. And venture capitalists provide careful governance and oversight to select a more promising model, rejecting models that no longer seem likely to be effective. In contrast, corporate governance tends to reinforce the corporate business model and inhibit a venture's ability to adapt to a different business model, even if it might work better for that particular situation.

Companies would do well to understand these VC processes far better than they typically do. Although corporate processes do an effective job of leveraging the corporation's current business model, these same processes impede the company's ability to envision and execute different business models. In some cases, it may well make sense for a company to partner with VC firms if the company wishes to commercialize technologies that do not seem to fit with its own business model.

The Business Model: A Double-Edged Sword

A business model is a double-edged sword for the corporation. It unlocks the potential value in a new innovation, but its very success can create a subtle, cognitive trap for the company later. An effective business model creates an internal logic of its own for how value is created and claimed. Every subsequent opportunity is evaluated in the context of this dominant logic: its target market, its market size, its margins, its value chain, its distribution channels, its use or neglect of third parties. Xerox's tremendously successful business model for its Model 914 copier later impeded its response to Japanese copier manufacturers. The strong internal logic of deep vertical integration, which worked so well for Xerox in the copier and printer business, cast a long shadow over the computer technologies developed at PARC. Xerox commercialized its PARC technologies through its copier and printer business model and lacked effective processes to create different business models for technologies that did not fit with that business model.

The separate spin-off examples reviewed here, with the exception of Metaphor, evolved their business model away from the proprietary value chains of Xerox toward models that made far greater use of external players and technical standards. Of course, the spin-off companies had to fill in many missing pieces to make their technologies work effectively as part of overall systems, but they did not strive for exclusive control over the entire system.

The success of 3Com and Adobe is ironic, because both spin-off companies had many fewer resources than did Xerox to commercialize their technologies. Yet they pursued business models that created much more value from those technologies than Xerox could. 3Com and Adobe created more value because they found a way to leverage these external resources. And each company's business model determined which internal elements were needed to connect with external technologies to capture a portion of that value, and what revenue mechanism would yield attractive returns for commercializing the technologies.

Metaphor serves as an illustrative failure in this context. The venture was built on a technology that seemed to embody an attractive value proposition. The leaders of this venture, however, failed to discover an appropriate business model capable of realizing the latent value in the technology. Like Xerox's managers, the leaders of Metaphor felt that in order to do anything, they had to do everything. They could not envision a business model for their offering that would harness the innovations of other firms as well as their own.

Crafting the Right Business Model
for Promising Technologies

Xerox, in managing its own labs, sought to extend its current business model rather than create a different one to respond to latent market opportunities in the PARC technologies. But a company like Xerox will not realize the value of its innovation investments at places like PARC until it learns how to craft business models to exploit the potential of the technologies it creates.

Crafting an appropriate business model may seem a daunting task for corporate managers, and Xerox's otherwise capable management team never did "get it." Yet, although it is indeed challenging, we will explore in chapter 5 how a very large, very successful company—the IBM Corporation—has managed to transform its approach to innovation. IBM now innovates with a very different business model than the one it used to pursue. Although it used to rely entirely on its own internal R&D, IBM today makes extensive use of others' technologies in its business. Its evolution points the way forward for many companies seeking to come to terms with the issues and opportunities posed by Open Innovation.

5

From Closed to
Open Innovation

The Transformation of the IBM Corporation

T HE VERY successful model of Closed Innovation within large firms
has gradually given way to a more diffused, more externally focused way of organizing innovation. Younger companies and start-ups have
eschewed the closed approach from the time of their founding, but the
question remains whether or how an established company might move
from a Closed Innovation mind-set to an Open Innovation mind-set.

The IBM Corporation has made such a transformation. Because of
the company's long and storied history, the account here will necessarily be selective and organized around the themes of Closed Innovation
and Open Innovation. IBM's transition was far from easy. In fact, it took
a near-death experience to force it to make the shift. And many thousands of people had to be laid off along the way, so not everyone in the
company was able to make this shift. Nonetheless, despite the layoffs
and the write-offs, IBM's experience shows that even large, successful
organizations from the days of Closed Innovation can (at some cost)
become far more open in their approach to innovation. What's more,
large companies can continue to profit from their innovation investments, albeit in different ways than they did before.

Closed Innovation Success at IBM: 1945–1980

It would be hard to overstate the impact that IBM has had on the computer industry. From the inception of computers during World War II
up until 1980, IBM was a central player—in fact, *the* central player—in

the industry. Up until the PC industry revolution in the 1980s, IBM was far and away the most successful company in the industry. It led the industry in practically any category you can think of: It had the largest sales, the most profits, the highest market capitalization, the largest research budget, and the most patents of any company in the industry. It is not an exaggeration to say that for many segments of the computer industry, IBM *defined* the industry and its environment.

IBM exercised its leadership during this period through the merits of the Closed Innovation model. In 1945, IBM dedicated its first research center, which was located adjacent to Columbia University in New York City. In a special arrangement with the university, IBM engaged Columbia and its faculty in the operation of the research center. IBM research staff collaborated with Columbia professors on research projects and taught some of the first computer classes to be offered in the United States at Columbia. The collaborative effort gave birth to a field that would later be known as computer science.

In the decade following World War II, the technology base for the data-processing industry changed dramatically. Mechanical and electromechanical counting and adding machines were replaced by vacuum tube electronics. Shortly after that, the transistor was invented in Bell Labs, and vacuum tubes were soon displaced by solid-state electronics.

IBM was directly involved in many salient inventions during this period. It was the first company to manufacture the core memory products invented by Jay Forrester at the Massachusetts Institute of Technology. These core memories created the first forms of electronic memory. They led to a new systems innovation, the Sage system for tracking military and civilian aircraft.[1] IBM itself had pioneered important innovations such as the first high-level programming language, FORTRAN, the RAMAC disk drive, and magnetic tape. These innovations promised to usher in still more advances in what was becoming known as the computer industry.

In 1956, Thomas Watson, Jr., assumed command of IBM from his father. The recent rapid pace of technical advance in the computer industry convinced him that IBM needed the capability to monitor, discover, and introduce new research discoveries. Until then, IBM had kept pace with the technical advances in its industry, but much of the core research had been conducted outside IBM. Watson felt that it would be risky to let this state of affairs continue. If the technical advances in the industry continued, and IBM lacked this technology research capability, the company could be overtaken by other firms that had mastered this new technology, as had happened to RCA. If, on the other hand, IBM could lead the industry in developing new technology, it could create an advantage for its products. Thus, research was both an investment in the future and an insurance policy against its many uncertainties.

For IBM at this time, research meant internal research, and the path to market for the output of this research was to be entirely within the firm. IBM established dedicated corporate research laboratories in New York and Zurich, modeled closely on how Bell Laboratories had been organized. These labs sought the very best graduates from the very best schools in the physical, mathematical, and computer sciences. IBM competed with Bell Labs, the National Weapons Labs, and the most prestigious universities for top Ph.D.'s in these areas. The company supplied these graduates with the very latest equipment and promised them substantial freedom in their research activities.

IBM's innovation philosophy at this time was to separate its research from its development. The fear was that if development were to be the primary focus of the scientists, they would become caught up in short-term problem solving and risk being blindsided by new developments driven by new bases of science. For example, as far back as 1961, IBM's research division focused its work on alternate materials to silicon, such as germanium and gallium arsenide. The development group for IBM's semiconductors was responsible for all of IBM's work in silicon from that time forward.

In 1964, IBM announced a revolutionary class of products, its System 360 family of computers. The System 360 was an enormous product development effort within IBM, one that required more than $4 billion and effectively "bet the company" on its results.[2] The 360 contained many new breakthroughs and would become the dominant design for mainframe computing for a generation. It was also a highly vertically integrated product, with IBM producing the key components, the key subsystems, the peripherals, the operating system, the software applications, as well as the overall system. IBM even produced such seemingly unlikely parts of the 360 as the keyboard, the punch cards, and the power supplies. And IBM sold the 360 to corporate America through its direct sales organization and offered financing, service, and support to its customers through its own staff.

This extensive vertical integration in almost every facet of the System 360's development and marketing was not a casual choice on IBM's part. The 360's design was based on a new architecture that IBM's engineers had developed. This architecture was different from that of other companies and also different from (and incompatible with) IBM's own earlier systems. It would take time and resources to teach this architecture to outside companies, and the capabilities of external vendors were decidedly meager at this time—particularly in comparison to Big Blue's own capabilities.

The 360 resulted in an enormous success for IBM, whose sales increased from $2.86 billion in 1963 to $11 billion in 1973. Its net earnings went from $364 million to $1.58 billion during the same period. In perhaps the most telling aspect of how successful this initiative was, the U.S. Department of Justice initiated an antitrust lawsuit against IBM in 1968. The company had grown so dominant that the Department of Justice now argued that IBM held an effective monopoly in the computer industry.

The success of the 360 ushered in a golden age for IBM's R&D. The company's philosophy was to encourage its researchers to pursue their own intellectual agendas, because IBM believed that this was the best way to elicit excellence in research. IBM's research division realized tremendous scientific discoveries, including five Nobel Prizes and six National Medals of Science. IBM also owned the patents that resulted from its research, and this was another source of value for the corporation. The research division directly contributed about one-third of IBM's patents and influenced about half of IBM's patents. As mentioned in chapter 3, IBM rose to become the single largest patent recipient of any company in the world.

In these years, IBM managed its patents with the goal of protecting its discoveries from being used by other companies. It licensed little of its technology, preferring instead to go it alone. In some cases, IBM did elect to cross-license a technology, but it did so to enable its developers to have more design freedom to pursue further advances in technology. Because IBM had deep pockets, it knew it would be an attractive target for some other company to sue, if the latter could plausibly claim that IBM had misappropriated its technology. A cross-license would remove that threat to IBM's treasury.

The business model for IBM was built on internal innovation, proprietary control over the architecture and all its key elements, and extremely high switching costs for its customers. The model also promised the customers a complete solution to their needs. IBM's internal integration assured customers that the company could be trusted with their most precious business information and could process that information for the customer without losing data. IBM's insistence on controlling every element of its products translated into peace of mind for IBM's customers. This perceived reliability was a huge benefit to IBM and an important part of its value proposition to its customers. This reliability was well voiced in the dictum "You'll never get fired for buying IBM." This model allowed IBM to invest in R&D with confidence, knowing that it would capture a significant portion of the value its R&D created.

Shifting Sands for IBM Innovation: 1980–1992

As IBM achieved tremendous dominance in its industry, some indications of what would later prove to be key erosion factors began to appear on the horizon. One trend was the growing acceptance of computer science as a legitimate academic discipline. This was a reflection in part of IBM's success and its impact on the field. As noted earlier, IBM helped Columbia create the first computer science program at a university, and the company structured its own labs like academic entities. IBM researchers actively participated in academic conferences around the world and even taught courses at many universities, thus assisting the creation of the academic discipline of computer science.

As computer science departments proliferated, the knowledge landscape from which innovation could arise in computing was transformed. IBM continued to hold a near monopoly in the computer market, but its near monopoly on ideas that could advance the industry began to erode. Put differently, the ability of other companies to access important ideas and commercialize new technologies began to grow significantly. The erosion factors discussed in chapter 2 began to impact mighty IBM.

These academic computer science departments began to drift away from the System 360 architecture offered by IBM. The end-to-end control of the 360 wasn't needed by many departments, which preferred to experiment with a variety of ways to utilize computing power. These departments were able to build their own primitive systems and write their own software and development tools to utilize those systems. They also proved to be an important early adopter of fledgling technologies from start-up companies such as Digital Equipment Corporation (DEC). Digital Equipment Corporation started out offering test equipment to academic and commercial clients, but soon launched what would be called a minicomputer. Academic computer science departments and engineering departments were avid purchasers of this new type of computer, because it freed them from the tyranny of the central computing organization at the university and from the queue of other projects awaiting computer time on the mainframe computer.

This market segment of customers gave further impetus to a second erosion factor, the VC industry. Digital Equipment Corporation would turn out to be an enormously valuable company in its own right. It went public in August 1966 and would grow into the world's second largest computer company by 1980. Digital Equipment Corporation was backed by the first VC organization, the American Research and Development Corporation (ARD), headed by Georges Doriot. The ARD's investment of $70,000 in DEC in 1957 would turn into a gain of $350 million by 1971, which certainly heightened the interest of other venture capitalists in the growing computer industry.[3]

Other new entrants in the minicomputer market also became profitable, valuable companies, such as Data General, Prime, Wang Laboratories, Datapoint, Four Phase, Pyramid, General Automation, and Computer Automation. These companies made significant returns for their investors as well. Although later investors' returns did not quite reach the heights that DEC achieved for ARD, the VC industry got a huge lift from its investments in the computer industry.

The combination of increased external knowledge and technology and the increasing availability of VC spurred the rise of a third erosion factor: the mobility of engineers and managers who were trained at IBM, but lured away to young start-up companies backed by VC. Chapter 2 showed the effect of this lure on the disk-drive industry. IBM's diaspora of departing employees manifested itself in start-up companies in many other areas of the computer industry as well, from hardware systems, tape drives, semiconductors, and printers, to software areas such as operating systems, databases, programming languages and tools, and applications.

The growing external knowledge base, the burgeoning number of start-up companies in various segments of the computer industry, and the departure of many IBM employees combined to put greater pressure on IBM's innovation process. IBM began to seek greater relevance from its research (relevance, that is, to IBM's businesses), and it wanted to get the results of its research into the market faster.

Joint Programs:
A Funding Mechanism for Greater Relevance

The pressure for greater relevance and faster time to market for its research efforts caused IBM to alter the way it funded its research activities.[4] Historically, research was funded from a central allocation out of IBM corporate. To IBM's business units, this was viewed as a tax on their businesses, which was used to fund new innovations. In the face of the mounting pressures, IBM decided to institute a second funding mechanism for its research, alongside the central allocation. IBM created what it called Joint Programs, which were funded out of R&D projects sponsored directly by individual IBM business groups. The term *Joint Program* reflected the joint participation of the research division with one of the development groups in the funding and development of a technology. In contrast to a tax, this was more of an internal contract between research groups and development groups within IBM.

The idea was to link the funding of a research project directly to a specific business group within IBM. That is, that business group actually paid for the research work. In these Joint Programs, teams of researchers from a lab and engineers from a product development division were put together to work on a project four to five years away from production. During the time that the researchers were located with the engineers, their salaries were paid directly by the business unit.

The use of a direct funding link from the business group created some important changes in how people within IBM approached the problem of transferring technology, according to James McGroddy, former IBM research director: "The Joint Programs caused researchers to take the problems of the businesses more seriously on the one hand, because this was a new source of research funds. It also forced the businesses not to treat research as a 'free good' on the other hand, and to work with the research division from the inception of the project, since they were paying for it."[5]

Despite initiatives like Joint Programs, the issue of more rapidly getting research discoveries out of the lab and into IBM's products remained a significant one for IBM. Part of this problem related to the people IBM employed in its innovation process. The company tried to hire the best and the brightest Ph.D.'s available, competing with universities and other leading industrial labs to get these people. These talents came at a cost, however. IBM's researchers were highly trained and highly skilled people, but these skills were often inflexible. If IBM could not accurately foresee the future innovations it would require, its researchers may not be able to switch to more promising areas in a timely way.

The issue of greater relevance for IBM's research implicated IBM's long history of separating research from development, a phenomenon discussed earlier in chapter 2. In the technology sector, for example, where Paul Horn had been the director of silicon semiconductor technology, there had been recurring problems with transferring research results into production. As Horn remembered:

> We in research thought that our job was to crack difficult problems, and then share our discoveries with the development group. They had smart people too, and knew things we didn't know about how to build chips. And we had a bit of an attitude too. There was a sentiment that, "I didn't come to Watson Labs to do fire fighting up at Fishkill" [where IBM had a semiconductor fab]. As a result, we would sometimes end up with competing efforts to do the same thing. In bipolar technology, for example, we had a research team working on prototype parts, utilizing some breakthrough discoveries that they had made which were resisted by the development organization. At the same time, a separate development team was trying to build the same parts using their process technologies from earlier products.[6]

In the software area, there was again a sense of missed opportunities. "We were inventing great technology," said Ambuj Goyal, then a manager in parallel process computing software, "but it wasn't converting into new business for IBM. For example, IBM invented the relational database, but companies like Oracle were stealing a march on us in the market, and taking most of the growth, to the point where in 1992 they had become the market share leader."[7]

IBM's Near-Death Experience

By 1992, IBM's business was facing tremendous competitive pressures on many fronts. Its high-end mainframe computers were serving a maturing market, and IBM's high market share meant that its revenues in this segment would likely decline over time. Its PCs were struggling to achieve profitability, and IBM's share had fallen behind other specialized

PC makers such as Compaq. Meanwhile, most of the profits from the PC business appeared to be accruing to Intel and Microsoft, not the computer manufacturers. IBM's workstation business, while profitable, was facing severe competition from Sun, Hewlett-Packard, DEC, and others. Its storage products continued to lead the industry in terms of performance, but had lost market share to dedicated OEM suppliers of disk drives and tape storage. IBM's semiconductor business was falling behind its competitors, despite the fact that IBM led the industry in semiconductor R&D spending. And IBM was losing momentum in many areas of software, such as its database business and its OS/2 initiative in PCs.

As a result of this myriad of pressures, IBM gave careful consideration to the idea of splitting up the company into smaller, more focused companies. Many observers felt that the technical synergy that joined IBM's businesses was weakening, while the market pressures that each business faced were different. IBM was considered too slow and too bureaucratic to respond in a timely way in each of its many businesses. Only by IBM's setting each business free on its own could each business continue to compete against more focused competitors.

This consideration had gone very far in certain areas. Within storage, IBM had recruited Systems Industries founder, former congressman, and venture capitalist Ed Zschau to become the general manager of the storage business. IBM renamed the business Ad*Star and hired investment bankers to explore the opportunity to spin out the company.

These pressures culminated in what can only be viewed as a near-death experience for IBM. At the end of calendar year 1992, IBM recorded what was then the single largest quarterly and annual loss in U.S. corporate history, a loss of $4.96 billion after taxes, resulting from a charge of $7.2 billion for restructuring. IBM had to make the first large-scale layoffs in its history (amounting to twenty-five thousand employees), bringing its tradition of lifetime employment to a brutal, abrupt end.[8] An outsider to the industry, Lou Gerstner, was brought in to lead IBM in April 1993—the very first time an outsider had been selected to head the corporation.

Surprisingly, Gerstner chose not to break up IBM. Although he orchestrated significant cutbacks in a variety of IBM's businesses and in IBM's central research organization, he decided to keep the company together as an integrated corporation.

To maintain IBM as an integrated organization, Gerstner and his lieutenants needed a vision for the firm, a new logic that would connect the many different parts, but would escape the logic of complete control that had pervaded the organization. As he later explained, IBM "had become a closed, kind of inward-looking organization."[9] Gerstner determined that IBM's dominant logic going forward would have to focus on IBM's customers, moving from an "in order to do anything, we have to do everything" approach to a "do whatever the customer needs us to do, and work with what the customer already has" approach. As a former IBM customer himself, Gerstner understood intuitively that customers needed help with incorporating the many technologies available in the industry and in creating effective solutions from these disparate pieces. If IBM could help customers solve those problems, it would have a strong value proposition to offer.

This new logic was reinforced by interactions with IBM's customers. McGroddy remembers well a key meeting he had held with a senior technical official at Citicorp, one of IBM's largest customers. The official drew a stacked bar graph of the value chain in technology and banking at Citicorp (figure 5-1). The graph started with atoms at the bottom, then put chips and devices at the next level, then put computers above those, then operating system software, then productivity software, and banking applications such as ATMs at the top. He challenged McGroddy, asking, "How much of this value chain are you helping me with? The company who is going to keep my business is the company that helps me compete in my part of the value chain."[10]

This was a revelatory meeting for McGroddy. As he looked at the Citicorp value chain, he immediately realized that the bulk of Citicorp's piece of the value chain was in the middle and top of the bar graph, whereas most of IBM's research spending was at the bottom. IBM's research commitments, specialized resources, and human capital were misallocated. Although IBM could offer Citicorp some impressive building blocks for the future at the bottom of the stack, it had surprisingly little to offer the bank at the top of the stack.

This revelation pointed the way forward for IBM's innovation system. While it would continue to address the building blocks in the value chain (e.g., semiconductors), IBM would increasingly win only if it could create new products and services at the middle and top of the value chain. This required McGroddy and his successor, Paul Horn, to manage a wrenching shift within IBM's Research Division. There simply wouldn't be as much need going forward for device physicists and physical chemists. There would be a much greater need for technologies that

FIGURE 5-1

Citicorp Value Chain of Information Technology

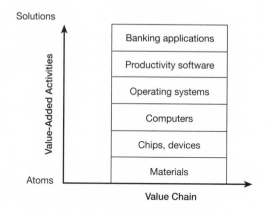

could provide systems integration capabilities for IBM's customers, products, and services that could enable businesses to do more with their computer infrastructure.

The Internet for IBM: Chaos or Opportunity?

As IBM retreated from atoms and molecules and advanced toward software and solutions in the mid-1990s, it had to confront the Internet. What should IBM's R&D strategy be with the Internet? The first thing IBM noticed was that hardly any of the core Internet technologies revolutionizing the computer industry were coming out of corporate R&D labs. In Horn's judgment, for example, Netscape had played a critical role in commercializing the hypertext markup language (HTML) and hyptertext transfer protocols (http) for the browser, yet had done little research itself in this area. Netscape adapted research that was conducted primarily at the University of Illinois, in the university's National Center for Supercomputing Applications (NCSA). The U.S. government, primarily through its Defense Advanced Research Projects Agency (DARPA), in turn had funded the NCSA. Tim Berners-Lee had created the actual HTML and http protocols while working at CERN, a particle physics lab in Switzerland.

Microsoft had become quite active commercially in the Internet as well. It had been actively hiring people from universities as well as redirecting its own staff to address the Internet technologies for its own browser product to compete with Netscape. But again, Microsoft was publishing little research of its own in this area; rather, it was absorbing and commercializing the fruits of others' research.

There were interesting research projects under way at a number of research universities across the United States. Horn and IBM were involved with these projects in various ways, ranging from the provision of funding, to collaborations between IBM researchers and university professors, to the hiring of graduate students as interns and new employees. But the universities themselves had no programs for the Internet; the faculty and students instead emerged from more traditional programs in engineering, mathematics, computer science, operations research, and the like. Thus the university work was good, but hopelessly fragmented.

Several consulting firms had set themselves up as information technology (IT) consultants, or business process reengineering consultants. Often, these firms would offer to manage the IT function for the customer, to enable the customer to "outsource" its IT needs entirely. While these firms could manage equipment from multiple companies, they did little research on their own either. Instead, their practice was informed by trial and error and assisted by some tools each firm had developed in the course of managing their customers' IT needs.

Based on the thinking of the Closed Innovation era, this situation seemed chaotic, to the point of being unmanageable. But inside IBM, there was a sense that, with a different approach to the Internet, the Internet could become a key building block within IBM and a core part of its future innovation strategy. Goyal remembered, "The more we looked at the Internet, the more we felt that we weren't solving the right problems as a company. Our re-engineering efforts were trying to reduce headcount and automate or outsource IT activities, which was what everyone was doing then. We thought that the Internet could be much more than that."[11]

Goyal's intuition was exemplified by some new projects that the research organization had undertaken around that time with some of IBM's clients, as IBM began to put much greater focus on the middle and top of its customers' value chains. One project was undertaken for Citigroup (the former Citicorp)—a project following up McGroddy's earlier meeting with the banking institution. Citigroup was struggling with the exploding complexity of the many financial instruments coming into use in its business. It knew that these instruments provided the potential to create valuable client offerings in the area of risk management for different interest-rate scenarios, currencies, and economic growth rates. But the sources of the necessary data were many and varied. Each customer had a uniquely different exposure to the movement of interest rates, currencies, and stock prices. Thus, an enormous amount of information access, data mining, and processing was required to locate the appropriate data and manage the risks for each customer. And these data existed on multiple vendors' computer systems. IBM researchers worked with their counterparts at Citigroup to integrate these disparate elements into an effective solution.

Horn recalled the impact of what Federal Express (FedEx) was doing with the Internet and its customers as an illustration of the potential value of the Internet for business processes: "One example we were very mindful of was the Fedex package tracking web site. This was a classic example of saving money through the intelligent use of information technology (since your customers performed the data entry activity themselves). At the same time that you're saving costs, though, customer satisfaction went through the roof. Now they had an ability to track their packages themselves throughout the Fedex system. When their boss wanted to know, 'where's my package?' the customer could provide an accurate, detailed answer."[12]

Another project was with a paper manufacturing company that wanted to optimize its supply chain. The project created an awareness of the need to coordinate information outside the paper company itself and to manage the information both at the company's suppliers and with the company's customers. Although this need had been identified with earlier technologies such as electronic document interchange (EDI), the Web provided a much easier and more uniform way to connect with outside companies. As Horn recalled, "These internet standards were standards you could get at. You could implement solutions on heterogeneous servers without having to rewrite the backend applications."[13]

This reflected a powerful shift in mind-set within IBM. The company had practically invented the computer industry and had created inside its own labs the core technologies in hardware and software that had powered the company's growth for more than fifty years. Yet, IBM's future would require it to go beyond this proud heritage. To deliver value to its customers at the top of the value chain, IBM would need to turn to external technologies, including those embodied in the Internet that were not created in any particular company's lab. In fact, IBM would leverage technologies that it did not own and could not control—technologies that were open to its competitors as well as to IBM.

In the language of chapter 4, IBM would need a radically different business model to create and capture value from innovation. The customer segment that IBM focused on remained the large corporate and governmental organizations that IBM had served for so long (though IBM added an important additional segment, discussed later). The value proposition to this customer segment remained one of delivering a complete solution: "You won't get fired for buying IBM." However, IBM—to its great credit—realized that the value chain it needed to utilize to deliver a complete solution to its customers had to transcend its own R&D. To deliver the best solution to its customers, IBM could no longer do everything itself. It would have to identify the best technologies out there from whatever source and develop the ability to connect these technologies into effective solutions. This was radical thinking within IBM.[14] The company had gotten beyond the not-invented-here mentality, which so commonly afflicts companies that maintain strong internal R&D organizations (see chapter 2).

IBM was able to create value for its customers through its embrace of open standards in a variety of areas, including the Linux operating system, the Java programming language, and the aforementioned HTML and http protocols. What is harder to understand in the context of its business model is how IBM captures value for itself when it leverages external technologies available to all companies and not controlled by IBM. This is an important issue within IBM and in all the other companies that seek to leverage Open Innovation concepts.

IBM cannot make money directly from these external technologies themselves. However, it can make good money helping customers integrate computing technologies to achieve their business goals. IBM does not obtain the 80-percent-plus gross margins of its deeply vertically integrated model on these integration projects. On the other hand, it doesn't need the same level of fixed investment and personnel to support those sales. The revenues for these projects are the fastest growing part of IBM's business, and IBM is changing its costs so that its return on investment will revert to the levels realized during the days of Closed Innovation.

IBM also created or amplified new revenue streams as part of its shifting business model. The company learned to charge for its management of customers' equipment, which is increasingly profitable for IBM as it transfers effective practices from one customer setting to other settings. IBM has even created a business to sell its knowledge management practices themselves, separate from their use within IBM for its management of customers' installations.

Innovation for Sale: Unbundling the Value Chain (*Out*)

IBM also initiated a second transformation of its business model. Historically, during its Closed Innovation period, IBM deployed all its technologies exclusively within its own systems and services. If you wished to buy a chip from IBM, you could only buy the chip inside an IBM component. That IBM component, in turn, was sold exclusively as part of an IBM subsystem, which was only available as part of an IBM system. The business model deployed all of IBM's innovations through IBM's own systems, which were sold only through IBM's own distribution, and serviced, supported, and financed by IBM—exclusively.

Gerstner's arrival caused IBM to rethink this insistence on internal integration. In 1993, IBM's storage division signed its first OEM agreement with an external customer, Apple Computer. In this agreement, IBM agreed to sell Apple some of its industry-leading 2½-inch drives for Apple to use inside its popular PowerBook laptop computers. Although IBM had its own laptop computer, the ThinkPad, which used its 2½-inch drive, the company decided that it would benefit more from selling extra volumes of its 2½-inch drives than it would gain in laptop market share from restricting the shipment of those drives to its own captive use. By 1997, more than half of IBM's production of 2½-inch drives was going into laptop computers produced by other companies, while IBM's ThinkPad laptop had less than 10 percent share in its market.

IBM also continued to invent new components within its disk drives, particularly its invention of magnetoresistive (MR) heads.[15] These heads were far more sensitive than the thin film heads then prevalent in the industry. Their sensitivity enabled drives to pack up to ten times more data on the same surface area of the drive. This boosted the capacity of the drive tremendously, with only a modest increase in the cost of the drive.

Initially, IBM shipped these heads inside its own 2½-inch drives, and their technical superiority helped IBM increase its share of the 2½-inch drive segment. Later, IBM decided to offer its MR heads as stand-alone components to other disk-drive companies, even though these companies used them to make drives that competed with IBM's. By offering its

MR heads on the open market, IBM enjoyed an even higher percentage of volume in the industry than what its drives had enjoyed, which were higher than the market share of IBM's laptop systems.

To observers steeped in a Closed Innovation mind-set, this seems to be madness: IBM is investing in superior technologies and achieving critical breakthroughs in those technologies, only to squander its advantage by selling the technologies to competitors on the open market. These competitors can use IBM's own technology to beat IBM, in building better 2½-inch drives or better laptop computers that use 2½-inch drives.

The logic of the previous paragraph only holds if an unspoken assumption holds true: that IBM can control and contain its technological edge for a significant period. This sort of exclusive, extended control may be possible in a rather barren knowledge landscape, but in an abundant knowledge landscape, it is increasingly the exception rather than the rule.

In an abundant knowledge landscape, IBM's actions are shrewd and farsighted commitments to innovation leadership. In the semiconductor market, for example, a new fabrication facility costs many billions of dollars. IBM continues to invest in building new facilities and designs and builds its own chips in these facilities. But it now also offers its chips to other systems manufacturers to use in their designs. It even offers to build the designs of other companies in IBM's facilities.

To restrict IBM chip-making capacity to IBM's own use would deny IBM's semiconductor division the opportunity to serve a much larger semiconductor market. By offering its chips to other manufacturers, IBM gains enormous volumes at the chip level, even as it sacrifices some differentiation for its own systems that use IBM's chips. These policies spread the high fixed costs of its fabrication facilities over more volume and give the company more leverage in its purchasing of fabrication equipment and supplies. On balance, this approach makes IBM's chips more cost-effective, which makes IBM's own systems more cost-effective and enables IBM to invest more in developing the next, even better, generation of semiconductors. This unbundling of the IBM value chain is depicted in figure 5-2.

More subtly, IBM's sale of its chips externally imposes some market discipline on its internal systems businesses. Those divisions cannot expect to win solely on the basis of superior chips; rather, they must win on their own value added. If a downstream business unit cannot meet

FIGURE 5-2

Unbundling of IBM's Information Technology Value Chain

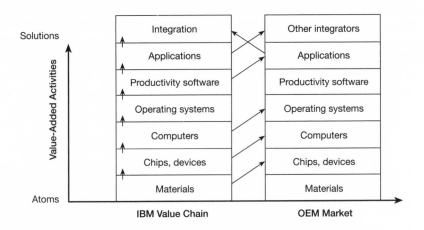

this test, then it is better for IBM not to "subsidize" it through exclusive access to a truly superior component. Indeed, it is better to sell that component to other system makers that can use it more effectively and grow their own business.

Licensing Intellectual Property: *(out)*
Another Key Profit Booster for IBM

IBM has still another way to profit from its innovation. Not only does it leverage external technologies in its own offerings, it also offers its own technology and IP for sale to other companies. The sale of IP is no small item; IBM received $1.9 billion in royalty payments for its IP in 2001. Even for a company of IBM's size, that is a lot of money. For comparison, IBM spent about $600 million in basic research that same year.

Managing IP will be explored more generally in chapter 8. Here, we will simply note the difference in this approach to managing IP from the approach IBM used in the days of Closed Innovation. Then, IBM was primarily concerned with preserving design freedom for its developers, so that it would not be the target of an infringement suit. This is a defensive approach. Today, the company still plays defense and still cross-licenses its IP to other companies (particularly when they too have potentially important IP). However, IBM now also plays offense with its

IP, seeking out infringing companies and not being shy about collecting significant payments for infringement. As a result, IBM may no longer maximize its own design freedom, but the freedom that it may forgo is compensated by the monies it receives in direct compensation.

The difference in the Closed Innovation and Open Innovation approaches to managing IP fits with the knowledge environment of the two periods for IBM. If IBM can expect to enjoy a long-lived advantage over its competitors, then it might prefer to give its developers as much freedom to work with as possible, since it expects to monetize its IP through the sale of its own products for a long period of time. If IBM expects its product market advantages to come under attack quickly, however, then it might prefer to obtain direct compensation from infringing competitors and monetize its IP more broadly and rapidly instead.

Learning from Customers: The "First of a Kind" Program

IBM has also crafted some processes to help it learn from its customers. One approach was a program IBM called First of a Kind (FOAK). This program was a contract between IBM's research organization and a leading-edge IBM customer to solve a commercially important and conceptually interesting problem. IBM would dedicate its own research staff, and the staff would work for an extended period at the customer site. IBM was careful to be sure that the customer understood that this would be an experimental effort, and the customer had to assign some of its own technical people to the problem.

The FOAK arrangement gave IBM a controlled environment for working out the solution—and the opportunity to fix any early problems with that proposed solution. The customer would get a solution to its problem. IBM would get the rights to use that solution in other settings and would own any IP its research staff created in the process of solving the problem. And IBM got something else: the chance to expose its own internal research staff to cutting-edge problems at its customers' sites.

As a result of the FOAK program, IBM has altered the research contract it makes with its own staff. Although IBM continues to hire academically strong Ph.D.'s into its company and continues to reward these people for academic conferences, papers, and awards, the company now also rewards its people for their ability to generate solutions to customers' problems.

IBM also has enlarged the duties of its research staff, turning them into knowledge brokers as well as knowledge generators. Every research manager is now assigned to be a relationship manager with one of IBM's businesses, in addition to supervising the activities of a research team with IBM's research division. Consequently, every research manager is responsible for an IBM business manager's relationship with the corporate research organization. Thus, a research manager assigned to the e-commerce business group is expected to facilitate the connection of useful IBM research output with the needs of the e-commerce business—regardless of whether those outputs come from the manager's own research area or from another part of the research division.

This broadened the mind-set of IBM researchers beyond their earlier focus on academically rigorous science. Brokering connections between an IBM business group and the research division forces the research manager to learn more about both. This builds greater breadth of knowledge in the manager about the various activities under way within IBM's research organization. It also increases the manager's knowledge of the needs of the assigned business group within IBM. Over time, he or she may envision more ways to link the outputs of the labs with the needs of the business group.

Winning in a World of Open Innovation

IBM's transformation demonstrates that even very large, very successful companies can learn new tricks. It also shows the shift in focus in locating ideas and how to take them to market, a shift discussed in chapters 2 and 3. In an abundant knowledge landscape, exciting new ideas can come from any number of places. The people searching for new ideas need to bring with them an open mind-set toward ideas and a broad perspective toward the needs of their organization. When IBM's researchers sit down now to establish their priorities for their next research initiative, they bring a greater breadth of knowledge and greater empathy for the customers, in comparison with IBM's traditional focus on academically important science. The resulting research outputs will likely have stronger connections to IBM's business model (or, in IBM's terms, greater relevance).

To win in a world of Open Innovation, IBM must know more about its customers' needs and learn more from its customers than its competitors do. IBM's success to date with the Internet and the expanded role of its researchers are allowing the company to learn about future market needs many years in advance of the mainstream market. This has expanded IBM's prediction horizon, giving it greater visibility into the future and the ability to plan research initiatives to exploit that vision. It also gives IBM's R&D units a context for reviewing the possible external technologies they might incorporate into that vision.

The Open Innovation approach requires IBM to focus on the value chain of its customers, rather than sticking with its traditional research heritage. IBM must inject market discipline within its own value chain by incorporating external technologies, in addition to its own, and by selling its technologies for use in other companies' (even competing companies') products. It means monitoring, detecting, enforcing, and selling IBM's IP to others. IBM has now embraced the second meaning of *not invented here:* Instead of reinventing wheels, IBM uses them to build new vehicles for its customers—and makes money doing it.

6

Open Innovation @ Intel

INTEL'S APPROACH to innovation differs substantially from that of IBM and provides a second example of how companies can pursue innovation opportunities in an environment of abundant knowledge. It also shows additional creative ways that companies can continue to profit from innovation, even when they don't own many of the underlying technologies they use. Like Xerox PARC, Intel operates smack in the middle of Silicon Valley, with all the erosion factors that diffused technologies out of PARC. Unlike Xerox, however, Intel exploits the reality of being surrounded by so much knowledge and venture capital. Intel creates programs to bring external technology inside and implements an aggressive program of investing corporate VC in start-up companies to extend Intel's markets.

Background on Intel

In 2001, Intel was the world's leading semiconductor manufacturer, with revenues of $26.5 billion, and more than eighty-three thousand employees working in eighty-plus countries worldwide. Despite its size, the company is actually rather young. Gordon Moore and Robert Noyce founded the company in 1968 and were soon joined by Andrew Grove. These three founders were veterans of the fledgling semiconductor industry and had worked together at Fairchild Semiconductor, a division of Fairchild Camera and Instrument. All three had left Fairchild in part because of their dissatisfaction with how Fairchild was running its semiconductor business.

The young company soon achieved commercial success. Its first significant product was the dynamic random access memory (DRAM) chip. In the early 1970s, the company invented the world's first microprocessor, the 4004. Over the ensuing years, Intel made a variety of semiconductor products, but the microprocessor product line became the bulk of the company's business. Intel gained an important design win in 1980, when IBM selected Intel's 8088 processor as the microprocessor in its first PC. As the success of the IBM PC grew, so too did the success of the Intel X86 architecture (the name given to the product family that originated with Intel's 8088 and 8086 chips), which became a de facto industry standard. In the mid-1980s, Intel decided to withdraw from the DRAM market, because of the razor-thin margins in that business.[1]

Although Intel had embarked on numerous initiatives to diversify beyond its microprocessor products, these products remained at the heart of the company. Intel had introduced a highly successful marketing campaign to brand itself and its Pentium-class microprocessors in the 1990s. Despite having gained a strong position in the microprocessor market segment, it faced direct competition from Advanced Micro Devices (AMD) and Cyrix, which made compatible microprocessors. In addition, Intel competed with alternative microprocessor architectures like the SPARC from Sun Microsystems; the PowerPC from a consortium of IBM, Apple, and Motorola; and Alpha from Digital Equipment Corporation.

Intel's ability to innovate and execute on those innovations allowed it to see off each of these challenges. In 2001, microprocessors accounted for approximately 81 percent of the company's revenues and an even larger share of the company's profits. As a result of the company's success and ability to execute the demanding tasks of developing and ramping up the manufacture of semiconductors, the company's market capitalization stood at more than $210 billion at the end of 2001.

What is more surprising and interesting is that Intel has achieved its success in this high-technology industry without conducting much basic research on its own. Although the industry is driven by Moore's Law, which predicts that the number of circuits that can fit on a computer chip will double every eighteen months, Intel has operated in this fast-moving industry by relying extensively on research conducted by others. Intel's experience demonstrates the use of Open Innovation principles for commercial success.

Managing the Gap Between Research and Development at Intel

The semiconductor industry arose from the invention of the germanium transistor at Bell Laboratories. Despite the rapid adoption of this revolutionary invention, the first commercial silicon transistor was shipped not by Bell Labs or its parent, AT&T, but rather by an oil-well services company, Texas Instruments. Later, the development of the first planar technology to enable the integrated circuit came from an aerial-survey company, Fairchild Camera and Instrument. This became a recurring pattern in the semiconductor industry: The inventors of a new technology often were not the first to profit from that technology.[2]

One of the reasons for this pattern was the difficulty of transferring new research discoveries into production. When Moore and Noyce worked at Fairchild, they saw firsthand how long it took Fairchild's research results to reach the manufacturing floor. Fairchild had invested significantly in R&D, creating a six-hundred-person stand-alone R&D organization. The organization was entirely separate from Fairchild's manufacturing facility (termed a *fab*, or fabrication facility, in industry jargon). Another early Intel employee, Paolo Gargini, recalled that, "while the lab and the fab were only five miles away, in practical terms they might as well have been 5000 miles away."[3] In the case of Fairchild's metal oxide semiconductor (MOS) technology, Fairchild researchers had been working on this in the lab since 1961. Yet, in 1968, Fairchild still had not transferred the MOS technology into production in its own fabs, even though other companies—including some that had spun off from Fairchild—were successfully shipping MOS technology products.

Noyce and Moore observed at Fairchild that the advanced R&D group had become completely separated from the production group. Similarly, the production group in turn had its own ideas about how best to build semiconductors. Each group had its own separate equipment, its own processes, and its own separate production lines. There were no common design rules or production practices, so that when the design group thought it had finished the design of a new chip, that chip was thrown "over the wall" to the fab to be built.

This separation was exacerbated by an attitude of intellectual superiority on the part of the lab scientists toward the fab engineers. Another example of this attitude was Paul Horn's recollection that he and his semiconductor researchers at IBM "didn't come to fight fires at Fishkill" (see chapter 5).

The experience of Intel's founders with this problem caused them to adopt a radical attitude toward internal R&D. Moore, along with Noyce, made an important decision: "Although the semiconductor industry depends on research breakthroughs for continued progress, Intel will operate without any formal research organization." [4] Instead, they chose to build Intel's organization around manufacturing and to utilize manufacturing facilities, equipment, and processes intensively for the necessary research required to advance their products. As Gargini phrased it, "The point is to make excellent chips, not to publish brilliant papers." [5]

This attitude also extended to the people they recruited for development activities. Most research departments wanted to hire the finest graduating Ph.D. students from leading computer science and electrical engineering programs. The companies would promise these academically trained people the opportunity to conduct their own research and publish what they discovered without the burden of having to teach.

At Intel the situation was very different, Gargini remembered: "All new researchers at Intel first had to work for six months in manufacturing. Then, if you were assigned to a development group, you could buy new equipment to develop new chips, but you had to operate that equipment yourself, and you had to get space for that equipment inside an existing production facility." [6]

Along with its manufacturing philosophy, Intel also conducted its research activities on the Noyce principle of "minimum information." As Moore explained, "This principle attempts to guess at what the answer is to a problem, and then goes back into the science only as far as needed to see if that guess was right or not. If this does not solve the problem, one makes another guess, and then goes back again. . . . One advantage of the minimum information principle is that Intel generates many fewer spinoff companies. Because it does not generate a lot more ideas than it can use, Intel's capture ratio [of ideas used to ideas generated] is much higher than Fairchild's ever was." [7]

Intel would develop a number of innovations with this process, but these innovations resulted from close observation of the transfer of technology into manufacturing, rather than from rigorous scientific investigation motivated by academic research. For example, Intel invented the erasable, programmable read-only memory (E-PROM) as a result of analyzing the source of "defects" in its DRAM chips. The defect was that certain aberrant chips would hold a charge, rather than dissipate it, after the power was turned off. Realizing that this defect could be turned into a product, because holding a charge would allow the device to store information even when a computer was turned off, Intel developed the E-PROM chip. The microprocessor evolved from a similar focus on reducing manufacturing costs. Intel was trying to respond to an order for control logic chips from a third-tier Japanese calculator manufacturer, Busicom. It turned out to be cheaper for Intel to combine several chips into a single device to meet the needs of the contract. Intel soon realized the commercial importance of its lower-cost solution, and created the microprocessor.

Thus, Intel was able to innovate effectively for many years without any internal research lab. In fact, Intel had no development facilities for a number of years; all the development activities occurred within existing production fabs. Moreover, there were significant limits on how much new equipment could be purchased for development at these sites, and this equipment competed for space with ongoing production activities. These barriers to development activity led Intel developers to minimize the amount of new process equipment for any given generation of new product, both to stretch the return on the equipment investment and to make it easier to use existing production lines for new products.

Copy Exactly

Intel's innovation focus—which relied chiefly upon development—finally changed when Intel decided to withdraw from the DRAM business. The DRAM fabrication facility, no longer active, became Intel's first development facility. Intel now faced a new risk: the risk that a separate development group would drift away from the production groups at the company and thus create a gap between research and development. Gargini recalled the issue that troubled Intel executives, who vividly remembered the earlier Fairchild example:

> How could we get the benefit of a dedicated development fab, without losing the production focus that had defined the company? Our answer was to invest in standardizing our equipment and processes between our lab and our fabs. In the first generation, we were able to keep 60–70% of our equipment identical between the units. This was the beginning of the methodology that came to be known as Copy Exactly.
> This evolved over time in stages.
>
> - in the beginning, we were trying to get purchasing economies from using the same equipment vendors and standardizing processes where possible
> - later, we began to insist on using the same equipment from the same vendors

- then, we were able to insist on using the same configuration options on the same equipment from the same vendor

- by 1989, Fab 9 in Albuquerque was built to receive the i486 from the development fab in Oregon. It had to buy all of the same equipment that was in place in developing the product in Oregon. And not just the same equipment, but also the same options, the same physical dimensions of the plant, even specifying the length of hookups for every intake valve, every water pipe. We did everything we could to make Fab 9 as close to an exact copy of the Oregon fab and process as possible.

Now Copy Exactly has become a religion for us. And it has had an important commercial benefit as well. Every process developed at the development fab transfers to two production fabs. Customers that qualify our products at the development fab no longer insist on also qualifying that part out of our production fabs. Thanks to our methodology, our yield at the first fab is equivalent to our yield at the new fab. It also allows us to leverage big improvements from our suppliers across all of our fabs.[8]

As Gargini observed, there also were limits to Intel's approach to R&D: "Copy Exactly has been a great methodology for us. It works very well, as long as the new technology being introduced is relatively incremental. It doesn't work as well when there are large, discontinuous changes in the underlying technology base."[9]

IBM and AT&T: Traditional Approaches to R&D

Other large, important semiconductor companies did not follow Intel's approach to R&D. Two leading semiconductor manufacturers, IBM and AT&T (and later, Lucent), maintained significant basic research capabilities. IBM conducted most of its basic research in semiconductors at its Yorktown Heights, NY, research laboratory, whereas AT&T's work was conducted primarily at Bell Labs in New Jersey. Researchers at both labs had received numerous scientific awards and were considered on par with the best of the university researchers. A few had even won Nobel Prizes for their research discoveries.

This leadership in research also pushed each company to make significant commitments to lead the industry into new technology platforms. For example, when the industry needed to increase the size of wafers from 150 to 200 millimeters to increase its yield of good chips and to lower its costs, IBM worked closely with all the leading semiconductor equipment suppliers to develop the required equipment specifications for the new wafer size. IBM even funded research activities at many of the equipment companies, to spur them to adopt the 200-millimeter wafer size—and IBM's proposed specifications for that size.

As a result of its work with these suppliers, IBM usually got the first working units of the new equipment, ahead of those companies—such as Intel—that had not invested in developing the new requirements and specifications. Access to early units of new equipment was vital for semiconductor makers to get their new processes up and running, which could enable more advanced products and greater competitive advantage in the market. Equipment suppliers in turn had to invest hundreds of millions of dollars (beyond IBM's financial contributions to them) to develop this equipment. Only a few equipment systems were available in any new generation of equipment, and it took substantial time to scale up the production of these units, each of which sold for tens of millions of dollars apiece. These high costs required the equipment makers to sell more units than IBM or AT&T could use for their internal production needs, in order to earn a return on investment for making the equipment. Suppliers would ship new equipment to companies like Intel six to nine months after the initial units were given to IBM or AT&T.

This was a wonderful situation for Intel. The company could focus on the effective transfer of technology into manufacturing and let IBM and AT&T fund the basic research for the industry, which would decide what the new technology would be. As long as Intel could get into high volume faster than other companies, it did not have to invent the core technologies it needed; it could afford to be a "fast follower."

The only problem was that Intel's approach was too successful to be sustainable. IBM and AT&T profited so little from their research investments that eventually they had to scale them back dramatically. AT&T's semiconductor business ran into problems in the 1980s, and the company cut back significantly on its work with equipment suppliers on next-generation semiconductor equipment technology. In 1993, Lou Gerstner joined IBM as CEO and mandated that IBM's semiconductor division become cash-positive. With this new mandate, IBM cut back on its pioneering research and its sponsorship funding with the equipment industry. The cutbacks noticeably reduced the amount of basic research funding in the semiconductor industry.

One indication of the impact of this reduction was the void created in technology sponsorship funding for the equipment suppliers. When IBM cut back its funding for new-generation equipment, the equipment companies came to Intel and asked what they should do to get money to develop the next-generation equipment. In the past, Intel had gotten its processes up and running ahead of IBM and AT&T, though Intel did not receive the equipment at the same time that the sponsor companies received it. Now the equipment suppliers were looking to Intel to fill the void.

Intel Innovates a New Approach to R&D

While Intel's approach to R&D was rather unconventional, the company nonetheless invested significant sums of money in R&D. Intel spent $3.8 billion on R&D in 2001, with one-third of that money going to process-improvement projects, and two-thirds going to new-product development. Intel had conducted some amount of research in component technologies as far back as 1985. By 1996, the consequences of AT&T's and IBM's retrenchment in semiconductor research, combined with Intel's own tremendous growth, dictated a change in Intel's approach to innovation.

Intel's experience and principles, however, caused it to eschew a traditional central research laboratory. Instead, the company decided to establish a decentralized, distributed model of research through the creation of three labs, each with its own specific areas of specialization. This arrangement was intended to give each lab greater focus and depth in its respective area.

The three labs were the Intel Architecture Lab (IAL), the Microprocessor Research Lab (MRL), and the Components Research Lab (CRL). The IAL facilities were located in Santa Clara, CA. Both the MRL and the CRL facilities were at two sites: Santa Clara and Hillsboro, Oregon. While there were smaller-scale research activities within Intel's development groups, the labs gave greater structure and focus to these research efforts.

These labs are organized roughly in correspondence with Intel's value chain in its microprocessor business model (figure 6-1). At the bottom of the chain is the CRL. This lab focuses on the technologies Intel needs from its suppliers and from its own operations to build excellent microprocessors and other chips. The CRL gives Intel access to leading knowledge from universities, suppliers, and the Sematech research consortium. It evaluates these external knowledge sources alongside internal Intel research initiatives and helps Intel build and evolve the supply chain for its core operational technologies.[10]

The second laboratory, the MRL, is the closest thing Intel has to a traditional central research lab. This lab does do some fundamental work in future microprocessor architectures and technologies. Yet, even here, the lab is careful to access and build on external knowledge in addition to the internal knowledge it generates. For example, the new Itanium 64-bit microprocessors are built on architectural knowledge contributed by Hewlett-Packard's own technologists. And the manufacturing process for the Itanium was informed by Intel's acquisition of the Alpha chip and its manufacturing facilities from the Digital Equipment Corporation.

The final laboratory, the IAL, conducts research into the future of computer architectures, where Intel's own products are used as components in a future computing solution. This lab corresponds to the top of the value chain that Citicorp shared with IBM's McGroddy (see chapter 5). The IAL enables Intel to access external knowledge from many sources and to develop architectures that integrate these future technologies into coherent solutions. It is a key resource that lets Intel retain the systems-level knowledge it needs to influence the future evolution of its ecosystem. The IAL also helps coordinate the activities of the

FIGURE 6-1

Intel's Research Laboratories, by Position in Value Chain

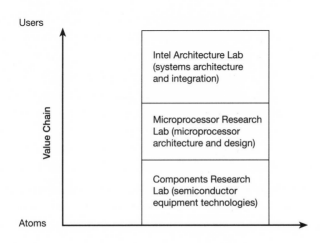

third-party developers. As with the CRL, the primary focus of IAL is on accessing external knowledge and internally focusing on architectural designs that integrate these parts effectively. Unlike CRL, though, Intel's IAL must plan its future systems-level architectures in conjunction with other companies (such as Microsoft), whose capabilities and resources also influence powerfully the direction of computing.

Intel's Additional Mechanisms to Access External Innovation

In addition to its internal research activities, Intel conducts a variety of activities to promote linkages between its labs and the external research community. The company organizes internal technology conferences each year, bringing researchers from each of the labs together. It also hosts a number of research forums and seminars, through which internal and external researchers come together and share their research. The company also puts out the *Intel Technical Journal*, which publishes research findings for the benefit of the Intel research community and the outside community.

The work of the labs is coordinated through Intel's Research Council, which includes members of Intel's executive staff, Intel's Research Fellows, and representatives from each research area of the company.[11] The council also manages Intel's external research program, establishing overall policies concerning external research, such as which projects to support and which schools and faculty to support. In 2000, Intel funded about three hundred external research projects, resulting in more than $100 million in research grants. This external effort has become increasingly international in its scope. In addition to its U.S. research activities, Intel has its own researchers working in Israel, Russia, and China, and had research projects with university faculty under way in eleven different countries.

Most companies support graduate student research by simply giving money and then checking back every year or so to find out what (if anything) had been done with their funds. Not Intel. Intel assigns internal employees to interact directly with the students they fund, as well as the students' professors. In 1999, in addition to thirty-one full-time assignees, eighty-seven voluntary "mentors" at Intel were assigned to students. In this way, students have access to a senior Intel manager in an area related to their research. Additionally, the Intel managers have an additional window onto current leading-edge research in areas of interest to them. The arrangement also gives these graduate students the chance to get to know Intel, and vice versa. Frequently, this relationship leads to new hiring by Intel.

Alongside these academic programs, Intel works with a variety of other external research channels and provides funding to the external researchers and students through them. The best-known channels are the Semiconductor Research Corporation and Sematech.[12] Intel also posts assignees to Sematech and directly sponsors lesser-known programs as well (these projects are included in the aforementioned external projects that Intel supports). One such program is the Robert Noyce Memorial Fellowship Program, which sponsors graduate students at leading computer science, engineering, and business administration programs around the United States.[13]

This combination of focused internal labs plus the blend of internal and external research embodies Intel's philosophy toward R&D. Sun-Lin Chou, the director of Intel's Components Research Laboratory, explained how his lab functioned in this philosophy: "The primary role of the Labs is to link Intel with the outside research community. We need to do enough internal work to be knowledgeable enough to talk with outside researchers, and to know which approaches seem most promising. We also need enough internal work to be able to transfer promising research results back inside Intel quickly."[14] In 2001, Intel expanded this model to bring itself even closer to selected university research centers. It has opened up new "lablets"—small-sized research facilities—which are located adjacent to three leading university research centers— Carnegie Mellon University, University of California–Berkeley, and University of Washington—instead of next to Intel fab facilities. As with other parts of its R&D system, Intel will manage these new entities in a decidedly nontraditional manner. Each lablet is led by a university faculty member who is on an academic leave and is not a permanent employee of Intel. Intel hopes and expects these new entities to connect it more closely to leading academic research, but Intel does not expect to "own" the output of this research. The company instead expects to win by having early access to promising new technologies.

On a more subtle level, Intel expects to win by using its collaboration with university researchers and its selective funding of other academic research to connect fragmented university research programs into larger research programs. These larger programs, in turn, will inform

Intel's future architectures and give the company the ability to coordinate external research more effectively at larger scale. This approach will also be fairly cost-effective, because Intel expects to leverage the research infrastructure at these leading university establishments instead of duplicating that infrastructure inside its own four walls.

As this approach reveals, it is no accident that Intel's research organization today is run by David Tennenhouse. Tennenhouse used to manage research programs at the Defense Advanced Research Projects Agency (DARPA). DARPA directed the research activities of numerous disparate research organizations and linked them into powerful research programs for the U.S. military. By many accounts, DARPA performed this role very effectively. And DARPA did this coordination without its own central laboratory. Intel hopes to apply much of the DARPA model to accessing, influencing, and coordinating university research for industrial purposes.

Evaluating Intel's Approach to Innovation

Intel's approach to managing innovation has a number of obvious strengths. It is efficient, because it launches few blue-sky investigations that might lead to dead ends. The approach is also efficient because it reinvents fewer wheels, instead building on the research discoveries of others (particularly university researchers) and transferring those discoveries into the company's own development process. Intel's approach to innovation saves money as well, because Intel leverages the facilities and personnel of other institutions. Although the company often pays to fund external research projects, these grants likely do not cover the full cost of the researchers, facilities, and other overhead expenses.

But efficiency is not the only desirable attribute of a company's innovation system. Intel must hire a different kind of researcher than those who IBM, Bell Labs, or Xerox PARC would traditionally hire. Intel's approach is unlikely to lure the star graduate students out of universities. If you were a hot, new Ph.D. in electrical engineering or computer science, graduating from an elite university, would you want to work at Intel? Instead of academic freedom, intellectual inquiry, and the thrill of scientific discovery, Intel offers its researchers six months on the manufacturing line, the Noyce principle of minimum information, and a career path that promises close coordination with manufacturing. Intel needs researchers who can work with and build on the research discoveries of others outside of Intel, or who can transfer the discoveries to the manufacturing line next door, or who can do both. It also needs systems architects able to construct new architectures that connect disparate and fragmented research activities into effective future systems. Arguably, IBM's knowledge brokering described in chapter 5 is carried even further here in Intel's approach, although Intel places comparatively less emphasis on knowledge generation.

Indeed, Intel's approach effectively assumes that others will continue to make the investments needed to assure the continued advance of the industry. When Intel was a comparatively small player in the semiconductor industry in relation to IBM and AT&T, this was a safe bet. Now that Intel has surpassed all the other semiconductor companies in revenue and profit, its very success calls this assumption into question. Intel's success and its relative lack of basic research have not escaped the attention of other leading semiconductor firms, and they too have shifted away from funding basic research.

Looking down the road, there is a real possibility of a crisis, in which the overall industry underinvests in the basic research needed to continue the progress predicted by Moore's Law. Moore's Law is not an iron-clad law; rather, it is an empirical result of technological advance that requires new fundamental technologies to arise fairly often, in order to realize the regular improvements predicted by the law. If the industry reduces its investment in basic research and shifts its public research dollars away from semiconductors and materials science, then the pool of available research to support the long-term growth of the industry will likely diminish. That, in turn, could slow down the industry's (and Intel's) ability to follow Moore's Law.

Intel Capital: Another Window on External Innovation

While Intel's model for R&D is interesting in its own right, the company's innovation system extends beyond its approach to internal and external R&D. Intel operates in the heart of Silicon Valley, and Intel managers cannot help but note the vibrant innovation community that surrounds it. As noted in chapter 1, being in the heart of the Valley is a mixed blessing, for the erosion factors that caused many Xerox technologies to diffuse out into start-up companies also put Intel at risk.

Intel, though, has found a way to benefit from venture capital (VC). It has created a farsighted program with corporate VC, which builds

strong connections between Intel and the start-up community that surrounds it. Intel's corporate VC program, now called Intel Capital, enables Intel to extend its own business strategy by leveraging the activities of these start-ups. The program even allows Intel to explore new
business areas beyond microprocessors by funding and observing the
experiments these start-ups conduct.

Moreover, the exploration that occurs inside Intel's R&D groups is
linked to the experiments that Intel funds in its corporate VC program.
In fact, the person who set up Intel's unique approach to research and
who ran Intel's Research Council for many years is the same person who
established Intel Capital: Leslie L. Vadasz. Vadasz's two roles would be
unthinkable in a Closed Innovation regime. Why would a person direct-
ing internal research activities be involved in investing part of the corporate treasury's funds in new start-up companies? Only in an Open Innovation approach would such a relationship become comprehensible.

The Strategic Role of Intel Capital

As of June 2002, Intel Capital held more than 475 investments in portfolio companies, with a market value of more than $1.4 billion.[15] But making
external equity investments is not a new practice for Intel. In the early
1980s, Intel began investing in its close suppliers, primarily to ensure a sta-
ble source of quality inputs for its design and manufacturing processes.
Target firms included software, microcode, component design, and equipment companies. While Intel intended to make a financial return on these
investments (i.e., the investments were not intended to subsidize their
suppliers), the goal of these investments was strategic: to give Intel the
technology supply base it needed to achieve its business goals.

By the mid-1990s, however, this focus expanded beyond Intel's supply chain, to include the "market ecosystem" of software and hardware
developers that supported Intel's microprocessor products. Intel recognized that more and better software and hardware offerings that ran on
top of the Pentium architecture increased the value of Pentium in the
market. Vadasz recalled the ecosystem insight as "obvious, but to us a
revelation," articulating what Intel already knew: that the existence of a
large pool of companies complementary to Intel helped everyone in the
Intel ecosystem.[16]

What became exciting to Intel was the idea of investing in this
ecosystem to accelerate the adoption of new, higher speed, Pentium

microprocessors. If more companies made products that were compatible with the Pentium processor, and that required faster processors to run effectively, that could increase the sales of Pentium chips. To this end, Intel began to expand its external investments aggressively, through joint marketing efforts, technology cooperation, and capital investments. Through the 1990s, Intel invested in literally hundreds of companies whose products—such as video, audio, and graphics hardware and software—required increasingly powerful microprocessors inside computers, thereby stimulating sales of Intel Pentium chips.

But expanding its microprocessor market was not the only purpose of Intel's VC investments. The company decided that its investments could not only help grow its current business, but also help explore new businesses beyond microprocessors. As Vadasz put it: "I want to invest in market success, to have more complementors, and a broader market, sooner. That is probably the most important step we've taken. The other step is the realization that investment can be a good way to understand new technologies that are not today's concern in the business units, but might become important in the future."[17]

Vadasz also oversaw an internal seed capital research program designed to fund internal technical investigations of technologies that did not yet intersect with the business units, but were thought to be important to Intel's future. These seed projects permitted experimentation with new technologies and ended within six to twenty-four months. Vadasz was eager to move projects that grew beyond this phase into other areas of the company for development: "You need to keep things turbulent. When [an internal] project becomes $10 million a year, even $5 million a year, I don't want my group to fund it any further. At that point, it needs to survive on its own—meaning that a business unit has to pick up funding for it. Our funding focuses on the initial phase, on technological investigation. You don't want 10-year projects. That may be good in a research lab or in a university, but not in an industrial environment."[18]

Sometimes, Intel would initiate an internal seed research program as part of its due diligence process for evaluating a corporate venture investment opportunity. Here is where the genius of Intel's combination of externally focused research and corporate VC becomes apparent. This combination of internal seed projects and external investments gave Intel a unique insight into future technology opportunities and enhanced its knowledge as a corporate investor. Vadasz elaborated: "Intel only makes investments that in some way help support Intel's strategic interests. As an added benefit, Intel can also use investments to gain insights into emerging trends. Traditional venture capital firms don't have the knowledge assets [in the form of thousands of engineers and marketing people] to do the level of technical due diligence that we do. I want to do more than simply invest money."[19]

Through Intel Capital, Intel has been able to invest in a range of areas to advance computing platforms in support of Intel's strategic interests. In 2001, more than half of Intel Capital's investment occurred outside the United States, helping Intel advance its strategy of globalizing its business and further developing its international markets.

Intel Capital's Investment Process

Ideas for external investments arrive at Intel in many ways. Intel managers within Intel Capital are assigned to specific business areas within the parent company, and work closely with the managers in those businesses. Together, the two sets of managers identify new trends, technologies, and start-ups that may be important to Intel's strategy in that business. Intel managers also consider the firsthand information about business and technology trends developed by their marketing staff or through internal research programs. Informally, Intel engineers and managers network with their opposite numbers in the technology and financial communities and keep their eyes open for new developments.

For companies that offered strategic and financial promise, Intel's next stage, "the hard work," as Vadasz put it, was negotiation with the target company on deal content. Progress in negotiations would lead to an investment project authorization (IPA) meeting at Intel to consider topics such as the target company's management, its competitors, and the terms of the developing deal. Most important, each IPA meeting would formalize answers to the three key questions posed of every deal: What do we get? What do we give? What is the measure of strategic success for this investment?

Guided by these strategic objectives decided in the IPA, Intel Capital would negotiate further with its target company and eventually close the deal, at which time it would establish processes for monitoring and managing company-to-company relations. Although Intel would seek board observation rights, it did not take a board seat in any company in its investment portfolio, primarily to prevent Intel employees from encountering fiduciary conflicts between their responsibilities to Intel and to the portfolio company. In any case, Vadasz noted, "If you don't have the 'gives' and the 'gets' worked out ahead of time, having a board seat won't matter anyway."[20]

From Intel's standpoint, the companies in which it invested could gain technology assistance that could improve product performance, and they could collaborate on the development of technical specifications. Moreover, these companies could receive insights into Intel's product roadmaps, participate in Intel's marketing programs, and access its distribution channels. The "gives and gets" decided in the IPA meeting could specify term-sheet warrants for additional shares in a company if Intel enhanced its product performance to specified levels.

If Intel Capital decides to invest, it generally manages the investment through the Intel business unit most relevant to the technology concerned, not through Intel Capital. In some cases, though, when financial issues facing the venture are of paramount concern, Intel Capital's own managers play a more active role in managing these relationships. Regardless of who fills that role, Intel revisits the IPA criteria of every company in its portfolio on a quarterly basis to assess the deal's postinvestment performance. "There's an old saying at Intel, I think it comes from Andy [Grove, Intel's former CEO and current chairman]," related Vadasz. "'Anything that you measure will get better.'"[21] Each quarterly review incorporates both trend and snapshot indicators to analyze how well the deal meets Intel's strategic objectives. "You need a 'forcing function' to make the relationship happen," stressed Steven Nachtsheim, Intel Capital vice president and director. "Managing the relationship does not mean making it work. It also can mean deciding that it's time to cut bait when it no longer makes sense. It's not a marriage."[22]

Although Intel seeks a return on its invested capital, it is primarily concerned about achieving the strategic objectives it negotiated into the term sheet. This is an imperfect solution to a difficult problem: Corporate venture investing should be driven by strategic goals, instead of purely financial goals. Yet strategically driven investments are inherently much harder to evaluate and measure quantitatively than financially driven investments. Intel's approach at least addresses one potential problem with evaluating the performance of a strategic investment, namely, the tendency to retrospectively redefine the goals of the investment so that the actual performance is considered more favorably than it should be. This retroactive redefinition moves the goalposts by removing the anchor that formed the basis for the investment in the first place.

But even Intel cannot answer the key question one would ideally want to ask about its corporate venture investments: How much did Intel's sales and profits increase as a result of its corporate venture investments?[23]

Intel Capital's enormous investment portfolio, which in early 2000 was valued as much as $8 billion and by June 2002 had fallen to $1.46 billion, has been the subject of some derision. Critics charge that Intel engages in "drive-by investing." They argue that the company cannot possibly coordinate with its own operations—or even effectively monitor—the more than eight hundred investments it has made in the 1990s and the 475 that it held in June 2002.

But this criticism misses the key point of Intel's investment strategy. An investment's strategic value to Intel may be justified simply if the investment increases demand sufficiently for Intel's own products. Intel need not closely manage every investment, because it typically coinvests alongside VC firms, which direct the venture's growth and monitor its performance. Moreover, the metrics that disclose the current market value of Intel's portfolio holdings take no account of any internal learning, development, or increased sales of Intel's own products as a result of its investment activities.

Intel itself may have added to the confusion about its investment rationale by widely touting the financial returns on its investments starting in 2000. This publicity about the financial returns obscured the fact that the high returns were secondary to Intel's strategic objectives; the (temporarily) high returns simply made Intel's investments more affordable at that time. Indeed, Intel continued to make corporate VC investments in 2002, despite its investment losses in 2001. Although the number of new investments in the United States has gone down, the number of its international investments has greatly increased.

Connecting Internal Knowledge with External Knowledge

Intel's approach provides a fascinating example of how Open Innovation principles can leverage internal and external knowledge in a very different way from the earlier Closed Innovation paradigm. Intel's research philosophy fosters an external orientation to the generation of knowledge. Intel looks outside first before determining what internal research activities to perform. And Intel thinks hard about how to connect the individual pieces of internal and external knowledge, to create new architectures and systems out of this knowledge. It is here where Intel's internal work enables it to capture a portion of the value it creates from its use of external knowledge.

Intel then employs corporate VC to build and extend the value chain of suppliers that it relies on to make complementary investments to support the architecture. And Intel's internal research capabilities allow it to conduct much deeper due diligence on the technical side of its investments than is typically done by most venture capitalists. These investments help accelerate the penetration of Intel's value network into the market.

Intel's approach would make little sense in a barren knowledge land-scape, because the company's primary emphasis is on accessing and lever-aging external knowledge. The internal knowledge-generation activities at Intel wrap around the externally available knowledge, rather than trying to compete with or ignoring it. Intel's corporate VC investing also ac-knowledges the potential latent in the myriad start-up ventures that arise in numerous areas of strategic interest to Intel. The choices made by these start-up firms' such as which technology platforms to support and which markets to target can influence the success of Intel's own ecosystem.

Intel can also use its corporate venture investing to explore new po-tential technologies and markets beyond its core business. Its extensive investment portfolio gives it tremendous visibility into the business plans of new and emerging companies, and this view can broaden its own vision of possible future directions for Intel's own business. Once Intel identifies a few areas that seem promising for further exploration, it can deploy its own internal research activities to deepen its under-standing of the technical risks and opportunities and find the leading external academic researchers in the area.

Intel's approach also provides a different way to think about the risks and rewards of vertical integration in an era of Open Innovation. Instead of forward integrating into the manufacture of computers, software, and other products, Intel obtains leverage for its core offerings at much lower cost by investing in companies that make these other products. Intel's model thus reaches far up and down the value chain and through-out the ecosystem, yet Intel's actual product offerings themselves remain highly focused on microprocessors and related semiconductor chips. Intel does not achieve the tight control via vertical integration that IBM achieved in the Closed Innovation paradigm. But Intel's funding of aca-demic research and its investing in complementory start-up companies gives it influence far beyond the scope of its own products.

Looking Ahead:
Clouds Gathering on the Horizon

Having given Intel's model its due, there remain important limitations and risks to its approach to innovation. Its strengths, such as its extensive use of external knowledge, are potentially limitations as well. Intel will need fundamental new discoveries in numerous areas of its business to continue to succeed. Within the next five to ten years, Moore's Law will lead the semiconductor industry into the domain of quantum computing. In this new way of computing, the size of individual circuits will become so small that quantum (i.e., subatomic) effects in materials will become critically important. Quantum computing will be an important research and technological challenge for Intel and the industry overall.

As noted earlier in this chapter, the funding that historically supported the creation of many basic discoveries in the semiconductor industry—from the military, AT&T, and IBM in particular—has diminished or gone away. Intel does not want to pick up the slack, yet it has a higher stake in continued discovery than does any other semiconductor company. If Moore's Law slows down, Intel will find itself competing more and more with other companies' products that got into production more slowly than did Intel's, and even against its own products from six or twelve months ago. The new Intel initiative on new "lablets" is a novel extension of Intel's model, but the initiative lacks the scale and scope to address the challenges of quantum computing that lurk on the horizon. And integrating the discoveries from the university research community in effective quantum computing architectures will require extensive internal research, even long-term research, of the kind that Intel has not historically had to perform.

Intel is aware of these challenges. Here is how Sun-Lin Chou described the merits and issues of Intel's innovation approach:

> There are limits to our model. We don't have a large pool of talent within Intel looking at brand new areas. This may cause us to miss a revolutionary breakthrough. You have to ask yourself, where is the next big idea, such as the next transistor, the next IC, the next successor to silicon going to come from? If you believe it will come from directed discovery, then you are well advised to invest in

focused internal research activities to increase your chances of finding it. If, however, you believe that the next big idea is likely to come from any one of a large number of areas, then you're better advised to structure yourself to be able to monitor a variety of research sources, and to respond quickly to research discoveries when and if they arise.[24]

7

Creating New Ventures out of Internal Technologies

Lucent's New Ventures Group

C HAPTERS 5 AND 6 have shown one company (IBM) with an internal research commitment to developing a different business model for leveraging its technology, and a second company (Intel) with an innovation system that connects internal and external research with corporate VC to grow its business model. These approaches bring external knowledge into the corporation (excluding IBM's licensing out its technology for the moment). This chapter will discuss a third approach to managing innovation, which involves taking internal knowledge out to the external market. This approach creates external venture organizations out of internal technologies, building new business models to commercialize those technologies in the process.

The importance of this process was shown in chapter 1, where, out of interesting internal technologies at PARC, Xerox created spin-off companies that it could not use in its own business. Chapter 4 showed the importance of discovering a viable business model to create new ventures out of promising technologies. Nevertheless, Xerox lacked a systematic process for exploring and evaluating alternative business models. A more systematic model for creating new businesses out of internal technologies has been implemented at Lucent Technologies, the home of Bell Laboratories. The architects of this new model studied the Xerox experience closely and have made a number of improvements on that approach. Lucent's experience is worth studying, both because of these improvements and because of the continuing difficulties Lucent has encountered.

Bell Labs

In the days of the Closed Innovation paradigm, Bell Labs was perhaps the preeminent industrial research laboratory in the world. This is where the transistor was invented. This is where the cosmic background radiation (or *dark matter*) in the universe was first detected. When you walk into the lobby of the main facility in Murray Hill, NJ, the walls bear plaques commemorating eleven Nobel Prize winners out of Bell Labs, and dozens of other researchers who have won other prestigious scientific awards.

Since the 1980s, this research institution has been breaking up. First, there was the breakup of AT&T and the Regional Bell Operating Companies (RBOCs) in 1984. This breakup caused part of Bell Labs to be placed into a separate lab called Bellcore, which later changed its name to Tricordia. Another portion of Bell Labs was split off in the trivestiture of AT&T in 1996, when Lucent, AT&T Longlines, and NCR were separated into distinct companies. Lucent Technologies now houses the largest remnants of Bell Laboratories. Finally, the micro-electronics business within Lucent was spun off in 2001 into a new company, Agere, and some of the lab went with that as well.

A Lucent Organizational Innovation:
Lucent's New Ventures Group

Lucent knew that it had a wonderful research organization in the portion of Bell Labs that it had retained.[1] It also sensed that it wasn't realizing the full potential of the labs in its own businesses and wanted to explore how it might do more with the labs and the research talent within. Out of this exploration emerged Lucent's New Ventures Group (NVG) in 1997. The NVG was created to commercialize any Bell Laboratories technologies that did not fit with any of Lucent's established businesses.

Lucent was careful to conduct extensive external benchmarking to determine whether and how to utilize corporate money to finance new technology ventures. Some of this benchmarking involved discussion with other companies that had experience with this activity, including Intel, 3M, Raychem, Thermo Electron, and Xerox. The planning staff also held numerous discussions with the private VC community, to understand how this group's approach to financing and commercializing new technologies worked. They learned that the history of corporate

VC has been a decidedly mixed one, and that there were plenty of pit-falls if they were not careful.[2]

Lucent determined from its planning that it needed to craft an operating model to blend the incentives, risk-taking, and speedy decision making of private VC with the deep technological resources and the culture of Bell Laboratories. The key challenge for the NVG was to graft a more entrepreneurial spirit onto the culture of the organization. This required faster decisions, more individual risk taking, and greater individual identification with the business opportunities latent in the deep technical resources of the company.

Lucent was well aware of the difficulties that it faced in trying to do this. It came across a challenge that was referred to as "the silicon paradox" and that David Liddle described so well: The companies most able to conduct research are the least able to profit from it.[3] In Lucent's mind, internal VC could address the silicon paradox by helping a new technology find another path to market.

The NVG's Innovation Model

The mission of the NVG was to "[l]everage Lucent technology to create new ventures that bring innovations to market more quickly . . . [and to] create a more entrepreneurial environment that nurtures and rewards speed, teamwork, and prudent risk-taking."[4] By following this mission, the team hoped to realize the objectives of building the ventures that they undertook into major new businesses using different business structures and outside partners. They also set a goal to achieve an overall 20 percent return on investment over time for their venture portfolio. As with the Intel Capital organization, NVG's investments had to earn their way; Lucent was not going to subsidize internal venture investments in its own technologies.

Yet, at the same time, Lucent had to take care that the NVG did not harm the innovation process within Lucent. Lucent did not want its researchers devoting all their time to creating projects that were intended to go to a new venture group; it wanted its innovation process focused primarily on supporting its own business. This meant that a delicate balance had to be struck between the creation of new pathways for established research to get to market and the need to focus research on the Lucent business as much as practicable.

To manage this balance, the NVG consciously created what became known internally as "the phantom world." The phantom world did not exist outside Lucent; it was a hybrid that was partly an internal VC organization and partly a business development activity within a large, technology-based company. It could be thought of as a halfway house that would enable people and ideas not ready to go out directly to obtain outside VC to develop their ideas further within Lucent. By being sensitive about the cultural gaps that had to be bridged, and by being sensible about the right mix of risk and reward to offer, the phantom world created a launching pad for ideas to move out of Bell Labs into markets outside of Lucent's traditional business channels.

Figure 7-1 shows a logic diagram for how the NVG balanced the protection of the internal innovation process with the development of external paths to market for Lucent technologies. The process started with periodic informal meetings between NVG managers and Lucent researchers. Ideas and projects were discussed between them, and occasionally the NVG manager would sense that an idea inside the labs might be brought to market via an independent venture. The manager could "nominate" that idea for external commercialization. Once a new idea or discovery was nominated, the internal Lucent business groups were given first priority over the technology. They would evaluate the strategic fit they perceived between the technology and their own business model. If a business unit wanted to use the technology in its own business and take over funding the technology, then that technology would migrate from the lab to the business unit. Essentially, the technology would go into that unit's business model or perhaps an incremental variation of the business model. The business would capture value from that technology through increased revenues and operating income. Importantly, the business unit had to make this determination within a fixed period, initially as long as nine months and later reduced to three months. Consequently, the business unit could not wait indefinitely for a nominated technology. This creatively addressed the budgetary disconnect between research and development described in chapter 2.

Some technology opportunities, though, did not fit strategically with a current business, perhaps because they were disruptive technologies, or addressed a "white space" that fell between the charters of current businesses. If, owing to these reasons, the business units declined to accept the responsibility and funding for the idea or technology, the NVG then had an opportunity to take the idea to market itself. First,

FIGURE 7-1

NVG's Innovation Model for Commercializing New Technology: Value Capture Structures

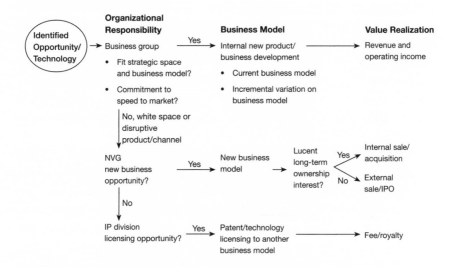

the NVG would develop a business model for this technology. Then, the group would consider the likely "exit" for the technology, particularly whether it would likely end up back in Lucent at some point or whether it was more likely to become an independent company. In the latter case, the new company might be sold at a profit to another firm or go public itself.

Of course, the NVG might well decide not to commercialize a technology, either. In that case, the technology would be available for external licensing to other companies through Lucent's intellectual property licensing office. In this instance, the licensee would utilize the technology in its own business model. Considering that Lucent received more than $400 million in 2001 in licensing payments, this option was frequently employed as well. Thus, the path to market for a Bell Labs technology depended in large part on where the most promising business model for that technology resided.

Sourcing ideas and managing these processes required extensive interaction between the NVG and the many managers within Bell Labs or the Lucent business groups. The NVG built an internal business development group, which developed its own set of relationships with the lab managers. These NVG staff became technology "scouts" and typically had both a technical and a management consulting background. They would find what they thought to be interesting leads from the various lab managers and then would bring these ideas back to the NVG senior staff for evaluation.

As noted in chapter 4, there is an enormous amount of technical and market uncertainty involved in commercializing an early-stage venture. The NVG addressed this uncertainty by carefully staging its investments in these ventures. During the *initial evaluation* stage, typical funding levels were limited to between $50,000 and $100,000 and normally lasted from two to three months. If the project looked promising, it then was subjected to a more thorough *market qualification* phase. During this period, the NVG put together the business team and concentrated on business plan development, product development, and customer testing and trials. Funding at this phase was usually between $50,000 and $1 million, and the timing was anywhere from three to twelve months.

The third, longest, and most expensive phase in the commercialization process was the *business commercialization* phase, which came after the approval of the business plan and venture review. In this phase, the venture team worked to establish the business structure and focused its efforts on product commercialization and market penetration. Initially, the NVG attempted to fund this phase on its own, but over time it chose to syndicate these investments with outside venture capitalists whenever possible. The involvement of external venture capitalists was regarded as a very positive signal of the commercial potential of an NVG venture, and the participation of external venture capitalists reduced the amount of funds Lucent needed for its internal ventures.

Once a venture was launched and funded, it began operations as a stand-alone entity. If things were going well, the venture went through a rigorous exit strategy review before the final phase—*value realization*, or exit—began. Options for this phase included internal acquisition, public stock offering, private sale, technology licensing, a technology-for-equity swap, or liquidation. The exit decision was based on a number of factors, such as strategic fit with Lucent or with its operational capabilities. For example, a venture that had little strategic fit with Lucent, required considerable operational capabilities not available within Lucent, or introduced entirely new customers and markets to Lucent would likely exit via an acquisition by a partner or a license. Ventures with the opposite characteristics might be reacquired by Lucent.

This process worked well for the group. By March 2001, Lucent had a portfolio of twenty-six companies, nineteen of which are shown in the following list:

Internal NVG Venture Companies	*Syndicated NVG Venture Companies*
• EC&S	• Face2Face
• Full View	• Lucent Digital Radio
• Lucent Public Safety Systems	• Persystant
• NetCalibrate	• Siros
• Savaje	• Talarian
	• Veridicom
	• VideoNet
	• Visual Insights
	• Watchmark

Ventures That Have Experienced Liquidation Events

- Elemedia (reacquired by Lucent)
- Lucent Digital Video (reacquired by Lucent)
- Maps on Us
- Noteable (reacquired by Lucent)
- Speech

Most ventures were in the Internet, networking, software, wireless, and digital broadcast spaces, which are of strategic interest to Lucent. Twenty of the ventures had been raw start-ups. The remaining six active ventures were started through technology-for-equity deals. In these latter deals, the team discovered a good technology in an attractive market space, but the product did not have enough critical mass to warrant a stand-alone venture. For these, the group partnered with an existing venture-backed company, licensing Bell Labs' technology in return for equity in the start-up.

The NVG Hybrid Model for Risk and Reward

In its daily operations, Lucent designed its NVG to balance the need to function like a venture capitalist with the need to connect to Lucent's overall business objectives. As table 7-1 shows, the NVG did not try to fully emulate the attributes of a private venture capitalist. Nor did it try to mimic entirely the attributes of an internal business development department. Consider, for example, the incentives paid to the managers of NVG-funded ventures. The NVG offered a pseudo-equity compensation system that provides greater rewards than commonly available through Bell Labs, and the system did impose some modest amount of risk on employees who wish to join a venture sponsored by NVG. But the risks and rewards were far less extreme than what are found in private VC-financed structures. The resulting balance of these factors on other dimensions such as financial discipline, monitoring, time horizon, and scale of capital invested, are shown in table 7-1.

The design of NVG's operating model had important implications for the Lucent people whom the NVG chose to lead each of the new ventures. Initially, many Lucent researchers were eager to become entrepreneurs, to push their ideas out of Bell Labs and into the market. They were thrilled to have the chance to see their ideas actually put into practice. And they thought that they could be at least as effective in commercializing their work as the Lucent businesses or the entrepreneurs who took VC money and started up new businesses. After all, the Lucent researchers were expert technologists, often with Ph.D. degrees.

However, Lucent rightly believed that the possibility of additional reward through stock options in a new venture should be accompanied with some additional risk. In order for any researchers to join a new venture, Lucent required that they forgo their annual bonus, which amounted to 10 to 25 percent of their annual salary. This sacrifice meant that the researchers bore some risk as well, though by the standards of many start-ups, this risk was rather small. Nevertheless, even this amount of risk was enough to discourage the majority of researchers from pursuing their technologies in new ventures. Other researchers, though, were excited about the opportunity to become entrepreneurs and were willing to carry their research out of the lab and into the market.

Over time, Lucent learned to bring in outside managers to lead its ventures. The NVG operating model depicted in table 7-1 also influences the type of people who can be brought in from outside. A pure

TABLE 7-1

Design of Lucent's NVG Operating Model in Comparison with Internal Business Development and Private VC Models

Attribute	Ranking[a]	Comment on Ranking
Incentive intensity	3	Pseudo-equity used
Financial discipline on downside	5	Staged funding used
Monitoring	4	Outside venture capitalists, board
Discovering alternative business models	4	Outside board, CEO
Time horizon	1	No specific fund length
Scale of capital invested	3	Shifting toward larger deals
Coordination of complementarities	3	Increasing reacquisitions
Retention of group learning	1	Limited career downside risk

[a]Ranking based on a scale of 1 to 5, with 1 representing an NVG most like internal business development models, and 5 representing an NVG most like private VC models.

entrepreneur having no experience with operating within a larger company would likely be unable to function effectively in the NVG operating model. He or she might never have seen corporate overhead charges; annual operating plans; or companywide occupational safety, environmental, or other corporate policy and personnel initiatives. Any entrepreneur who recoils from the very mention of these terms would have found it enormously frustrating to work with Lucent's organization to commercialize new technologies.

The NVG model in table 7-1 emulates some of the governance features of private VC. The money is given to individual ventures through staged financing increments, very much like rounds of investment by VC firms. In nine of the ventures, NVG even syndicated later rounds of investment with outside venture firms and invited the outside venture partners onto the board of the venture. This helped provide diligent monitoring and oversight and allowed NVG ventures to access some of the external VC network of contacts in order to help identify appropriate CEO candidates and promising business model approaches.

However, the NVG also leveraged some potential structural advantages of corporate venturing. NVG managers were particularly interested in projects that could exploit any complementarities with Lucent's assets. As was the case with Intel's corporate venture investing in chapter 6, much of the NVG's due diligence process involved extended discussions with internal Lucent business managers and Bell Labs technologists. Their expertise helped the NVG identify important industry trends and missing elements in Lucent's internal offerings and understand Lucent's customers' needs for new product and service offerings. These discussions also helped validate the business potential of a new venture and align the ventures with the overall strategic direction of Lucent's businesses. They also broadened the perspective of technology managers within Bell Labs to the directions and opportunities in the wider world.

Lucent Digital Video:
An Example of the NVG Process at Work

An example of how a venture worked its way through all the phases of commercialization can be seen through the Lucent Digital Video business (LDV). In the fall of 1996, Paul Wilford, a researcher within Bell Labs, was working on building a technology that could convert analog signals to digital signals, in the hopes of shipping digitized video content around on digitized networks, which were the next generation of networks being built. Victor Lawrence, the Lucent vice president of advanced technologies, encouraged Wilford to keep at his research, even though there was currently no demand for it in any of the business units. At an internal Lucent Technologies exhibition where the different researchers pitched what they were doing to senior management, Wilford's research came to the attention of the NVG.

As a result, Steve Socolof, one of the partners in the NVG, started working with the product and the team. At that time, the small market for the new product was incurring early forecasts of a $30 to $40 million market. Since this estimate was not large enough to interest Lucent, its business units passed on funding further development internally, and the NVG got the chance to commercialize this technology. As a part of that process, the NVG tried to find a sponsor within another business group to cosponsor the activity (though this group would not have to fund the development). The NVG president, Tom Uhlman, put the team in touch with an executive who was running Lucent's North American marketing for all channels other than the core telephone companies and who was therefore tuned into the marketplace then emerging. Through a series of meetings with this cosponsor, the team developed several iterations of its business plan.

This connection between the new venture and Lucent's marketing channels was mutually beneficial. The venture received extremely valuable feedback on its ideas from a very knowledgeable market participant that might be an eventual customer or distribution channel for the technology. This feedback was typically hard to obtain for most Bell Labs projects while they were still in the laboratory. Most market feedback to lab projects was filtered through Lucent's business units, which were constrained by annual P&L concerns in their evaluation of new technologies. The connection was also valuable for the Lucent marketing channels. They got a fresh look at early technology before they normally would see it from within the labs, and this new technology provided a window on new, emerging possibilities that might affect their business in the medium term.

The initial investment round in October 1997 was an internal round of investment at a valuation of several million dollars. The NVG recruited an outside executive, Andreas Papanicalou, as the CEO and established a board of directors that included Uhlman and Socolof. After two years, the team had between $15 and $20 million in revenue coming in and was projecting between $25 and $30 million for the next year. At this point, Socolof noted, "it was the summer of 1999 and we decided that it was now time to take this venture out of Lucent. We had several external evaluations of the business done and there were some merger discussions along the way, which were informally held with an external business partner. We then came back to Lucent and said we were thinking about where to take it next."[5]

As it turned out, Lucent's Optical Networking Group now voiced interest in the business. In the period between 1997 and 1999, several multimillion-dollar sales of Lucent's fiber-optic transmission systems to China were enabled by Lucent's ability to bundle LDV's digital encoders into the offers. At that point, the Optical Networking Group began a negotiation with the NVG to reacquire the venture. After doing its due diligence on the venture, the Optical Networking Group came back with a business case for the acquisition that they presented to the Lucent acquisition-oversight committee. Lucent's mergers and acquisitions group also solicited outside bids for the venture to help establish a fair market price. A short negotiation over value ensued, a price was agreed, and the Optical Networking Group acquired the business. Lucent would have been a much later entrant to the digital network video market without this internal acquisition of the LDV venture.

Because of the NVG structure, this acquisition wasn't simply an internal reorganization of the digital video team from one group to another. Instead, the Optical Networking Group wrote a check to the NVG for the venture. The venture managers and key employees actually got a large premium for their portion of the equity, so that their reward was similar to what they would have received if LDV had been acquired by an external company. Similarly, the NVG's managers received credit for a large gain in value created in the venture in their own compensation. However, since the NVG owned most of the venture, Lucent effectively wrote a check to itself for the bulk of the acquisition.

A "Second Opinion" for Lucent Technology: Correcting the False Negatives

Note how much Lucent learned about the optical video coder market between 1997 and 1999. A technical project that was deemed to address a small niche market actually came to market, and its sales were indeed initially small, but growing nicely—and pulling in sales of other Lucent products. What was a business unit planning conjecture in 1997 ("It's just a niche market and therefore not interesting to us") was replaced by some hard facts two years later: The venture had already done $15 to $20 million in revenue, and it would do $25 to $30 million next year. Moreover, it was helping Lucent close big deals with its other equipment in key accounts.

This alternate path for LDV constituted a powerful "second opinion" that most Bell Labs technologies never received. If the business unit didn't want to fund a technology, there was no court of appeal for the technology. The initial judgment served as the last word on the matter. And the initial judgment is made on little hard data, in an environment of high technical and market uncertainty. Errors are likely to happen in such circumstances, but usually there is no opportunity to correct them.

More specifically, Lucent's commercialization process (absent the NVG) provided many ways to correct *false-positive* errors, that is, errors in which the projects were initially judged to be promising and later discontinued. What Lucent *lacked* was a process to manage *false negatives*, namely, projects initially judged to lack promise, but which later turn out to be valuable. There was no way to reconsider these initial judgments within Lucent. The NVG offered a process to deal with such errors. Of course, the NVG made errors in its judgments too, but Lucent overall was more likely to correct false negatives with the NVG as part of its process than it is without the NVG.

Similarly, Lucent's business groups could get involved with a NVG venture anywhere along its development timeline. The larger business units would not have had the appetite for risk to fund many new ventures from the beginning. However, as a result of the NVG's investing in and developing these ventures, the business units reaped the benefit of being able to watch the new businesses grow. The units also could internally acquire the business at any point, as long as the business was purchased at fair market value.[6] The NVG could thus serve as a second source of technology for Lucent's business groups.

Another benefit of the NVG's presence on Lucent's innovation system was that many Bell Labs researchers valued the presence of another group that might potentially be interested in their ideas. Lucent even found recruiting advantages to its NVG program. The company's biggest competition for new Ph.D. hires often comes not from other research laboratories, but often from start-up firms. The NVG helped Lucent recruit new Ph.D. scientists and engineers, who appreciated joining a world-class research organization that also provided a second path to market for their ideas down the road, via start-ups.

Another major benefit reaped from the NVG was, as Uhlman put it, "the strategy of syndication." The NVG's ability to create high-potential ventures enabled it to encourage a large number of very smart and respectable VC firms to invest. In 2000, the NVG had thirty external venture capitalists perform due diligence and invest more than $160 million of external capital in their ventures.[7] This level of investment signals the quality of the technology associated with Lucent. In addition, these external coinvestors injected additional knowledge and expertise into the NVG's judgments about potential markets and exerted financial discipline on the further funding and development of NVG ventures. In environments of high technical and market uncertainty, it helps to have additional informed, independent actors involved in planning the future of these technology-based ventures.

The biggest potential benefit of the NVG process to Lucent, though, was also the most elusive: the NVG's acting as an impetus for Bell Labs technologies to move faster off the shelf. In the past, Lucent's business units could wait and see whether a Bell Labs technology would become important before deciding whether to fund its further development.

The NVG's model put pressure on the other business groups to make up their mind about new potential technologies. Once the NVG found an interesting technology in the lab, the group jumped on it very quickly. The NVG would then go over to the business groups and tell them to "speak now or forever hold your peace," which would force the business groups to take action much faster then they normally would on many emerging technologies.[8] The reactions from the business groups could vary from a decision to invest and bring the technology into their group, to a decision to say no and decline on further rights to the technology. Either way, the NVG would provoke them into a decision. The NVG vice president, Andrew Garman, recalled:

> I think the biggest practical benefit of the group was increasing the clockspeed of the system. One of the differences between the philosophy and spirit of the venturing world versus the corporate world is that in the venturing world, the more exotic and differentiating the technology, the better. Immediate cost is often not of major concern, and speed to market is the basis of competition. In contrast, the corporate world is used to winning by volume, reliability, and brand name. In this new age of rapid technological change, that old model does not necessarily work so well for the corporation. In order to win, they need to be able to move faster than that old system taught them. We inject that new level of speed into the Lucent system.[9]

This argument is powerfully appealing in the context of Open Innovation. Lucent's NVG provided a second path to market, and this second path probably influenced the actions of the first. The presence of the NVG likely increased the search space for new business models, and it incorporated many desirable attributes of VC into the commercialization of Bell Labs technologies. The NVG even teamed up with leading venture capitalists to fund many of its ventures, bringing in additional capital, expertise, and connections from those investors.

The NVG Issues: Measuring Strategic Benefit, Compensation, and Shareholder Value

Despite its achievements, the NVG model was nonetheless controversial within Lucent. Some of this controversy was due to unfortunate timing and bad luck, which must be understood by others if they hope to emulate what the NVG has done. Yet some of the controversy stemmed from deeper issues, which are more challenging to address.

One issue is that the most important benefits of the NVG process are difficult to quantify. Lucent cannot tell, for example, how much faster its technology has gotten to market as a result of the NVG's presence. Nor can it determine how much its own sales have increased as a result of the ventures that the NVG spawned. Furthermore, the NVG cannot claim that none of the technologies it commercialized would have gotten to market if it had not been involved. These strategic benefits are extremely challenging to quantify, a problem also affecting Intel Capital (chapter 6).

What is easy to quantify is the return on capital that Lucent has earned from investing in the NVG's ventures. This figure was very attractive during the boom years in the telecom sector, rising to more than 70 percent return on invested capital through 2000. That figure has fallen, as the telecom sector declined dramatically in 2001 and 2002. As this quantifiable figure lessens, the ability of the NVG to justify its continued strategic value to Lucent became more open to question.

This difficulty in quantifying strategic benefits poses a fundamental challenge to utilizing internal VC to fund new external ventures. When times are good and returns are high, this approach provides an additional path to market for underutilized technology. In addition to creating new ventures, this path can accelerate the commercialization of technology internally. In fact, when returns are high, the cost of this additional path to the originating company is quite low. When times are bad and returns fall (particularly if they become negative), the costs of this approach rise, and the inability to quantify the strategic benefits makes the continuation of the approach problematic.

There are political costs to the NVG model as well, and these likely intensify when returns decline. Some people inside Lucent argued that the competition to commercialize technology created by the NVG's nomination process was not healthy for the company; that it spawned a culture of deal making and closed-door politics based on personal relationships. For example, a lab manager who had invested his lab's resources into applications for a given second-generation technology could potentially be upset with the NVG for supporting a new venture with a riskier approach using a fourth-generation application of that same technology.

And the second opinion that the NVG process provided to technologies can prove embarrassing to the manager whose initial opinion was shown (at least in hindsight) to be in error. Lucent has reacquired three of the ventures that the NVG started, paying market price for these ventures and giving substantial equity gains both to the venture leaders and to the NVG's principals. Yet the NVG received these technologies only after a Lucent business chose not to commercialize them internally. The managers of these businesses had to go back to their top management and explain why the reacquisition was desirable for Lucent. Presumably, they had to reconcile this with their earlier decision to let the technology go outside into a new venture. This conversation likely was awkward at best for those business managers.

These political costs increased when the fruits of the NVG's labors began to materialize for its principals. By early 2001, the NVG portfolio had created more than $200 million in value, measured through Lucent's reacquisition of the technologies just mentioned, two other external sales, and the current value of private ventures as of their last financing. The NVG's principals were compensated on a carried-interest basis, meaning that their compensation was directly tied to the equity gains in the NVG portfolio.[10] The large gain in the value of the NVG's portfolio triggered large payments to its principals. In 2001, Uhlman, the NVG president, was among the most highly compensated individuals within Lucent.[11]

This payout to the NVG's principals, moreover, came at an extremely awkward time. Lucent as a corporation fell on very hard times in 2001, taking charges of $11.4 billion pretax for restructuring. As part of that write-off, the company had to lay off thirty-nine thousand employees.[12] Senior managers within Lucent who kept their jobs did not receive a bonus that year. Although Uhlman, Socolof, and the other NVG managers did not receive the healthy bonuses that Lucent managers obtained from 1997 through 2000, this omission was forgotten in the carnage of 2001. The company had a hard time paying NVG principals big bonuses in 2001 while it was laying off employees elsewhere.

Of course, the NVG principals received their payouts only after they had created a large amount of value for Lucent. Nonetheless, it was hard to show that the value that existed in the NVG portfolio was also accruing to the Lucent stockholders. As Socolof noted, "Value has clearly been created. The issue is whether that value is being translated to Lucent's shareholders or not."[13]

Wall Street analysts themselves did not know how to best translate this value to Lucent's shareholders. Edward Snyder, a senior analyst at Chase H&Q for the wireless equipment and software industries, observed, "Companies like Lucent need to try to define what metrics they are measured on in the public markets and try to translate the value from these new [NVG] spin-offs into those metrics."[14]

What Snyder means is that, if Lucent is valued in the market through the growth in revenues and earnings from its own operations, simply adding a bit of cash to the bottom line through the NVG's activities would not change his estimate of the intrinsic value of the company. The NVG portfolio would be a nonoperating activity that would be treated as nonrecurring income.

Snyder's comment reveals the difficulty of converting a corporate portfolio of new technology ventures into value for the company's shareholders. To escape from the ghetto of nonrecurring income, the company would have to change the metrics by which its portfolio is valued. This would include, among other things, providing guidance to Wall Street about the *future* performance of its technology venture portfolio. Yet, these ventures are highly uncertain and terribly difficult to predict.

These difficulties became more salient in late 2000, when Lucent's financial turmoil had resulted in great turnover in its senior-level management. As a result, the NVG team lost the strong support from top management that the team had enjoyed earlier within Bell Labs and Lucent corporate headquarters. The NVG principals had to resell the value of its approach and justify the differences of the new venture investment cycle and the different compensation mechanism to an entirely new set of senior managers. The lack of a clear, direct link between the rise in the NVG portfolio's value and any increase in Lucent's shareholder value made these sales efforts even more difficult.

Requiem for a Promising Innovation Model

The tensions between the NVG process and Lucent's businesses, combined with Lucent's continued financial difficulties, finally culminated in a divorce. In January 2002, Lucent sold off its 80 percent interest in the twenty-seven remaining NVG ventures to an outside investor group led by Coller Capital. Lucent received just under $100 million for its interest.[15] The NVG principals will leave Lucent and continue to manage the portfolio of ventures for Coller as a group called New Venture Partners (NVP). It remains to be seen whether the NVP principals will work with Bell Labs to form any additional new ventures out of Bell Labs technologies. The NVP will also attempt to work with the R&D laboratories of a select few additional companies, to broaden their access to emerging, cutting-edge technologies.

Garman, who has extensive experience on corporate VC at both Xerox and Lucent, reflected on the ongoing challenge of managing additional paths to market for internal technologies:

> Operations like this, where a new ventures group is part of a larger organization, are often victims of their own success. The more successful new ventures you do, the more the other business groups want to do it themselves, and the more the corporation is liable to criticism from shareholders who say, "Why didn't you own 100 percent of that instead of only 25 percent of it?"
>
> History has shown that it is very hard to sustain this type of model over time, and I think the trend in corporate America is to decrease R&D investment. Wall Street apparently values the Cisco model, where you effectively outsource R&D by making venture investments and doing acquisitions, so I think the natural forces are that there will be less R&D expenditure over time and it will be harder to retain researchers as well. That being the case, one business model would be to amortize this venture experience base that we have established over multiple corporations. Thus, we could serve Lucent, as well as other noncompeting companies that do not have the critical mass of research to justify an [internal] investment in a group like this.[16]

Garman may well be right—there may be an attractive business model for NVP to partner with other firms to create new ventures out of underutilized internal technology. And some of the internal tensions may lessen if NVP works for multiple noncompeting companies.

But something has been lost for Bell Labs. Although Lucent sold off its past portfolio of ventures for some much-needed cash, it no longer has a process for generating any new ventures out of its internal technologies going forward. Given the financial realities of Lucent's situation and the growing discord between the NVG's process and Lucent's internal businesses, this outcome was perhaps inevitable, but is a pity nonetheless. Bell Labs will continue to make important research discoveries and breakthroughs. The disconnect between the labs and Lucent's business units will also continue, impeding the path to market for many promising Bell Labs technologies. Lucent will need a catalyst to spur the movement of its technologies out of its labs and into the market. It will need ways to obtain second opinions about new technologies and ways to explore alternative business models for these technologies. And these technologies should go not only to Lucent's current markets, but also to the new, emerging markets of tomorrow. When the general telecom marketplace is so depressed, there is no better time to search for new business opportunities to create additional growth for the company.

Creating Value for the Shareholder from Internal Innovations

The question of whether a company's shareholders participate in the gains of an internal VC portfolio remains a deeper problem. Companies cannot translate a portfolio of ventures into shareholder value until new venture formation activities in a company somehow connect with the external capital markets of that company. This is challenging for new venture creation. The high uncertainty of early-stage R&D makes it hard to predict revenues, profits, and cash flows well in advance. Such predictions would thus be difficult to communicate to the external capital markets. Companies with significant industrial R&D that have the potential to create such ventures will need new business and financial innovations to bridge this gap.

One possibility for addressing the issue of creating shareholder value for internal innovations would be to create an *innovation bond*.[17] This bond would be an instrument that a corporation would execute with an outside capital supplier (ideally, a private equity company unconcerned with reporting quarterly earnings and better able to bear the vicissitudes of new-venture financial performance). The innovation bond would assign to the holder the revenues from the activities of a portfolio of venture firms created to commercialize a corporation's technology. The bondholder would also govern the portfolio of ventures. The corporation, in turn, would receive from the bondholder a steady stream of payments over the expected period of the ventures, say, perhaps seven to ten years. In future years, additional bonds to additional ventures could be issued.

This future predictable stream of payments for a company's innovations that do not go to its own businesses might then be valued by analysts and might therefore increase the value for Lucent's shares—

establishing a direct link between new ventures and shareholder value. The private equity partner would bear the equity risk of the portfolio so created, since its privately held structure means it needn't worry about quarterly and annual profits or the volatility of earnings streams.

In a sense, this is what Lucent has achieved through selling its NVG portfolio to Coller. Lucent, however, received a onetime (and therefore nonrecurring) payment of $100 million. Although the payment gave Lucent immediate cash, it forfeited the steady stream of payments that the market might have capitalized into Lucent's own share price. If the NVP can create new ventures out of other companies' R&D, the NVP will likely continue to realize attractive financial gains from utilizing its processes. Those companies, though, will also confront the question of whether any monetary gains they receive from these ventures will pass through to their shareholders.

Lucent deserves tremendous credit for having the vision to create and implement the NVG model. It is regrettable that the parent of Bell Labs lacked the resources to sustain the model through an admittedly brutal set of market conditions, so that the world might enjoy more Bell Labs technologies, faster.

8

Business Models and Managing
Intellectual Property

IN CHAPTER 7, we saw how Lucent created alternative paths for its
Bell Labs technology to get to market through internally financed
venture spin-offs. In this chapter, we will examine another alternate
path for technology to get to market, the path of licensing technology.

Licensing technology is an important part of managing intellectual
property (IP). How companies manage IP depends critically on whether
they operate in a Closed Innovation paradigm or an Open Innovation paradigm. The Closed Innovation paradigm assumes that you must "make"
your ideas and monetize them through your own products (see chapter
2). A company manages IP to create and maintain control over its ideas
and to exclude others from using them. The Open Innovation paradigm
assumes that there is a bountiful supply of potentially useful ideas outside
the firm and that the firm should be an active buyer and seller of IP (see
chapter 3). A company manages IP not only to leverage its own business,
but also to profit from others' use of the company's ideas.

The business model also influences the management of IP. Chapter
4 documented the ability or inability of companies to create and capture
value from their own technology through their business model. This
chapter extends that analysis to show how accessing external IP can create value and how understanding the limits of other companies' business
models can help capture value from IP.

The link between IP and a company's business model is overlooked
by many proponents of managing IP. Consider the following claim:
"[C]orporate America is wasting a staggering $1 trillion in underutilized
patent assets. Given the pressures on companies these days to maximize
shareholder return, this underutilization of technology assets represents

either a stinging myopia regarding intellectual property or the greatest opportunity to be handed to chief financial officers in a generation."[1]

This claim is typical of many made by enthusiasts of IP. They claim that IP has enormous potential value, if only companies would pay proper attention to managing it. These proponents have half a point. There is indeed latent economic value in companies' IP, and some of that value has not been realized. Yet as I will discuss on the following pages, most patents are worth very little, and it is hard to know in advance which patents are valuable and which are not. Moreover, the claim as it stands is incomplete, because it assumes that technology assets have some inherent value, independent of any business model used to employ them. Chapter 4 explained that technology by itself has no inherent value; that value only arises when it is commercialized through a business model. As with xerography and some other PARC spin-off technologies, the same technology commercialized through two different business models will yield two different economic outcomes. An awareness of the business-dependent value of technology is a crucial insight for this chapter, because much of the work on managing IP *assumes that there is some objective value* for a technology, separate from how it is commercialized.[2] As a result, the enthusiasm for more proactive IP management, such as that noted in the preceding quote, misses some key issues—and opportunities—in managing IP.

We will start by exploring the market for ideas in general and then will discuss how a company's business model can motivate the company to be a seller as well as a buyer in this market. Once we understand the overall market for ideas, we will discuss how companies can manage IP in this environment. A great deal of the conventional wisdom on this topic fits with the logic of control and exclusion that characterized the Closed Innovation paradigm. Using the logic of Open Innovation, we will sketch out a very different approach to managing IP. To create value from a technology, companies must create a business model for it, or else allow someone else's business model to govern the value realizable from the innovation. Alternatively, a company's business model might dictate that the company would be better served by publishing its knowledge, whereas at other times, a company would be better off protecting it instead.

The Market for Intellectual Property

We need to start by defining our terms and clarifying what IP is and is not. Not all ideas are protectable as IP, and many ideas that might be protectable are not protected (figure 8-1). Intellectual property refers to the subset of ideas that (a) are novel, (b) are useful, (c) have been reduced to practice in a tangible form, and (d) have been managed according to the law.[3] Although IP encompasses patents, copyrights, trade secrets, and trademarks, this chapter will focus primarily on patents. Patents are the leading source of trade in IP, and many of the issues in managing patents will also apply to the management of other types of IP.

By some measures, the market for patents and licenses is enormous. The dominant players in the worldwide patent and licensing markets, the United States, Japan, and the European Union (EU), accounted for more than 90 percent of the $142 billion global royalty receipts in 2000, according to the Bureau of Economic Analysis in the U.S. Department of Commerce.[4] The United States was the largest net exporter of royalties, with royalties and fees received from foreign firms in 1998 amounting to $36 billion, which was three times the $11.3 billion spent by U.S. firms on offshore technology. This surplus was driven by trade with Asia, where Japan, the single largest consumer of U.S. IP, accounted for 45 percent of all royalties and licenses, with South Korea, in second place, making up 18 percent.[5] ⟩ *SHEB, NSK*

While the overall market for this exchange is huge, the majority of exchange occurs between affiliates of the same firm operating in different countries, rather than in the open market. In the United States, 73

FIGURE 8-1

Ideas and Intellectual Property

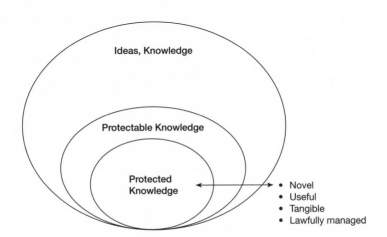

percent of all international licensing volume in 1998 was due to these transactions between affiliated firms.[6] This exchange is driven by many considerations outside the scope of this chapter, such as tax rates and where firms wish to take profits in their activities.

Nonetheless, the amount of arm's-length transactions in patents and licenses is also substantial and growing. The estimated $66 billion in 1996 in U.S. corporate royalty receipts from unaffiliated entities both foreign and domestic has been growing at an estimated 12 percent each year. Individual corporations profited significantly from these receipts. The IBM Corporation reported receiving more than $1.9 billion in royalty payments in 2001. Lucent also received $400 million that same year. Texas Instruments received more than half its net income in such payments during the late 1980s.[7] As the overall market size suggests, and as individual companies have found, there can be big money in licensing one's IP.

Although big money is at stake, the management of IP seems to have substantial room for improvement. According to a survey conducted in 1998, only about 60 percent of patents held by the top patenting firms around the world were utilized in mainstream businesses.[8] Many responding companies had hundreds of nonperforming patents, which were neither used in their own business nor licensed to any other business. As companies learn of the profits of the exemplars just noted and survey their own patent portfolios, they sense that they can do more with their IP than they are currently doing. As will be discussed in the following paragraphs, however, most patents are not worth much. Consequently, there may not be as many valuable patents among the 40 percent of nonperforming patents as IP management proponents think.

In addition, companies are paying more attention to selling their own IP to others than they are to buying more IP from outsiders. This is a serious oversight. Companies can realize a great deal of value by accessing an external technology, instead of inadvertently reinventing it internally. Both the buying and the selling perspectives are necessary to improve the management of IP.

Strategies for Managing Patents

Patents traditionally played a protective role in business strategy through their legal ability to exclude rivals from using a company's own technology. Other strategies such as vertical integration—the dominant mode of organizing innovation assets in the twentieth century during the Closed

Innovation era—had also defended a company's business by allowing safe, efficient transfer of specialized knowledge within a close-knit group.[9] In this era, patents were valued primarily as a barrier to entry, not as a source of revenue and profit in their own right.

By the 1990s, CEOs and CFOs began viewing patents and other IP as revenue-generating assets that could directly increase a company's market value. Licensing out one's own IP during this era elevated patents and other IP assets to the domain of corporate strategy. Businesses with underutilized patent portfolios began taking their IP off the shelf and using it to generate profits. Companies such as Dow Chemical also sorted through their patent portfolio and donated a sizable portion of it to reduce portfolio maintenance costs (primarily filing fees, language translation, and annual renewal fees to cover administrative costs), which could be quite high, and received a tax benefit for doing so.[10]

However, these maintenance costs are only the tip of the iceberg in the costs of managing IP. The darker side of creating additional value from one's IP is the cost of enforcement: In the United States, 6 percent of patents incurred some form of legal challenge, leading at times to costly judgments.[11] In the 1990s, awards were often in the $10 million range, although several passed the $100 million mark.[12] The costs of litigation can truly add up: In the United States, they were estimated to be as much as 25 percent of aggregate R&D costs of U.S. industries.[13]

Companies would prefer not to pay royalties for IP if they don't have to, and the thicket of competing claims of dozens or hundreds of patents can create genuine confusion about exactly who owns what. Moreover, the validity of a patent's claims is not truly known until after it has been tested in court in an infringement suit. For this reason, companies that might be infringing on another company's patents understandably do not volunteer their money. Indeed, if the IP owner is not engaged in a business activity that uses the IP, the owner may not even become aware of the infringing activities of other firms.

Litigation is only the last step in the process of monitoring, detection, enforcement, and value realization. Preferable outcomes for IP owners usually include reaching a settlement through cross-licensing, alliances, or retroactive royalty fee payments with or from the infringing partner. According to Jeff George, VP of AT&T's Intellectual Property Management Organization, "when someone infringes on one of our patents, we take action—but that doesn't necessarily mean litigation. Usually it means negotiating royalties, cross-licensing or even strategic alliances."[14]

Where Patents Come From

Most analyses of managing IP start with the patent-issuance process, that is, the stage at which the company has already received a legal patent. Unfortunately, scholars often pay little attention to the process that most R&D organizations go through prior to obtaining an eventual patent. Yet this is where any useful approach to managing IP must start.

Here is a simplified view of the process that results in a patent. The first step is the report of a discovery or an invention by one or more employees in the organization. In some organizations, these reports are termed *invention disclosures*. Once a discovery or an invention is reported, the organization in which the invention took place (which is the legal owner of the discovery) must decide whether to file a patent on the idea. Sometimes, the idea may be kept as a trade secret, or it may not be protected at all. As discussed in the later section on Intel, publication even may be the best path for the discovery to follow in some cases.

If a decision is made to file a patent, then the inventor must spend time with a patent attorney, who will file the patent claim with the U.S. Patent and Trademark Office. The USPTO reviews the claim and often asks for additional information, such as other relevant prior art, or how the claims of the patent application differ from the claims of prior patents. If the invention is determined to be novel, useful, nonobvious, and adequately explained, the USPTO may then issue the patent. The USPTO estimates that it takes an average of twenty-five months for a patent application to wind its way through to issuance, and the process costs $15,000 to $50,000 per patent, on average, to complete.[15]

To understand the process of managing patents once they are issued, we must start with a point often overlooked in discussions of managing IP: Most patents are worth very little financially. For example, in studies of patents from six leading U.S. universities, the top 10 percent of those patents accounted for 92 percent of the royalty payments those universities received. Put the other way, 90 percent of patents from these universities accounted for only 8 percent of royalty payments. These results are consistent with other studies of the distribution of payments for patents in universities and from society at large.[16] These studies also conclude that most patents are worth very little.

Another related, also overlooked point is that it is very, very difficult to know the value of a patent beforehand. Since filing patents is expensive,

companies would doubtless prefer to save the costs of filing the worthless ones—but they have no way of knowing which are worthless.

Chapter 4 provides a context to interpret these facts. Technologies
acquire economic value when they are taken to market with an effective
business model. When research discoveries are driven by scientific inquiry and are not connected to any business purpose, the commercial
value of the resulting discoveries will be serendipitous and unforeseeable. Unsurprisingly, most of these discoveries will be worth very little,
although a few may be worth a great deal—once they are connected to
the market through some viable business model.

The implication from this is that companies should manage IP to
enhance and extend their business models and should seek out new
business models for discoveries that don't fit their present models. Research discoveries from within the company should be evaluated not
only on their scientific and technical merit, but also on their ability
to strengthen the company's ability to create and capture value in its
business. This in turn suggests that companies should educate their
R&D personnel on their business model, so that the researchers can
understand the potential connections early on in the research process.

In an informal survey of a number of high-technology companies,
I found that companies generally do not educate their researchers
about the business side of their innovations.[17] They do little to share
their business model with their researchers, and usually locate their
R&D personnel away from the people who plan and execute the business strategy.

A more specific finding in the same vein is the way rewards are given
to employees who discover patentable ideas within the company. In a
company I used to work for, Quantum Corporation, any employee who
came up with an idea that the company decided to submit for a patent
received $500. He or she got another $1,000 if the patent was subsequently granted by the patent office. The employee also got a plaque,
which replicated the cover page of the patent in bronze, if the patent was
granted. That was it. There was no assessment of whether or how the
invention helped Quantum advance its own business, and all patents
were rewarded in the same way.

Nor was this a unique case. At the time of my survey at Xerox, an
employee who came up with a patentable idea received $500—period.
And if the Xerox employee came up with ten such ideas, he or she not

only received ten $500 payments, but also was invited to a dinner with other Xerox inventors who had ten or more patents. Again, there was no discrimination between patents that directly applied to Xerox's businesses versus those that had no applicability to Xerox. Other companies have similar symbolic observances for a person's receiving patents, such as hall-of-fame awards. These companies also make no distinction between patents that have direct connection to the business model and those that do not. Only in the cases of IBM and Lucent did companies take any note of the strategic effect of a patent, and this was only recognized in a few cases long after the patent was received. Table 8-1 shows the rewards that other leading technology companies in my survey provided to their inventors.

For comparison, I have included Stanford University's policy on rewards for its inventors.[18] The difference in incentives is striking: Stanford pays no reward for a patent filing, nor does it pay any award for a patent's being issued. However, Stanford shares with its inventors a sizable percentage of the royalty stream that its patents generate. Interestingly, Stanford also shares a similarly sizable percentage with the academic department that housed the inventor, and the school retains a final third for its own purposes. (The amounts paid by Stanford are net of Stanford's costs of obtaining the patent and a charge for its costs of operating its technology licensing office.)

These incentives inside the companies in the table (excluding Stanford) are not very large, to say the least. If the enthusiasts of IP are correct in saying that IP is a critical source of value for companies in the twenty-first century, then one might expect these incentives for inventors to be much larger, to spur them to create more IP. If, on the other hand, the value of a patent depends primarily on its being commercialized through a business model, then the weak incentives make more sense: The value comes from the party that has a business model to create and capture value from the patent, *not* from the invention of the patentable technology itself.

This also implies that companies should find ways to search for, and reward, the creation of effective business models that leverage technologies they seek to license. Absent an effective business model, a technology may be worth little indeed. With an identified business model, the owner of IP has a better idea of where to look for potential buyers and some idea of the value of the idea to those buyers. The importance of the

TABLE 8-1

Informal Survey of Patent Rewards to Inventors by Selected High-Technology Companies

Company	Award for Patent Filing	Award for Patent Issuance	Other Rewards	Other Rewards Comment
HP	$1,000	None	NA	
IBM	$1,500	$500	$25,000	Exceptional patents (in hindsight)
Lucent/Bell Labs	$500	None	$10,000	Strategically important patents (in hindsight)
Microsoft	$500	$500	NA	
Quantum	$500	$1,000	$5,000 $10,000	Plateau awards at 5th, 10th, 15th, and 20th patents
Seagate	$500	$1,000	$5,000	Hall of fame for 10th patent
Sun	$500	$2,000	NA	
Stanford University	None	None	33% net royalties	1/3 to inventor 1/3 to department 1/3 to school

business model in managing IP will be illustrated further with Millennium Pharmaceuticals in the next section.

Notice that something else is missing in these reward policies. Nowhere in these companies' reward policies is there any incentive for employees to identify and access useful *external* IP. This omission would be perfectly understandable if owning the IP were the key to generating value in today's economy. Then the external technology would be of little importance to a company's value and so would not warrant any particular incentive to find it.

If, however, accessing external knowledge is also critical to creating and capturing value, then the omission is a mistake. If external technologies can also support and extend a company's business model, then companies ought to encourage their R&D staff to survey the landscape to identify potential outside technologies. They could even provide a "bounty" to their staff when a promising external technology is identified and brought into the firm. And they should do this survey *before* launching next year's internal R&D projects.

Intellectual Property Strategies in Action: Millennium Pharmaceuticals

A few leading companies discussed in this section exemplify Open Innovation principles in action for the management of IP. Each company has a logic behind its approach, which is not a logic of control and exclusion, but instead a logic that connects IP to business models and leverages internal and external IP through those models.[19]

Millennium is a very young company that has catapulted itself into a surprisingly strong position in the pharmaceutical industry. Founded in 1993, the company achieved a market value of more than $11 billion by the end of 2000 and split its stock twice that year.[20] Moreover, Millennium achieved this valuation without selling a single product or pharmaceutical compound; all the company's activities through 2000 involved delivering information and analysis of potential biological compounds and licensing its technologies for doing this analysis.

Millennium is an instructive example of how IP takes on exciting new possibilities when managed in an Open Innovation mind-set. Many companies act as contract research organizations (CROs) that supply information and analysis of biological compounds to pharmaceutical manufacturers. Prior to Millennium, though, most of these CROs lived from research contract to research contract and essentially charged their customers for the time and expenses of their employees. As small organizations with no control over their IP, these CROs had no way to grow out of what is a low-margin business that lacks economies of scale.

One crucial limit for most CROs is that the knowledge generated from their work belongs contractually to the company paying for the research. This is a typical control mentality over IP that characterizes so much of the Closed Innovation paradigm. Because of the prevalence of this contractual provision, CROs cannot themselves build on or otherwise use the knowledge that they generate from their work.

Millennium started out doing contract research as well.[21] How did it escape from the CRO rut of living from contract to contract, with no control over the knowledge that it generated? It did so by creating a powerful technology platform that allowed it to rapidly discover and validate biological targets and chemical compounds, and by using some highly astute deal making with its pharmaceutical customers. I will discuss the technology platform later, but will analyze the deal making here.

Millennium recognized that its customers would use the results of the contract research within the confines of their business models. Millennium exploited the fact that their customers placed little value on knowledge that did not fit these business models. This was the pattern the company established from its first major deal, with Hoffman-LaRoche (now called Roche) in 1994. Millennium agreed to provide Roche with a number of *targets* (genes or proteins linked to diseases through various tests that both companies agree on in advance) for obesity and Type II diabetes. Roche had strong interests in both areas and was developing a variety of initiatives to treat these health conditions.

However, Roche was *not* particularly interested in other possible uses of the targets in diseases outside its chosen focus, such as cardiovascular disease. Because of the capabilities Millennium had established with its technology platform, it convinced Roche that it could identify and screen potential targets more effectively and more quickly than rival CROs. Millennium then assigned Roche the rights to those targets within the domains of obesity and Type II diabetes, but *retained* the residual rights to those targets for other possible diseases.

This arrangement was a good deal for Roche. The company needed additional targets to feed into its business model, and it had decided to focus on obesity and Type II diabetes. Roche had the scientific expertise to convert the most promising targets into drugs. The company had the clinical and regulatory expertise to manage the Food and Drug Administration (FDA) testing and approval process for these drugs. And it had the sales and marketing assets needed to call doctors' attention to its drugs when they were approved for use. As we saw earlier with Xerox, Roche assigned little value for a technology (here, a specific target) outside the scope of its business model. And giving away the residual rights to these targets in areas of little interest to it, Roche may have gotten a better deal from Millennium than it would have had it insisted on complete control over all possible uses of the targets. Indeed, Millennium probably accepted less money from Roche than it ideally would have liked. Steven Holtzman, Millennium's chief business officer, commented after the deal, "We gave a little more to Roche because we were younger."[22]

Nonetheless, the Roche deal enabled Millennium to break out of the CRO mold and established two vital parameters for what would become Millennium's business model: First, Millennium's technology platform was a valuable asset, even for large pharmaceutical companies. And second, companies could access this platform profitably for their particular business needs, but would not obtain complete ownership over the resulting IP.[23]

Over time, Millennium has established a variety of research partnerships like the one it established with Roche. Millennium advances its technology platform through some up-front funding from the partner and retains residual IP rights to targets, leads, and compounds beyond the areas of interest to its partner. In addition to the Roche deal, Millennium has signed similar agreements with Eli Lilly, Astra AB, Wyeth-Ayerst, Monsanto, and Bayer.

In deciding how to structure and price these deals, Millennium thinks hard about the partner's business model, Holtzman said: "We spend a lot of time thinking about how the poor man or woman on the other side of the table is going to have to go sell this deal to his or her boss. We spend a lot of time trying to understand how they are modeling it, so that we know whether we can fall within their window."[24]

This awareness of, and empathy for, the customer's business model enables Millennium to identify where value will be realized for its partner. That understanding, in turn, helps it capture residual value from the deal outside the partner's business model.

Another important deal was reached with Bayer in 1998. In that deal, Millennium agreed to deliver 225 targets over a five-year period for Bayer, which amounted to the responsibility for nearly half of Bayer's drug development pipeline. In return, Bayer gave Millennium $33 million up front, committed to another $219 million in licensing fees and research funding, and promised another $116 million in performance incentives. In addition, Bayer committed to returning to Millennium almost 90 percent of the 225 targets after selecting those that fit their business model. As these deals have accumulated, Millennium has developed a growing base of IP built from the "leftovers" that its customers didn't particularly value or had no clear way to use.

Millennium has also taken an Open Innovation approach to the management of its technology platform. As discussed, the company's ability to develop processes, equipment, and software to enable it to rapidly evaluate potential targets was a powerful selling tool for its research partnerships. In a Closed Innovation mentality, Millennium might have chosen to keep this platform exclusively to itself, since its capability was winning it new research partnerships.

But it took a different, more farsighted approach instead. Eli Lilly approached Millennium in 1995 with an interest in licensing the high-throughput DNA sequencing technology that Millennium had developed. Eli Lilly also wanted to license Millennium's technology for rapid analysis of differential expression, which shows which genes are expressed in different tissues and organs in the body. Millennium knew that these technology areas were evolving rapidly and that it would have to make major investments to keep up with the leading edge. The company also knew that it lacked the resources of many larger companies to do this. A deal with Eli Lilly would compromise Millennium's exclusive control over its current technology and processes, but the proceeds from a deal could support Millennium's continued investment in building its future technology and processes. Thus, Millennium made the deal, licensing two key technologies to Eli Lilly. According to Holtzman, who also championed this transaction, Millennium looked at its competitive advantage when considering the deal: "We sat down internally and said, 'Wherein lies our competitive advantage?' And what we concluded was that our success would lie in the application of our technology, not in the technology itself. In order to stay ahead of the curve technologically, we needed to find a reliable source of funding. So . . . we said we would be willing to license the technology.[25]

A related philosophy governed the arrangement that Millennium reached with Monsanto in agricultural products. Millennium realized that its own business model was not going to exploit its technological prowess in the agricultural domain in the foreseeable future. Although its technology doubtless had potential value in that area, Millennium itself had no practicable way to exploit that opportunity. When Monsanto approached it about licensing its platform in 1997, Millennium saw another opportunity to trade its technology platform for additional funds to advance that platform. The companies agreed to a deal that delivered $38 million up front to Millennium and promised a potential additional $180 million over five years. This gave Millennium additional resources to build out its platform and to keep up with the rapidly advancing technology. Millennium's ability to advance its platform, in turn, would enable it to enter future partnerships on attractive terms.

Do these deals work not only for Millennium, but also for its partners? One way to answer is to evaluate whether the objectives of the partner are achieved. In the case of Bayer, the objective can be measured by the delivery of the expected number of targets. By 2002, Millennium had delivered more than 180 targets. From these targets, Bayer has found six promising leads and has taken one into clinical development.[26] The Monsanto partnership has been set up to "pay for performance," with payments of $20 million per year for Millennium's reaching predetermined milestones. To date, Monsanto has made every milestone payment to Millennium. The results suggest that at least these partners are reasonably satisfied with the relationship.

By 2000, Millennium judged that it had accumulated enough of these rights to shift its business model. No longer would Millennium simply act as a sophisticated CRO with a state-of-the-art set of screening processes; it would now become a full-fledged drug development company that would operate from "gene to patient," in the words of its CEO, Mark Levin.[27] This new business model escalates the capital needs of the company and entails significant new risks. But the company could never have gotten this far without its deep understanding of the uses and limits of business models in managing its IP.

Intellectual Property Strategies in Action: IBM

Because IBM was the leading U.S. patent recipient from 1995 through 2001, it is not surprising that it may have learned a thing or two about how to leverage its IP. IBM received an estimate $1.9 billion in licensing revenues in 2001, which was about 17 percent of its pretax income that year. To put this amount in perspective, consider that IBM would have had to generate an addition $15 billion in revenue (at its 2001 operating margins) to generate the same amount of pretax income.[28]

Although IBM receives the most U.S. patents of any company in the world, IBM uses its IP not to exclude rival firms, but instead to grow its own business. The full scope of IBM's strategies could take another entire chapter in its own right. What I will focus on here is how some of IBM's strategies map so well into the Open Innovation paradigm. I will start with how IBM manages the actual patents it receives.

U.S. patents are granted by the U.S. Patent and Trademark Office. The office has begun electronically publishing all the patents that it issues; anyone wishing to search for a patent can now find it online at http://www.uspto.gov. Since this material is maintained and published by the government each year, you might conclude that there is nothing of value to be done by a profit-seeking business in this area at least. Yet anyone looking for a patent online would soon realize that the search process is incomplete at best, and frustrating or even hopeless at worst. As a result of this difficulty, one initiative IBM undertook early on was to offer its own patent database for online searches. Although the core data are the same U.S. patents that are located in the USPTO database, IBM added additional search features to make the patents easier to locate.

Why would IBM seek to add value to a public database? Consider that IBM receives more patents than anyone else and that it receives substantial licensing and royalty patents for its patents. A better search process may create more such receipts for IBM. More subtly, better search processes may help patent examiners and attorneys identify the relevant prior art, including IBM's own prior patents. Such knowledge may increase the impact of IBM's patent portfolio on the issuance of new patents. This is akin to Intel's use of its capital to grow its Pentium ecosystem. Here, IBM is using internal resources to grow the ecosystem for IP management.

More recently, IBM realized that a Web service with enhanced search features for patent data could become a stand-alone business in its own right. It has chosen to team with the Internet Capital Group, which invested $35 million to spin off its patent database into a new company, Delphion. Delphion believes that its Intellectual Property Network is "the world's most popular online destination for researching patents." IBM continues to be a customer of the service, but no longer has to fund it with its own internal resources.

A second aspect of IBM's management of its IP draws on the IBM discussion in chapter 5. As discussed, IBM does a thriving business in selling technology and technology components to the computer and communications industries. For example, IBM utilizes some of its semiconductor fabrication capacity to serve as a foundry, where it manufactures chips for other companies to their stated specifications. This increases the capacity utilization of IBM's fabs, which spreads the enormously high fixed capital costs over a larger production volume, improving the economics of IBM's own products.

IBM is also able to charge a healthy margin for the external use of its fab capacity, and part of that margin is earned by IBM's IP portfolio. When a start-up company like Tensilica, for example, wishes to compete with a powerhouse like Intel in the low-power microprocessor market, it has to worry a great deal about Intel's ability to impair its business through the threat of patent infringement litigation. Given the complexity of microprocessors and the complexity of their manufacture, it is difficult at best to assure a young start-up's investors and prospective customers that the start-up's activities will not infringe another company's IP rights. What's more, Intel is known to be aggressive about litigating any perceived infringement of its IP.

This is where IBM's IP enters in. IBM has a wonderful portfolio of semiconductor patents, earned over many years of R&D in the industry. IBM has leveraged this portfolio to enter into cross-licensing agreements with virtually all the major industry players (including Intel), often receiving payments in addition to access to other companies' IP in return for access to its own. This network of agreements and strong internal IP makes IBM a safe foundry for younger companies seeking to enter the industry. IBM signed an agreement to make Tensilica's chips, and likely earns a healthy margin doing so. Tensilica is not merely buying foundry capacity, or even the supply of high-quality chips in the volumes it requires. By using IBM as its foundry, Tensilica is also buying an IP insurance policy.

IBM has used its IP portfolio to sign up long-term contracts with large companies as well, such as Cisco Systems and Dell Computer. IBM agrees to supply important component parts to these customers over a long period, and these long-term customers receive both the parts and an IP assurance that these parts are free from potential infringement actions of other companies. While IBM must compete with other companies to supply Cisco and Dell, those companies competing with IBM do not have the same depth of IP that IBM enjoys. This ownership of extensive IP gives IBM an edge in the competition to supply complex products, where the possibility of IP infringement is real and hard to discern in advance. Put differently, companies that do not buy from IBM are taking some amount of risk in their IP. They may find that they infringe on IBM's rights and will have to pay some amount of money to IBM anyway.

Intellectual Property Strategies in Action: Intel

Intel has not traditionally invested in internal research in the way that IBM or AT&T used to do. Nonetheless, it too has a significant patent portfolio (though nothing as extensive as IBM's), and it has innovated some creative ways to make use of its IP as well. Part of Intel's approach to IP is to aggressively defend its rights against direct competitors, as its decade-long battles with rival AMD attest. Intel seeks every opportunity to slow down AMD in AMD's attempts to copy Intel's Pentium architecture, and Intel has also gone after departing employees when those employees have joined start-up companies that sought to compete with Intel.[29]

see also p. 122

But Intel's approach to managing IP goes far beyond the Closed Innovation approach of playing hardball with its direct competitors and its departing employees. As described in chapter 6, Intel has been able to leverage external IP in its business quite effectively as well. It is this latter aspect of Intel's approach to managing IP that I will focus on here.

One important example of leveraging external IP comes from Intel's approach to university research, which was discussed in chapter 6. Intel underwrites a substantial amount of university research, but not by handing universities a blank check. Instead, Intel insists on making upfront agreements that govern its access to technologies that emerge out of university research that Intel funds. These agreements stipulate that, should an Intel-funded project later be patented by the university, the university agrees to give Intel royalty-free access to that technology.

Note the logic of this approach from Intel's perspective. Intel does not own or control the outcome of university research that it funds. However, it does assure itself of the ability to use the research output of projects it funds, whatever the eventual IP protection of that output. As noted previously, Intel also benefits from this approach in gaining access to the research agendas of leading university researchers. By reviewing research proposals that seek to obtain Intel funding, Intel learns about the "technology frontier" in a variety of academic domains *before* it spends a dime. And Intel's funding also allows the company to monitor the progress of the university research, giving it early access to any promising results arising from that research.

This access isn't free for Intel. Not only must it put up the funding for this work, but the company must spend additional funds on Intel staff that manage the relationships Intel has with leading universities. Then Intel spends more money on its internal labs, trying to transfer the most promising results into its own processes. But Intel's investments give it the knowledge and the connections to become an enlightened sponsor of university research and an intelligent user of promising results emanating from the universities.

Intel's strengths as a manufacturer of semiconductors and its control (with Microsoft) over the Wintel PC architecture position the company well to continue to leverage external knowledge in its business. Intel is so strong in these areas that it can win in its business by playing for a tie in the IP domain. That is, Intel can win if it can continue to access leading knowledge from whatever sources are available, provided that it can gain access to that knowledge on reasonable terms.

Intel's strengths enable it to influence the knowledge landscape that it relies on to advance its business. One mechanism it uses to shape the landscape is to publish research discoveries, rather than patent and protect them internally. Intel maintains a technical publication, the *Intel Technical Journal* (Web site http://www.intel.com/technology/itj/index.htm), whose primary purpose is to document Intel discoveries that the company would prefer to put into the public domain, rather than to patent for itself.

The logic of the publish-versus-patent approach here is a wonderful example of Open Innovation thinking. In a Closed Innovation regime, firms that make new discoveries would think first about how to own and protect this knowledge, so that they could exclude rivals from this knowledge. They would prefer to patent the knowledge to gain the legal entitlement granted by the U.S. government in excluding their rivals from this knowledge. These patents might also allow Intel to entice rivals into cross-licensing agreements that prevent them from holding up Intel's business by threatening IP infringement litigation.

In an Open Innovation world, though, this logic is but one of many considerations. Sometimes, firms will choose to patent core knowledge, but carefully consider the "publish" alternative as well. Companies ask themselves, If knowledge in this area is abundant, can we really hope to exclude our rivals for very long? Can they invent around whatever protections we can claim? Is our own business better served by protecting this knowledge, or would it be better for our business to propagate the knowledge widely? Is it in our interests *to make sure that no one can fence this knowledge in*—that this knowledge will be available to everyone without cost? After all, if it is firmly in the public domain, then a rival cannot threaten us with some version of it later on.

When should the firm patent its knowledge, and when should it publish it instead? This issue hearkens back to the business model being used by the firm. The model helps the firm create value throughout the value chain and then positions the firm to capture some portion of that value.

These twin roles of the business model inform the patent-versus-publish decision. Knowledge that grows the value chain, which enhances the ability of firms in the ecosystem to advance the complementary products and services they make, is exactly the kind of knowledge that the Open Innovation firm wants to make public. Knowledge that helps the firm position itself to capture a portion of the value within that chain, by contrast, is the kind of knowledge that the firm wants to claim for itself. The firm's own complementary assets also help the firm claim a portion of the value in the ecosystem for itself. In Intel's case, its manufacturing prowess, its Pentium brand, and its Wintel architecture all help Intel profit from advances in its ecosystem, even from advances that it does not own or control.

Intel incurs some risks when it publishes its knowledge instead of patenting it. For one, rivals such as AMD also benefit when Intel's knowledge expands the Wintel ecosystem. If Intel fails to maintain a lead over AMD in its business, its knowledge could help AMD overtake Intel. And Intel certainly forgoes any opportunity to collect licensing and royalty payments from its knowledge when it chooses to publish it.

But there are risks on the other side facing Intel as well. Perhaps the biggest issue is what happens to Intel's business model if Moore's Law "slows down," that is, if the industry fails to make the technical advances predicted by Moore's Law at the same pace in the future. Intel's advantages in manufacturing, marketing, and architecture are worth much less when the technology base advances only slowly. Then, the high-quality chips that Intel made last year, and the year before, become increasingly effective competitors to Intel's sales of chips in the current year. Users would have less and less reason to replace their old systems, because these systems would become obsolete much more slowly. And competitors would have an easier time competing against Intel, since they would enjoy more time to catch up to Intel in producing high volumes of chips with the latest technology. As the PC market shows signs of maturing, Intel likely thinks that the risks of its technology slowing down greatly outweigh the risks of publishing its knowledge.

Incidentally, other companies can also benefit from the publish-versus-patent approach without incurring the costs of creating their own journal. Recall that it costs tens of thousands of dollars to file a patent application and takes an average of twenty-five months to see it through to issuance. That's a lot of time and money for small companies, particularly when they operate in industries with accelerating product cycles and shorter time-to-market pressures. Companies may prefer a mechanism that allows them to make immediate use of their knowledge and protects them from some other company's investing the time and money to stake a claim to that knowledge later on. The "publish" option allows companies to do this, and third parties now provide various means to do this at a very low cost.

One such mechanism is IP.com (Web site: www.ip.com). For as little as $155, a company can post a document on the company's Web site and effectively ensure that the document becomes part of the public domain of prior art. Since IP.com maintains links with the U.S., European, German, and Hungarian patent offices, subsequent applications for patents to these offices will be searched against any documents of prior art on IP.com. This greatly reduces the chance of another company's patenting this knowledge later on, and it provides an inventing company with an affirmative defense in the event that another company does receive such a patent and then tries to sue for infringement.

Valuing Intellectual Property: It Takes a Business Model

Companies that have invested significant R&D resources and have received a number of patents along the way understandably would like to know what the patents are worth. They rightly sense that most patents are worth very little—so little that the companies would actually save money if they donated the patents (and their subsequent maintenance costs) to some worthy institution. But these companies also hear the stories of how much money an IBM or a Texas Instruments or a Lucent is making from its patents, and think, What about us? How much could we make from our own patents?

A thriving cottage industry of IP valuation consultants has arisen to respond to this demand. For a fee, they will evaluate the entire portfolio of patents that a company holds and tell the company what this combined portfolio is worth. One such exercise occurred at Xerox PARC, where an external IP valuation in 1997 determined that the PARC patent portfolio was worth more than $1 billion. This valuation made intuitive sense to PARC research management, because Xerox had invested more than $1 billion cumulatively in funding PARC since its founding in 1970.

But valuing IP is more problematic than this assessment would imply. The ideal measure of IP is what a willing buyer would pay a willing seller in a market of many buyers and sellers, where all parties are well informed about what is being transacted. Calculating what a technology costs to be produced is only one means of valuing IP, and not usually the most appropriate means. Another measure is what it would cost a potential buyer to invent around the technology, since this is the opportunity cost of not purchasing the IP. A third measure would be to gauge comparable sales of IP—what "similar" buyers have paid for "similar" technologies in the recent past.[30] There is no reason to think that these measures would yield the same valuation, and in practice, most IP consultants triangulate on a final figure by employing analyses of all three. Moreover, none of these methods takes any account of the business model into which the technology will be placed.

In fact, Xerox found that when it came time to actually engage in IP transactions the consultants' assessments of its patent portfolio were overly optimistic. In one case that I have documented, Xerox had some patents in the area of interactive collaboration using shared public electronic domains.[31] It sought to obtain value from this IP by spinning off the research team that developed the concepts within PARC into a company called PlaceWare. It did this because Xerox had determined that its own business model had no further use for the technology, and Xerox wanted to stop any additional funding of the project. The company also wanted to get some financial return on the IP it had created.

The core issue for obtaining value for this IP, though, was the business model that would be used to commercialize the technology. The generic ideas had commercial potential, but the company was uncertain where and how to use the technology. Many alternatives were considered, but none seemed a clear winner. When the PlaceWare project sought external capital, these considerations became crucial to its *pre-money* valuation (i.e., the value of the company before any additional external capital was invested into the company).

At that point, Xerox had invested at least $5 or $6 million into the technology, having funded a team of five or six people for the previous four or five years. Xerox initially hoped to receive $8 to $10 million for it. This is fairly typical of most IP sellers' perspectives: We have done all this work for years now, and we'd like to make some return on the investment we have made in the IP.

To the IP buyers, though, who in this case were venture capitalists, this perspective seemed ludicrous. There was no proven business model for the IP to create value, nor was there even a potential business model in view. The IP itself was fairly general, and the specific software that had been written over the past four or five years would have to be entirely rewritten before it would be useful. This perspective is fairly typical of that of IP buyers: How much more do I have to invest in this IP to get something of commercial value?

The actual valuation that resulted from the bargaining between Xerox and the venture capitalists who eventually financed the spin-off of PlaceWare was far lower than Xerox had hoped. The premoney valuation of the enterprise was put at $3 million. Xerox received a 10 percent equity stake in the firm in return for a nonexclusive license to the IP in the venture. Xerox also received a promissory note for $1 million, due in four years' time. This note was valuable—if the company remained viable four years down the road. Thus, Xerox received somewhere between $300,000 and $1.3 million for its IP in PlaceWare, depending on how one valued the note.

This valuation is far below what any IP valuation firm would have judged to be the value of Xerox's IP. Yet it proved to be the value that a buyer was willing to pay Xerox for the IP in question, which is the only true measure of what IP is worth. This is a cautionary tale for firms that seek to capitalize on the treasure hidden in their patent portfolios, and a sobering reminder that conceptual valuation exercises can stray far from a technology's actual value in the market. Licensing a technology outside is essentially hiring an external business model to create value for that technology. Unless and until a business model can be identified for a technology that is available for sale, you are likely to receive a surprisingly small amount for that technology. For this reason, companies seeking to leverage their IP will need to work hard to identify prospective business models that could profitably employ their technology, even if the company has no plans to use that business model itself.

9

Making the Transition

Open Innovation Strategies and Tactics

IN MANY INDUSTRIES today, the logic supporting an internally ori-
ented, centralized approach to R&D has become obsolete. Useful
knowledge is widespread in many industries, and ideas must be used
with alacrity if they are not to be lost. These factors create the new logic
of Open Innovation, which embraces external ideas and knowledge in
conjunction with internal R&D. This logic offers new ways to create
value, along with the continuing need to claim a portion of that value.

The presence of many smart people outside your own company is
not simply a problem for you or a fact of life to be regretted. It poses an
opportunity for you. If the smart people within your company are aware
of, connected to, and informed by the efforts of smart people outside,
then your innovation process will reinvent fewer wheels. What's more,
your internal efforts will be multiplied many times through their embrace of others' ideas and inspiration.

This is a powerful value creation engine; it will not, however, enable
you to capture a portion of that value. For that, you will need your internal R&D activities. They help resolve complex interdependencies in
nascent technologies to create architectures and to advance them later
on. Your business model will define what portions of the value chain you
will need to provide internally, and it will link those portions to the surrounding value network that creates and delivers that value to your customers. Buying and selling IP is a powerful way to establish and accelerate the realization of your business model. And mechanisms such as
corporate VC, licensing, spin-offs, external research projects, and IP are
today important levers in the innovation process.

There remains, however, the significant problem of transition: How can you and your company move from a mentality of Closed Innovation to one of Open Innovation? In a related vein, how can you persuade your organization to give up a certain amount of control, to access and utilize the wealth of external knowledge? This chapter offers a number of ideas to help you begin this transition, to begin the journey toward a more open innovation process.

Taking Stock: Survey Recent Innovation Activities

A good place to start on Monday morning is to take stock of recent innovation activities in your own company and in other companies in your industry. The goal here is to build a strategic map that shows the sources of recent innovative ideas for your company and your industry. Ask yourself these questions as you build your map:

- Where have the important ideas in your company and your industry come from in the past five years? How have they fit with your business model?

- What role have start-up organizations played? Have they been able to penetrate the market and gain share? Where have *their* ideas come from? What is their business model?

- What role do venture capitalists and other private equity investors play in your industry? Are they active investors? What explains the bets that they are making? How do these bets compare to the bets your own company is making?

- What role do universities play in contributing knowledge and understanding to your company and your industry? In what areas of importance to your company are the key departments in those universities working? Who are the top professors in those areas?

Consider the first question, the source of recent innovations in your industry. In workshops with executives, I invite them to list some of the key innovations that have come into their industry in the recent past. I then inquire about the source of these key innovations. Often, many important innovations that really changed the industry actually came from some rather surprising places, places one wouldn't initially expect. I also find that many companies' own R&D staff members are so busy meeting shorter-term objectives with incremental innovations that they contribute fewer fundamental insights than their budgets would initially suggest.

Defining your own business model using the constructs of chapter 4 is an important related exercise. What is your target market? What are your key value propositions to that market? How do you get paid? How do you create and capture value? Who are the key third parties? Many companies lack clear, consistent answers to these questions. It is valuable to capture your business model and then share it within your company. Among other benefits, your business model provides a language for connecting technical activities and business activities in your innovation process.

Once you have defined your own business model, look at which companies have recently started up in your industry. Are any of these entrants experiencing success? If so, why? What is their business model? How does it differ from yours? These start-ups can be important sources of experimentation with business models, technologies, and markets in areas that established companies often neglect. Many large companies don't follow start-ups very closely or take them very seriously. In a world of Open Innovation, it is a mistake to ignore start-ups, and it is a virtue to study and learn from their experience.

Another exercise is to take a venture capitalist to lunch.[1] This is harder than it may seem. Most venture capitalists lead hectic lives and are very hard to schedule. And many of them find little in common with company executives. So be prepared for a skeptical reaction. You'll find that thoughtful venture capitalists will make time for you, though, if you're willing to share information about market and technology trends in areas in which they are actively investing. And you'll find that they have well-informed opinions about these issues as well and have "put their money where their mouth is" by investing accordingly. Don't be surprised if these opinions differ from your own, and resist the tendency to defend your views. Instead, listen and see whether there may be some merit in their perspective. Remember that you do have something of value to offer: Your company may be a coinvestor, a technology or marketing ally, or even an eventual acquirer of a venture capitalist's portfolio company. These days, in the collapse of the stock market bubble, savvy venture capitalists are seeking to build stronger relationships with corporations.

Finally, you should assess the state of relations between your company and any universities whose faculty are doing research in areas of interest to your industry. A good relationship involves far more than simply donating some money when the development office comes calling. It requires you to build personal relationships between your technical staff and individual faculty members and their students. You will need to share information, ideas, successes, and failures with them. You should be prepared to learn from them, as well.

This inventory of your current innovation activities will help you perform two critical tasks that will define your company's future: First, it will advance your current business. Second, it will define and grow your new business.

Advancing Your Current Business:
Building Your Innovation Roadmap

It is helpful to create a roadmap that details your future R&D projects and shows roughly when they will appear. Examples of such roadmaps include the Sematech roadmap in the semiconductor industry (table 9-1). This roadmap specifies how and when smaller, more powerful chips will be developed in the industry. It allows a wide variety of companies to coordinate their own investments, so that they fit better with the investments of other participants. Another example of this future planning is the product pipeline of a major pharmaceutical company, which shows what products are in the market, which are in clinical testing, and which are still in the laboratory.

Filling the Gaps in Your Current Business

The roadmap provides a window on the future and makes it more concrete. It often brings to the surface the gaps in that future as well, where the company is missing a product that is necessary to maintain sales and momentum in the market. It is critical for a company to identify these gaps in advance, so that the company can address these gaps before it is too late. External technologies and ideas are highly useful sources of "gap-filling" projects, which can keep the company moving along its roadmap. They can also hedge against the possibility of a slip in some internal project and take up the slack to keep a company's product line moving forward if an internal R&D effort should stumble.

TABLE 9-1

Semiconductor Innovation Road Map

	YEAR OF FIRST VOLUME PRODUCTION							
	1991	1993	1995	1997	1999	2001	2003	2006
Circuit Line Width (in microns)	0.80	0.50	0.35	0.25	0.18	0.15	0.13	0.10
Maximum-Size DRAM	4Mb	16Mb	64Mb	256Mb	1Gb		4Gb	16Gb
Intel Processor	i486 50Mhz	i486 100Mhz	Pentium	Pentium Pro	Pentium III	Merced (Itanium)		

Source: Semiconductor Industry Association Industry Roadmap (1994, 1996).

This roadmap is based on a detailed extrapolation of Moore's Law, which predicted that the circuit density of a semiconductor would double every eighteen months in a very predictable fashion. Gordon Moore made this observation in the 1960s and it has proven to be a remarkably accurate predictor of the resulting circuit density of semiconductor devices.

Achieving these smaller and smaller circuit line widths requires close coordination between a wide variety of complementary semiconductor manufacturing technologies, including photolithography (the process of using light to etch a circuit pattern on a chip), the mask (the device that contains the circuit pattern), the chemical agents used to impart the pattern, the physical size of the wafers used to hold the etched pattern, and the equipment used to measure these tiny distances reliably and accurately. This roadmap helps the semiconductor industry stage its innovations so that these technologies are produced at a time when other required technologies will also be available, instead of being delivered too early or too late.

Finding the Blind Spots in Your Current Business

Your business model also provides a context for how external ideas and technologies will be viewed within your company. Where does your business model focus your innovation efforts? Where are your blind spots, areas on which you are *not* likely to focus to find possible future opportunities, because of the dominant logic of your business model? The more successful your model has been, the more likely you are to have blind spots. These blind spots are where some of the external sources of ideas, technologies, and business models can be the most helpful to you. Because they are created and tested outside your company, external inputs are less susceptible to being culled out within your organization before they get a real chance to demonstrate their value.

Review External Technologies with External Experts

Once you have identified possible gaps and blind spots in your future, you have the context to initiate a careful review of external technologies and ideas. Create a scientific advisory board (SAB) for your company. If your company already has an SAB, bring it into the discussion of your future roadmap and business model. Use this SAB to expose some of your company's own thinking about future trends, opportunities, and other issues. Share your thinking and assumptions with the SAB, and see if the members agree with your views. Do they know about any external work that might help advance your own projects? Can they come up with more powerful, less risky, or potentially cheaper ways to approach a project? Include your senior R&D leaders, so that they can incorporate the resulting feedback into their own planning. It is very inexpensive to redirect internal R&D projects early in their life, whereas it is very expensive to do so later on.

Licensing in External Technology

Look for external technology you can license into your organization. Many companies have never done this. If you haven't, ask yourself why not. Is there truly no external knowledge of any use to your company? Or have you not had a process to seek it out, identify it, evaluate it, and then transfer it into your company?

Some companies rely on their legal counsel to manage the licensing process. While the legal counsel has to be an integral part of this process, it is a mistake to treat licensing as solely a legal matter. There are vital business issues that licensing can influence, and you cannot delegate these issues to your legal staff. One such issue is the not-invented-here (NIH) virus, which makes some internal R&D organizations allergic to any externally sourced technology. They can identify all the problems and risks of an external technology, and they discount the ability of the technology to overcome these limitations. While they may have valid concerns, the NIH virus causes their assessment to be biased. Your business objectives must balance the potential benefits against these potential risks. If you rely on your legal staff to overcome this, you're likely to be greatly disappointed.

Other important business issues are the financial terms of a possible license, how much exclusivity you receive for the use of the technology, and how well protected the ideas are legally. These issues require you to work closely with your legal staff to manage the trade-offs. More exclusivity, for example, typically will cost you more money as a buyer. Similarly, specifying certain fields of use, and retaining others, may bring you more money as a seller. These questions strongly relate to your business model and cannot be delegated to the legal team.

The process of filling gaps and overcoming blind spots is illustrated in figure 9-1. In addition to funding external research and licensing, figure 9-1 shows other vehicles for accessing external technology, such as venture investing and technology acquisition. Note that the figure depicts external technologies at various stages of development. Very early stage research projects are highly uncertain and will take a long time to get to market. Acquisitions, by contrast, typically transfer ownership of established products and services already in the market. Start-up ventures and technology in-licensing fall in between these two sources in terms of their time to market. Depending on your roadmap, you may need more than one type of external project. Each type needs to be evaluated differently, in terms of its timing, its risks, and its rewards.

FIGURE 9-1

Filling the Gaps with External Technologies

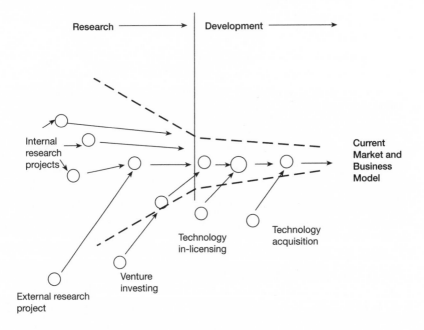

Filling these gaps in your R&D portfolio should not exclude your internal R&D leadership. These leaders can often be highly useful in evaluating an external company's technology, as long as you guard against the NIH virus. *Offer a bounty program* to reward anyone (including R&D staff) who identifies an external technology that the company decides to use. After all, external technologies that support your business model can create value for your business as well as internal research can.

Funding Start-Ups to Fill Unmet Needs

Your knowledge of your business and your markets also may give you valuable insights into unmet needs that you cannot or choose not to address internally. In these instances, consider participating in financing the entry of start-up organizations that can go after these opportunities. You'll be able to watch them by participating on the board of directors (either as an observer or as a voting member), and you'll learn what is working and what is not working in that space.[2] A relationship with a start-up is more valuable than the best market research, because you'll be observing a real company that is making a real product and selling it to real customers, who pay real money. You can be an early customer of these companies' offerings as well, and use your experience with them in planning the strategic direction of your own business. Occasionally, you may decide to work more closely with them in an alliance or even acquire one of them if their activities become crucial to realizing your own strategy.

The general principle in leveraging external technologies is to utilize internal and external ideas to *create* value for your customers and to rely on internal technologies and assets to *claim* a portion of that value. If other companies' offerings can help your business go farther and get there faster, then this may be the best way to proceed. These external technologies are particularly useful if you can define an architecture that connects others' offerings with your own, instead of waiting for your internal R&D efforts to get you there. You will need to invest yourself, though, in the core technologies and complementary assets that support your own claim to a portion of this value. Don't rely on others to claim your value for you.

Growing Your New Business

Filling the gaps to advance your current business is only half of the value in becoming more enlightened about the external knowledge environment. Innovation isn't just about finding new and better ways to grow your current business. It also represents a process for discovering a new business to expand your company beyond its current business. This process is fraught with risk; most innovations fail. But every current business eventually reaches a limit. Companies that don't innovate, die.

There are two ways to develop a new business: You can buy it, or you can build it. The former option, of mergers and acquisitions, is outside the scope of this book. But keep in mind, though, that when you buy your new business, you are paying someone else for the work to date spent on creating that business. Your value only comes from any *further* growth you can realize from that business, *not* from the growth already achieved.

The external knowledge landscape is a vital resource for discovering and recognizing new business opportunities not currently reflected in your roadmap. These new opportunities can enable you to launch new initiatives that could lead to a stronger position in the industry. These initiatives might even help you stretch industry boundaries to exploit converging trends that will one day transform the industry.

New opportunities are where new entrants, particularly new start-ups, can be the most revealing. Start-ups that are merely joining the industry by advancing along the current roadmap don't provide much new insight about where the industry is going. Instead, look at the more visionary start-ups that are challenging the boundary of the industry. These ventures are often funded because they have identified some future opportunity not being well addressed by current industry participants. Take the time to understand their beliefs, and see if you might have an opportunity to fold some of that thinking into your own future.

If you don't know whether the start-ups are right about the opportunity, don't write them off prematurely. Take steps to monitor their activities, and learn from their experience. As they pursue their vision, they have to meet a variety of tests: to recruit people, solicit customers, and define a business model that may clarify the real magnitude and character of the opportunity. In emerging markets with novel technologies, such risk taking is the only way to elicit meaningful market information. The companies that take these risks will be the first to find out what the market potential really is. The companies that closely watch these start-ups will learn this well in advance of companies that ignore them.

Playing Poker with Your Own Technologies

Your internal innovation process is another potential source of the seeds that you can use to build a new business. Here, you don't have to pay someone else for the initial growth, but you must use different processes to nurture young seedlings from those you use to manage your mature businesses. Remember Xerox's experience with its PARC technologies, and the comparison of playing poker instead of playing chess. Xerox managed to create a number of technology advances for its mature copier and printer business out of PARC, but its management processes (designed for playing chess) stifled its ability to create any new Xerox businesses out of other PARC technologies (which required processes for playing poker). The processes that VCs use to manage their portfolio companies provide important guidelines for the processes that companies should use to nurture their seedlings. It may even make sense to bring in VC firms to invest along with you in this process, as Lucent's NVG did.

To build a new business out of your innovations, you will need to determine whether a particular R&D project should go to market through your own organization, or whether it should go to market *outside* your current organization via an alliance, a spin-off venture, or a license. The hardest problem you will have in deciding will not be which structure is best to go outside; rather, it will be the allergic reaction of the business side of your organization to going outside at all. This is the not-sold-here (NSH) virus, the business counterpart to the NIH virus in R&D. The NSH virus says, "If we're not selling it in our own sales channels, we won't let anyone else sell it either." Your sales and marketing people will undoubtedly insist that they must have exclusive use of the technology and must restrict the technology to their own channels of distribution. You can imagine their point of view:

- Using an external organization risks losing control over the technology

- If we lose control, competitors could steal the technology

- Outside companies will make money with our stuff

If your current business units are willing to fund the technology going forward, then give them control over its use. If they fund it directly, they are likely to utilize it in the market in a timely way. They also might want to consider licensing the technology later on themselves to increase their revenues and reach parts of the market they cannot serve directly (as IBM often does), but you can leave that for them to decide. At least they're using the technology.

If, however, the business is not ready to fund the technology directly, but *still* insists on vetoing any external use of the technology, you will need to intervene. The business unit is essentially asking you to shelve the technology, unless and until it decides to use it. As Xerox and many other companies have learned to their financial detriment, the business can wait a long time before deciding if it will use the technology. If you try to shelve it, you are at risk of losing it altogether. So what the business unit is asking for is ultimately unrealistic. If the business won't fund the technology itself, it likely will have to compete with some variant of it from another company within a short time in any case. Shouldn't the company profit from that alternative use, if it cannot profit from its own use?

Finding the Best Business Model for Your Innovation

Once you have overcome the NSH virus, the question of which path to use for any given innovation becomes one of, where is the best business model for that innovation? If your own business has an effective business model for the technology, then your business should fund its further development, which should be the preferred path to market. If your business has the necessary complementary assets, then perhaps the new technology can enable you to extend your current business. If these are lacking, and if an external company has a business model that can profit from using the technology, then that may be an attractive path to market for the technology. This need not be an either-or decision: IBM makes extensive, internal use of technologies that it also licenses to other companies, including competing companies. It finds this particularly helpful when the fixed costs of developing these technologies are high.

If the technology lacks any obvious business model, internal or external, then it either must be abandoned, or some start-up company will have to take on the challenge of searching for a viable business model for the technology. This will require a spin-off venture, as we saw with Xerox PARC's many technologies and with Lucent's NVG. These spin-off ventures could lead to new businesses for the company, particularly if the company possesses useful complementary assets. So a venture that moves outside may not necessarily remain outside. These paths to market are shown in figure 9-2.

FIGURE 9-2

Alternative Paths to Market

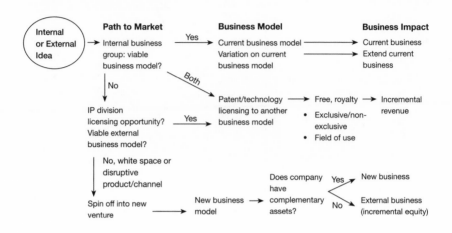

Increase the Velocity of Your Innovation Process

Increasing the rate of movement of these projects, or the velocity of your innovation process, is another benefit of employing an Open Innovation approach. Utilizing the process shown in figure 9-2 will refresh your overall R&D project portfolio. Moving ideas into and out of the company can motivate your company to get its ideas faster to market, either inside your own business or outside through the business of others. Faster to market means faster feedback from the market and, hence, faster learning within your organization. Over time, organizations that learn faster will outperform even quite capable organizations, if those latter organizations are slow to adapt to a changing environment.[3]

Figure 9-3 shows the outcome of the processes in figure 9-2, as projects flow to the business model that best fits the technology. This is not an automatic process; rather, it must be closely managed. A company must overcome important tensions and resistance, but can realize significant rewards at the end of the process.

Harnessing University Research

Your innovation process requires new research breakthroughs periodically, to sustain the flow of ideas to fuel your current and new businesses. To be sure, you can continue to innovate for some time by

FIGURE 9-3

Growing New Businesses and Profiting from Others' Use of Your Technology

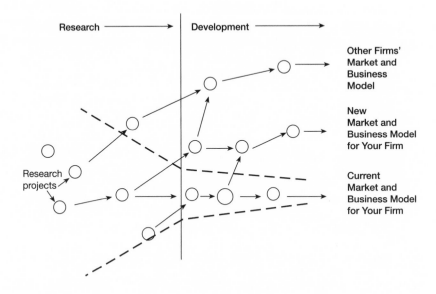

recombining the others' ideas into new and useful products and systems. And, as we saw with Intel, you can craft creative business models to stimulate the use of new breakthroughs from other parts of society, such as universities and even nuclear weapons laboratories. Harnessing the ideas of others is a powerful way to create value.

Intel provides a useful model of how to sponsor and support rigorous and relevant research within a university, which is one way to ensure that new discoveries continue to arise. And you don't have to have $200 billion in market value to follow Intel's approach. Most science and engineering schools have numerous individual research centers, and each center is eager to receive financial support. Can you afford to donate some of your equipment or services to an individual faculty member within one of these centers? Wouldn't you want an expert to train future experts using some of your technology (rather than that of your competitors)? Once you find a faculty member who will work with your technology, help him or her learn how to use it. Then, pay attention to what the researcher does with it. Come give a lecture in one of the professor's classes. Invite students to do class projects at your company.

Offer yourself as a member of the industry advisory board of one of these centers.

If that seems too expensive, then consider sponsoring a graduate student's tuition for a year. Graduate students are very, very expensive for universities to train, and you will find your sponsorship well appreciated. But don't just give money. Take a page from Intel's book, and invest the time to meet the student and learn about his or her studies. See how the student's interests might connect with work inside your own company. And there are always summer opportunities to have students and their professors come visit or work with you, to share what they're learning and see what you're doing. You might even find that it is a low-cost way to recruit highly capable employees.

The Continuing Need for Internal R&D

But to claim a portion of this value and to transfer external discoveries into your company, you will still need to invest in internal R&D, which will need to be housed within your company. But don't approach this with the closed mind-set of chapter 2. Instead, borrow from some of the ideas in IBM's playbook by creating closer links between research and development, and by occasionally placing your researchers at the locations of your most demanding customers, who are the real customers driving the development organization. Borrow from Intel as well by using your internal research staff to evaluate external research projects and potential investments. Let them see firsthand that some excellent research and technology exists outside your own company.

Take the time to educate your researchers on your company's business model and your future roadmap. Many of your research staff may be unclear or confused about these business aspects of your company. A few may disagree with them. Occasionally, one may have an insight about how to improve them. In any case, it is far better to address these concerns than to have the researchers proceed in ignorance of these issues. It is no bad thing to have researchers pursue research agendas that are informed by the company's business model, as well as by what others outside the company are doing. And it can also be useful to create alternative paths to market for your technology, so that the researchers get the satisfaction of seeing their ideas put into action, one way or another.

Business +

Public Policy and Open Innovation

Open Innovation will enable knowledge and ideas to find greater use, in a wider variety of possibilities and configurations, than was previously possible. Overall, this can be a source of further value creation in society and can enable new ways to capture some portion of that value for firms in the society. Notwithstanding these opportunities, this new paradigm will also raise new issues that were less salient in the earlier period.

One issue of greater importance will be funding the "seed corn" for the next generation of scientific discovery. The new division of labor between industry, government, and academia will witness less basic research inquiry being conducted inside corporate research laboratories. The strength of the diffusion mechanisms, and the resulting breakdown in the virtuous circle, mean that industry can no longer be expected to underwrite the bulk of the costs of early-stage research. The wealth of innovations that diffused out of these laboratories since the 1960s is not likely to recur from those labs in the future, given the labs' shift in orientation away from basic research. The seed corn that will create the innovations of twenty years hence will have to be provided elsewhere in the society.

Governments and universities will need to address this imbalance. Increasingly, the university system will be the locus of fundamental discoveries. And industry will need to work with universities to transfer those discoveries into innovative products, commercialized through appropriate business models. *— but if they undermine non-commercial drive, openness, ren the risk of*

The Role of Government in Open Innovation   *Killing the golden goose*

The shift in the location of basic research will mean that government will need to fund a good deal of basic research, though that research need not be conducted by government scientists, but instead could be performed at a university. But spending a lot of public money on research is not enough. Even more important is how that money is spent.

Programs awarded on merit, which aspire to scholarly excellence and publication, are far more helpful than those awarded on the basis of *earmarks* political connections and those whose results do not get published. Without publication, the government may lack any ability to monitor and benefit from research that public tax monies have funded. Worse, without publication, private companies and other researchers may lose the opportunity to build on those ideas in their own businesses. This restricts the flow of knowledge, and reduces the multiplier effect that arises from the use and reuse of ideas in a wide array of situations, often in areas never envisioned by those who made the initial discoveries.

Businesses are sometimes their own worst enemy in this regard. Although collectively they are far better off to have government funds expended on research and technology projects with the highest merit, individual businesses often prefer to lobby for their own pet projects, which might yield a higher profit for them, at least in the short run. But devoting your internal resources and personnel to projects that do not make economic sense, except for a government subsidy, is no way to position your company to make the best use of internal and external ideas in an abundant knowledge landscape. Supporting more neutral, meritocratic processes for awarding government grants and projects will help challenge your staff to pursue excellence in their work—and to demand it from others who receive government assistance.

Similarly, businesses sometimes resist the publication of scientific results from government research projects that they execute. This resistance reduces the company's chance to learn from external criticism of the research and may even slow down the pressure within the company to make use of the research findings. Open publication promotes the vigorous exchange of ideas and creates a powerful stimulus to apply the ideas before someone else applies them instead. And since the most valuable application of a discovery may be far distant from the uses currently envisioned by the company, society again suffers from such unwarranted secrecy.

For knowledge to remain abundant and for companies to make effective use of external as well as internal knowledge, government institutions will be needed to further the exchange of IP. One way that governments can further this exchange is by maintaining processes for awarding patent protection that are transparent, widely understood, and predictable. Patent awards need to be clear, and limited, in their protection.

Another role for the government is to adjudicate competing claims to IP. The government needs to resolve efficiently the inevitable disputes that arise around infringement, the level of damages arising from infringement, and the appropriate remedies for such infringement. The goal should be to remove the elements of chance and caprice from IP litigation, so that innovating companies can trade their ideas in confidence.

The ambiguity and complexity that attends the current process taxes the innovation process, and small companies and start-ups may suffer disproportionately as a result. Their suffering results in fewer experiments with novel combinations of knowledge in our society.

A further and more nettlesome issue is whether and how the government should assign IP rights to the results of research that the government itself funds. In the United States, for example, the Bayh-Dole Act of 1980 allowed universities that conducted research with government funds to file for patents on results from that research. These patents are owned and then licensed by the university. Some evidence indicates that universities have been able to profit substantially from this institutional experiment, particularly in the life sciences sector. However, many university licensing programs do not even cover their own costs. The latter licensing programs quite likely slow down the diffusion of useful basic knowledge to the rest of society.

These restrictions on the diffusion of publicly funded research results may sound like a technicality, but they are not. If industry in the future is going to rely increasingly on university research for its seed corn, issues of this sort become critical policy levers that can enable or thwart the advance of a country's innovation system. In a similar vein, faculty at universities should be encouraged to interact with industry, rather than be treated as another type of civil servant of the state. Some countries prohibit university faculty from working and receiving funds from private companies, or "moonlighting." This prohibition drives a wedge between the needs of industry and the research of faculty, effectively slowing down the diffusion of ideas from the university to industry. Increased relevance need not come at the expense of scientific rigor. It is far better to encourage some amount of interaction, as long as the amount of time spent does not exceed some specified amount.

Innovative companies will need to involve themselves in this debate, because they are likely to require greater access to the results of university research in the future than what they have in the past. They should promote government policy that furthers the production and dissemination of the basic research discoveries that will propel the innovations of twenty years hence. They should support the broad disclosure of these results, which will enable them to experiment with creative combinations of new and existing knowledge to deliver more innovative products and services. They should create win-win agreements with universities, where companies offer research funding to universities in return for early access (on a nonexclusive basis) to research results. Such agreements can accelerate a company's research agenda and focus academic researchers on important industry problems, without compromising society's goals of broader diffusion for the research output down the road.

The Value of a Multiplicity of Business Models for Innovation

Companies will still have to perform the hard work necessary to take promising research results and convert them into products and services that solve real customers' problems. This hard work will integrate the ideas of others with the firm's own ideas and deliver the result through the company's business model. Society will benefit if these ideas flow through multiple business models, as there is unlikely to be a natural monopoly on the single best way for a technology to get to market. And it is difficult for even the best-run companies to manage multiple business models. Inevitably, the technologies will evolve to serve the needs of the dominant, successful business model of each of the companies, even if another, better model might be developed for the use of the technologies.

Indeed, there is little justification for monopoly in a world of Open Innovation. The economies of scale that may have existed in the R&D of a generation ago (when Closed Innovation thinking accepted monopolies as a necessary price for discovery-oriented industrial research) are weaker now. Correspondingly, the diffusion opportunities that exist to reuse and recombine knowledge will yield more innovation sooner for society than will keeping this knowledge locked up inside the silos of monopolist firms, where the technology is made available to society through a single business model.

Consider the perspective of Robert Metcalfe, the Xerox PARC researcher who departed the Xerox monopoly to commercialize Ethernet. He is a seasoned researcher as well as a veteran observer of many innovations in the computer industry. "The old approach to innovation was based on a social bargain with large companies," he once told me. "Give us a monopoly in our markets, and we will invest in basic R&D. That's a bad bargain."[4]

It may have been a necessary bargain at one time, when knowledge was not widely distributed throughout society and a company needed to do a great deal of discovery-oriented work internally to do anything useful externally. But today it is not necessary or even feasible to lock up vital knowledge and ideas in silos, where they will only be used when and if a company's internal business needs dictate. A world of opportunity awaits the company that can harness ideas from its surrounding environment to advance its own business and that can leverage its own ideas outside its current business. A society of such companies, provided that it invests in increasing the stock of its knowledge, the skills of its people, and the institutions to support the exchange of that knowledge, will realize a bright and prosperous future for its citizens.

Notes

Foreword

1. See Ilkka Tuomi, *Networks of Innovation: Change and Meaning in the Age of the Internet* (Oxford: Oxford University Press, 2003) for a detailed discussion of innovation, changing social practice, and technology in use.

Introduction

1. I use the term *paradigm* to refer to a widely accepted model for how a group of professionals pursue a complex activity, here industrial R&D. Kuhn's notion of a paradigm can be found in Thomas Kuhn, *Structure of Scientific Revolutions* (Chicago: University of Chicago Press, 1962). In chapter 2, I elaborate on the origins of the Closed Innovation paradigm and why it has gained such prominence as a way of organizing innovation.

2. See Richard Schonberger and Edward Knod, *Operations Management* (Boston: Irwin, 1994), 59–61, for an example of this view.

3. Nabil Sakkab, P&G's senior vice president for R&D for global fabric and home care, described P&G's new innovation strategy in an address to the Industrial Research Institute: Nabil Sakkab, "Connect and Develop Complements Research and Develop at P&G," *Research-Technology Management* 45, no. 2 (2002): 38–45.

4. Larry Huston, director of external innovation, Procter & Gamble, telephone conversation with author, 5 August 2002. He noted as well that the Connect and Develop initiative had strong support from P&G's board of directors, and that a board subcommittee has been working on the issue.

5. Sakkab, "Connect and Develop."

6. The maxim that "not all the smart people in the world work for us" first came to my attention from a talk given by Bill Joy of Sun Microsystems in the early 1990s. See, for example, Alex Lash, "The Joy of Sun: The Most Important Person Building the Software That Makes the Internet Tick," *The Industry Standard*, 21 June 1999, <http://thestandard.com/article/0,1902,5171,00.html> (accessed 27 September 2002).

Chapter 1

1. This response by RCA may seem myopic in hindsight, but is actually quite typical for companies encountering radically different technologies. In his careful historical studies of technological evolution, James Utterback, *Mastering the Dynamics of Innovation: How*

Companies Can Seize Opportunities in the Face of Technological Change (Boston: Harvard Business School Press, 1996), recounts a number of cases in which the leaders in an earlier technology, when confronted by a potentially radical new technology, made significant improvements on their established technology. They underestimated the ultimate potential of the new technology, however, and were eventually overtaken by it. Two examples of this reaction, which Utterback recounted, were the response of sailing vessels to steamships, and the response of ice manufacturers to early refrigeration.

2. For Goldman's perspective on Xerox's challenges and the need for it to commit to significant internal R&D, see Jacob Goldman, "Innovation in Large Firms," in *Research on Technological Innovation, Management, and Policy*, vol. 2, ed. Richard Rosenbloom (Greenwich, CT: JAI Press, 1985).

3. See D. Smith and R. Alexander, *Fumbling the Future* (New York: William Morrow and Company, 1988), for an indictment of Xerox's corporate management of PARC. Michael Hiltzik, *Dealers of Lightning* (New York: Harper Collins, 1999), revisits the same events described in *Fumbling the Future* in a more sympathetic fashion and explores the sharp divisions between key research managers within PARC, in addition to the tensions between PARC and Xerox corporate managers.

4. Although both companies are large today in relation to Xerox, Apple Computer had just gone public in 1979, and Microsoft was a small, private software company in Redmond, WA, in 1980. Both were tiny in comparison with the mighty Xerox at that time.

5. For an academic history of thirty-five companies that spun off from all five of Xerox's research centers to commercialize Xerox's technology outside the firm, see Henry Chesbrough, "Graceful Exits and Foregone Opportunities: Xerox's Management of Its Technology Spin-off Companies," *Business History Review* 76, no. 4 (2002).

6. This accommodating attitude is typical of many large companies. They actively cultivate a reputation for treating people well as part of how they recruit scientists and engineers into the research organization. When these companies must cut off research funding for projects, they don't want to force people out of the company when those projects are terminated. Graceful exits allow researchers to continue their work, preserve the company's reputation, and save money for other research projects.

7. Companies that are still operating independently are measured using the average of their opening and closing stock prices for that year. Acquired companies are measured by the pro rata portion of their shares in the new company. For example, SynOptics merged with Wellfleet to create Bay Networks, which was later acquired by Nortel. The market value assigned to SynOptics in figure 1-1 assumes that its pro rata portion of its stock was held throughout these transactions.

8. Stanford economist Nathan Rosenberg has an apt description of the challenge of envisioning the best use of a new technology: "There is often a gross failure to anticipate many of the eventual specific end uses of an innovation. A great deal of creative intelligence and social imagination is necessary to perceive new possibilities at that vague interface between new technical capabilities and social needs." Nathan Rosenberg, *Inside the Black Box: Technology and Economics* (Cambridge, England: Cambridge University Press, 1982), 185.

9. An ironic example of the difference between the intended use for an idea and its eventual use comes from Gordon Moore, the founding CEO of Intel. He reflected that,

when IBM awarded Intel the design win for the Intel 8088 microprocessor for IBM's new PC, Intel did not regard the IBM computer design win as one of the top fifty market applications for the product. Yet today, most of Intel's revenue and practically all of its profits come from its Pentium microprocessors, which descended from the original IBM design win. See Gordon Moore, "Some Personal Perspectives on Research in the Semiconductor Industry," in *Engines of Innovation: U.S. Industrial Research at the End of an Era*, ed. Richard Rosenbloom and William Spencer (Boston: Harvard Business School Press, 1996).

10. My colleague Stefan Thomke has written a wonderful book on experimentation, and some of his points that were focused at the project level apply here at the company level as well. The ideal experiment is quick to run, doesn't cost much, and tells you a great deal of information. The ideal test also faithfully reflects the actual conditions that the real product or service will encounter. Technologies that pass a highly faithful test are very likely to be real successes in the market. See Stefan Thomke, *Experimentation Matters: Unlocking the Potential of New Technologies for Innovation* (Boston: Harvard Business School Press, 2003).

11. Nathan Rosenberg, in *Exploring the Black Box: Technology, Economics, and History* (Cambridge, England: Cambridge University Press, 1994), 87–88 and 95, also writes about the importance of experimentation for societies as well as firms:

> The freedom to conduct [economic] experiments has been the essential element accounting for the fact that industrialization has been, uniquely, an historical product of capitalist societies. . . . The freedom to conduct experiments is essential to any society that has a serious commitment to technological innovation. . . .
>
> . . . There is an additional advantage to a system that encourages, or at least tolerates, multiple sources of decision-making. Not only do human agents differ considerably in their attitudes towards risk; they differ also in their skills, capabilities, and orientations, however those differences may have been acquired. This heterogeneity . . . constitutes a valuable resource that is much more readily enlisted into the realm of potentially useful experimentation by an organizationally decentralized environment. An economy that includes small firms and easy entry conditions is likely to benefit from this pool of human talent far more than one dominated by centralized decision-making.

I would add that a firm that monitors and selectively accesses the decentralized environment will have an advantage over even very capable firms that do not.

12. James McGroddy, telephone interview with author, 23 July 1999.

13. John Seely Brown, telephone interview with author, 6 April 1999.

14. Other research in other contexts has noted the myopia that can afflict companies' forecasts and their resulting impact on the allocation of resources. This shortsightedness can entrench the current customers at the expense of potential new customers. See, for example, Clay Christensen and Joseph Bower, "Customer Power, Strategic Investment, and the Failure of Leading Firms," *Strategic Management Journal* 17, no. 3 (1996): 197–218.

15. Figure 1-2 shows Xerox's process in 1996. For an analysis of how Xerox's process evolved from 1979 through 1998, see Chesbrough, "Graceful Exits and Foregone Opportunities."

16. An example of this problem within PARC was a project involving software to enable interactive collaboration over the Internet in the mid-1990s. The PARC research project manager spent several months visiting various Xerox businesses to see whether the technology could be applied internally. To his surprise, he found that the Xerox sales organization did not even use e-mail at the time, to communicate either internally or externally. As a result, these Xerox personnel were singularly unhelpful in identifying the potential value of Internet collaboration. Consequently, Xerox could not even use its own organization as a test bed for future innovation. While PARC made sure its researchers "ate their own cooking" by having them use many of the emerging technologies, it was far less successful in motivating other parts of the Xerox organization to try them out as well.

17. Amar Bhidé, *The Origin and Evolution of New Businesses* (Oxford: Oxford University Press, 2000), also contrasts corporate processes for evaluating new projects to those of venture capitalists. He recounts many differences between these two groups that are consistent with my argument here, particularly the much greater depth and objectivity of corporate evaluations, relative to those of venture capitalists. He also notes the high level of inertia within corporate decision processes, relative to the rapid adaptation of the VC decision processes.

18. This has a powerful implication that derives from complexity theory. When companies must take action in highly complex environments, the companies that can adapt more rapidly will fare better than companies that start in a more favorable location, but are less able to move from that location. See Giovanni Gavetti and Dan Levinthal, "Looking Forward and Looking Backward: Cognitive and Experiential Search," *Administrative Science Quarterly* 45 (2000): 113–137. If VC-backed companies are more adaptive to their environment than are similar ventures housed inside large corporations, the VC-backed companies may fare better in the market, even if they start with inferior technology or fewer resources.

Chapter 2

1. The work of Edith Penrose, back in 1959, provides one of the first academic explanations for why firms conduct their own internal research. "After all, the specialized firm is vulnerable. Its profitability and very survival as a firm are imperilled [sic] by adverse changes in demand for the types of products it produces and by increased competition from other producers." Edith Penrose, *The Theory of the Growth of the Firm*, 2nd ed. (Oxford: Oxford University Press, 1995), 112–113. In this view, internal industrial research is both an option for future growth and, even more, an insurance policy against adverse changes in the firm's environment.

2. Rowland's rant is quoted in David Hounshell's entertaining account of the rise of U.S. industrial research laboratories, "The Evolution of Industrial Research in the United States," in *Engines of Innovation: U.S. Industrial Research at the End of an Era*, ed. Richard Rosenbloom and William Spencer (Boston: Harvard Business School Press, 1996), 16.

3. Leading business historians such as David Hounshell and John Kenly Smith date the first establishment of industrial research laboratories to 1856, when William Perkin discovered how to synthesize a mauve dye from aniline. This was augmented by the discovery of alizarin dyes in 1868 and the azo dyes in 1876. By 1890, the German

firm Bayer had constructed a modern laboratory with books, lab equipment, and a dedicated staff. Bayer's laboratory was soon copied throughout the chemicals industry, and many firms in the United States took their cues from Germany, which was then the acknowledged leader in industrial technology. See David Hounshell and John Kenly Smith, *Science and Corporate Strategy: DuPont R&D, 1902–1980* (Cambridge, England: Cambridge University Press, 1988), 4.

4. Alfred D. Chandler, *Scale and Scope: The Dynamics of Industrial Capitalism* (Cambridge, MA: Harvard University Press, 1990); Chandler, *The Visible Hand: The Managerial Revolution in American Business* (Cambridge, MA: Harvard University Press, 1977); Chandler, *Strategy and Structure: Chapters in the History of American Industrial Enterprise* (Cambridge, MA: MIT Press, 1962).

5. Some of the castle walls were occasionally knocked down by government enforcement of the Sherman Antitrust Act, enacted and enforced after 1898. Even this antitrust enforcement, though, further encouraged firms to invest in proprietary research to create new products as they sought to maintain their market positions. In hindsight, then, the Sherman Act motivated dominant firms to retain their position through horizontal mergers (instead of vertical monopolies) and by investing in new innovations. See David Mowery and Nathan Rosenberg, "The U.S. National Innovation System," in *National Innovation Systems*, ed. Richard Nelson (Oxford: Oxford University Press, 1993), 37.

6. Mowery and Rosenberg, "The U.S. National Innovation System," 37.

7. Franklin D. Roosevelt, quoted in Vannevar Bush, *Science: The Endless Frontier* (Washington, DC: U.S. Government Printing Office, 1945), xi.

8. Bush, Science: *The Endless Frontier,* 14.

9. Bush, 133.

10. In Henry Chesbrough and Clay Christensen, "Technology Markets, Technology Organization, and Appropriating the Returns to Research," working paper 99-115, Harvard Business School, Boston, 1999, Christensen and I provide an extended discussion of the history of IBM's shifting policies toward external and internal supply of critical components in its disk drives. We show that when IBM tried to use outside suppliers and found them unreliable, IBM took the supply of these components in-house. Later, external suppliers became far more capable, but IBM chose not to utilize them even when it now could rely on them. Starting in 1993, IBM has changed this behavior, a transition I discuss in detail in chapter 5.

11. The many challenges of integrating technologies are thoroughly explored in Marco Iansiti, *Technology Integration: Making Critical Choices in a Dynamic World* (Boston: Harvard Business School Press, 1998).

12. Suppose, for example, that a Merck research scientist developed a chemical compound whose molecular structure became quite valuable. If that scientist chose to go to a new start-up company, the compound would incontestably remain Merck's property, and Merck could appropriate its value without fear of leakage. However, in other industries in the information technology sector, similar employee defections have been associated with substantial diffusion of valuable knowledge without any compensation received by the former employer.

13. Henry Chesbrough, "Environmental Influences upon Firm Entry into New Sub-Markets," *Research Policy* (in press), shows that firms with former IBM executives

were associated with higher rates of entry into new market segments in the hard-disk-drive industry, compared to U.S. firms that did not have these former executives.

14. This is not the end of the story in many industries. Research by Jae Yong Song, Paul Almeida, and Geraldine Wu, "Mobility of Engineers and Cross Border Knowledge Building: The Technological Catching-Up Case of Korean and Taiwanese Semiconductor Firms," *Comparative Studies of Technological Evolution*, vol. 7, *Research on Technological Innovation, Management, and Policy* (Oxford: Elsevier Science, 2001), 59–84, shows that many of these foreign national professionals eventually return to their home countries and bring substantial knowledge and know-how with them when they return. Using patent data in the semiconductor industry, Song and his coworkers show how Korean and Taiwanese semiconductor firms were able to catch up to the leading-edge U.S. and Japanese firms through these "returning brains."

15. National Science Foundation, *Science Resource Studies: Survey of Graduate Students and Postdocs* (Washington, DC: National Science Foundation, 1998), <http://srsstats.sbe.nsf.gov/> (accessed 23 October 2002).

16. For a well-done, accessible introduction to VC and its role in financing innovation, see Paul Gompers and Josh Lerner, *The Money of Invention: How Venture Capital Creates New Wealth* (Boston: Harvard Business School Press, 2001).

Chapter 3

1. J. Thursby and S. Kemp, "Growth and Productive Efficiency in University Intellectual Property Licensing," *Research Policy* 3, no 1 (2002): 109–124, concluded that U.S. universities were becoming more commercially productive with their research. They report that university patents have risen from 250 in 1980 to over 1,500 annually in 2000, and provide interesting evidence that universities are getting more output, as measured by the number of licenses they receive for these patents, per unit of "input.

2. Samuel Kortum and Josh Lerner, "What Is Behind the Recent Surge in Patenting?" *Research Policy* 28 (January 1999): 1–22.

3. In the earlier era, large companies also looked down on the quality of R&D activity conducted by smaller companies, but no more. Today, the quality of technical personnel in start-up firms can be surprisingly high. Managers at corporate research centers such as PARC report that their biggest competition in hiring brilliant new researchers out of leading university Ph.D. programs is not other research centers, such as IBM's Watson Research Center, Lucent's Bell Labs, or even a federal lab. It is start-up firms and universities. When these groups can lure the best and the brightest to their organizations, away from the large company laboratories, the perceived historic superiority of large-firm R&D can no longer be taken for granted.

4. National Science Foundation, *Science and Engineering Indicators*, NSF/Scientific Resource Study (Washington, DC: National Science Foundation, 1998), <http://www.nsf.gov/sbe/srs/seind98/start.htm> (accessed 23 October 2002).

5. The overall length of tenure remains at three and one-half years, from 1983 to 2000, but this understates the mobility of the workforce because of its aging in those years (older workers are less mobile than younger workers). Within age groups, the

length of tenure has declined for *all* age groups, between 1983 and 2000. See <http://www.bls.gov/news.release/tenure.nro.htm>, table 1 (accessed 27 September 2002).

6. Even now, after the VC bubble has popped and investing has returned to 1998 levels, VC remains a powerful force to be reckoned with, relative to what companies are spending overall in their R&D. The VC world invested $48 billion in the United States in 1999 (Venture Economics Web site, <http://www.ventureeconomics.com> [accessed 29 October 2001]). By comparison, the total amount of money that U.S. companies spent on industrial R&D for 1999 was $160.3 million (National Science Foundation, <http://www.nsf.gov/sbe/srs//databrf/nsf01326/sdb01326.pdf> (accessed 29 October 2001).

7. I heard many variations of these concerns at the annual meeting of the Industrial Research Institute in Williamsburg in 1999, <http://www.iriinc.org> (accessed 27 September 2002). See also Richard Rosenbloom and William Spencer, eds., *Engines of Innovation: U.S. Industrial Research at the End of an Era* (Boston: Harvard Business School Press, 1996), for a wonderful collection of viewpoints on industrial research in this vein, past and present. A more recent lament in this vein comes from Carver Mead, a renowned semiconductor researcher and professor emeritus at CalTech (in Dean Takahashi, "Sounding the Alarm," *Electronic Business* [November, 2001]: "The whole funding of research is screwed up. That's why I got out of the business of research. It's very sad that it's all gone wrong" (56).

8. Merck & Co., Annual Report (2000), 8.

9. Ibid.

10. See the Venture Economics Web site, <http://www.ventureeconomics.com>, for the most recent data on the amount of VC investment being made. The site reports that $19.2 billion was invested in 1998, which rose to more than $81 billion in 2000 and fell to $36.5 billion 2001.

11. In Henry Chesbrough, "Making Sense of Corporate Venture Capital," *Harvard Business Review*, March 2002, 90–99, I explore how companies can utilize corporate venture investments to advance their own strategic goals.

12. The use of the ecosystem as a metaphor for how businesses compete and survive was well employed earlier by James Moore, *The Death of Competition: Leadership and Strategy in the Age of Business Ecosystems* (New York: HarperBusiness, 1996). The point I am making here is how venture capitalists play a very positive role in creating, shaping, and developing the ecosystem.

13. See Eric von Hippel, *The Sources of Innovation* (New York: Oxford University Press, 1988), for a superb account of the powerful role that lead users can play in the innovation process.

14. Internal competition should not be avoided, but it will need to be managed. For a useful approach to managing such competition, see Julian Birkinshaw, "Strategies for Managing Internal Competition," *California Management Review* 44, no. 1 (2002): 21–38. Internal competition cuts both ways. Internal technology groups may move faster to respond to the needs of their marketing and sales divisions when marketing and sales have recourse to external technology sources as well. Internal technology groups ignore their downstream division's needs, or are late to respond, at their own peril. If the downstream business can access an alternative technology outside, it

chastens the internal upstream group while protecting the overall firm from being late in the market. A better mousetrap tomorrow may not be as valuable as a good mousetrap available today.

15. The argument about the relationship of technical complexity to organizational integration is developed at length in Henry Chesbrough and Clay Christensen, "Technology Organization, Technology Markets, and the Returns to Research," working paper 99–115, Harvard Business School, Boston, 1999. In that paper, we also show that modularity need not be the end state of a technology's evolution. There can be cycling between vertical integration and modularity, followed by a return to integration. The role of internal R&D in resolving complex technological interdependencies was also discussed in Henry Chesbrough and Ken Kusunoki, "The Modularity Trap: Innovation, Technology Phase Shifts and the Resulting Limits of Virtual Organizations," in *Managing Industrial Knowledge*, ed. I. Nonaka and D. Teece (London: Sage Press, 2001), which discussed the Japanese hard-disk-drive industry.

16. See also Michael Cusumano and Annabelle Gawer, *Platform Leadership: How Intel, Microsoft, and Cisco Drive Industry Innovation* (Boston: Harvard Business School Press, 2002), for other examples of how companies coordinate the architecture of a system without making each of its parts. The book does a good job of conveying the need for coordination within a platform, which specifies the relationship between the interdependent parts, as well as the need to evolve the platform, so that its performance does not stagnate over time.

17. Henry Chesbrough and David Teece, "When Is Virtual Virtuous? Organizing for Innovation," *Harvard Business Review*, January–February 1996, recounted the experience of IBM in the PC industry. IBM behaved very virtually for a company of its size, creating an independent business unit to develop an open architecture for its IBM PC. As part of its drive to move fast and remain flexible, the company outsourced the microprocessor from Intel and the operating system from Microsoft. However, IBM subsequently lost control of its architecture, and today the profits from the PC architecture that IBM created flow through to Intel and Microsoft. Chesbrough and Kusunoki ("The Modularity Trap") explore how companies need to shift organizational modes as an industry becomes modular. They explain that companies must nonetheless retain enough systems knowledge to shift back to a more integrated mode when an architecture reaches its performance limit and a new generation of architecture must be created.

Chapter 4

This chapter draws heavily from Henry Chesbrough and Richard Rosenbloom, "The Role of the Business Model in Capturing Value from Innovation," *Industrial and Corporate Change* 11, no. 3 (2002): 529–556. My colleague Dick Rosenbloom has been a student of managing innovation for many decades and has had the opportunity to work with Xerox and PARC for many years. I found it extremely valuable to compare the insights I had gained from studying the commercialization practices of "the ones that got away" with Dick's deep knowledge of Xerox's processes for commercializing technology in its own businesses.

1. See Chesbrough and Rosenbloom, "Role of the Business Model," for a more academic treatment of this definition and its roots in the earlier business strategy literature. That paper also points out the importance of the cognitive element of the business model, which is absent from most definitions of the topic. I will discuss that aspect later in this chapter, in the context of Xerox's evaluation of its PARC research technologies.

2. In still other cases, a more modest technology advance may yield a better business model comparison with a better technology. An example of this anomaly comes in antipiracy software. The music and media businesses are in turmoil over the potential loss of revenues from pirated versions of CDs, videos, and the like. They would like a technology that prevents illegal copying. But this is technically very challenging: According to Ed Felten, a computer science professor at Princeton University, "I tend to doubt that you can build a system that's unbreakable in this area" (*Boston Globe*, 8 April 2002). What able technologists like Felten miss, though, is that antipiracy developers might make *more* money from an *imperfect* technology than they would from a foolproof one. Why? A foolproof technology would get sold once, and that would be the end of its revenue. Because an imperfect technology can always get better, a company can sell the initial technology and then sell upgraded versions back to this already-installed base for a stream of payments over time.

3. Michael Porter, *Competitive Strategy* (New York: Free Press, 1980).

4. See David Teece, "Profiting from Technological Innovation: Implications for Integration, Collaboration, Licensing and Public Policy," *Research Policy* 15 (December 1986): 285–305, for the seminal paper that first articulated this concept and demonstrated its utility in capturing value from technology commercialization. Michael Cusumano and Annabelle Gawer, *Platform Leadership: How Intel, Microsoft, and Cisco Drive Industry Innovation* (Boston: Harvard Business School Press, 2002), show Teece's original concept in practice. The book provides in-depth explanations of how each of these companies leverages its own technology with complementary technologies from other companies that utilize the same "platform."

5. For more background on the concept of the value network, see Clayton Christensen and Richard Rosenbloom, "Explaining the Attacker's Advantage: Technological Paradigms, Organizational Dynamics, and the Value Network," *Research Policy* 24 (1995): 233–257.

6. What enables a company to sustain its strategy is a rapidly evolving area in academic business strategy. A good place to start in considering what the strategy field has learned since the seminal contributions of Michael Porter is David Teece, Gary Pisano, and Amy Shuen, "Dynamic Capabilities and Strategic Management," *Strategic Management Journal* 18, no. 7 (1997): 509–533.

7. James March and Herbert Simon's pathbreaking book, *Organizations* (New York: Wiley, 1958), is a great place to start in understanding how organizations structure their knowledge. R. Daft and K. Wieck, "Toward a Model of Organizations as Interpretation Systems," *Academy of Management Review* 9 (1984): 284–295, provide a useful review of more recent scholarship on this topic. Rebecca Henderson and Kim Clark, "Architectural Innovation: The Reconfiguration of Existing Product Technologies

and the Failure of Established Firms," *Administrative Science Quarterly* 35 (1990): 9–30, link this cognitive structure to the structure of complex technical systems.

8. C. K. Prahalad and Richard Bettis's award-winning article, "The Dominant Logic: A New Linkage Between Diversity and Performance," *Strategic Management Journal* 7 (November–December 1986): 485–511, lays out the concept that a company with many employees needs an internal, dominant logic to organize and coordinate the actions of the many disparate actors inside the firm. Absent such a logic, any company of any size would find itself in constant meetings to coordinate even trivial tasks. A strong internal logic enables individuals and groups to anticipate the appropriate way to consider various actions and to make a choice that will fit with the initiatives of others in the firm. Mary Tripsas and Giovanni Gavetti's analysis of Polaroid's struggles in digital imaging, "Capabilities, Cognition, and Inertia: Evidence from Digital Imaging," *Strategic Management Journal* 21 (October–November 2000): 1147–1163, point out the downside of this dominant logic. Polaroid's dominant logic from the earlier era of instant photography dictated that the real money was made on the film, rather than the camera. This logic did not suit digital imaging and thwarted the company's many attempts to profit from its substantial investments in digital imaging technology.

9. Arthur D. Little, quoted in "The Role of the Business Model in Capturing Value from Innovation," *Industrial and Corporate Change* 11, no. 3 (2002): 529–556.

10. Ibid.

11. For an interesting account of this model from a manager who became a CEO of Xerox, see David Kearns and David Nadler, *Prophets in the Dark: How Xerox Reinvented Itself and Beat Back the Japanese* (New York: Harper Business, 1992). The particulars of the original Model 914 business model are described on page 34.

12. Kearns and Nadler, *Prophets in the Dark*, 88.

13. The Japanese entry at the low end of the market with a seemingly inferior technology is an example of Clay Christensen's concept of a disruptive technology; see *The Innovator's Dilemma* (Boston: Harvard Business School Press, 1997). As this example shows, it wasn't the technology *per se* that was disruptive; rather it was the impact of that technology on Xerox's own business model that complicated Xerox's attempts to respond to the threat.

14. An interesting alternative interpretation to the commercialization of PARC technologies, discussed in the next section of this chapter, is offered by Amar Bhidé in his stimulating book, *Origin and Evolution of New Businesses* (Oxford: Oxford University Press, 2000). In chapter 5 of his book, Bhidé attributes Xerox's failure with PARC to his central thesis, that large corporations are unable and unwilling to underwrite small, uncertain losses and prefer instead to make large but more certain bets. This view is consistent with a finance perspective, which regards projects as fully described by the mean and variance of their expected returns. The Xerox experience and the business model concept interpret the data somewhat differently: Companies evaluate projects (particularly early-stage technology projects) through the lens of their prevailing business model, and any calculations of mean and variance are cognitively biased as a result. Consequently, investments large and small are accurately gauged in the current business, whereas estimates of their value are downwardly biased in a potential

new business. Bhidé also notes that large companies face strong growth pressures, because of the VC market and the mobility of labor. These are two of the erosion factors that I described in chapter 3 and that have shifted the innovation paradigm toward Open Innovation.

15. The Star system was a marvelous synthesis of many technologies that would later become central elements of personal computing. The Star innovations included the bit-mapped screen, the integration of the mouse with the point-and-click user interface, the Ethernet networking protocol, and the PostScript font-rendering technology, among others.

16. D. Smith and R. Alexander, *Fumbling the Future* (New York: William Morrow and Company, 1988), 238; M. Hiltzik, *Dealers of Lightning* (New York: Harper Collins, 1999), 366–367.)

17. Henry Chesbrough and David Teece, "When Is Virtual Virtuous? Organizing for Innovation," *Harvard Business Review*, January–February 1996, 76–86, recount the hazards of IBM's outsourcing strategy in the PC business. It is fascinating to recall that IBM was initially praised for its ability and willingness to outsource its key technologies. Only many years later would the praise dim, as it gradually became apparent that IBM had lost its ability to control the direction of the PC architecture that it did so much to launch.

18. The account in this section is based primarily on a personal interview with Robert Metcalfe, on 1 July 1999 at his residence in Boston, MA. Additional information comes from Robert Metcalfe, 1994, and Urs von Burg's account of the development of Ethernet. Urs Von Burg, "Plumbers of the Internet: The Creation and Evolution of the LAN Industry" (Ph.D. diss., University of St. Gallen, Switzerland, 1999).

19. One can see the effects of Xerox's dominant logic at work in this decision. In the context of Xerox's established business, it made strong business sense to form an alliance with DEC to pursue Ethernet. The terms of the $1,000 license made good sense with the context of Xerox's established business. However, these terms accorded little or no value to the additional commercial opportunities that might arise from the technology. One can infer that Xerox managers may have filtered out any consideration of alternative business uses for Ethernet.

20. Although this sort of strategic alliance around an "open" standard was commonplace in the 1990s, it was highly unusual in the computer industry in 1980. IBM, DEC, Apple, Xerox, and others all built their computers around closely guarded, proprietary technologies. Xerox could have discerned Ethernet's huge ultimate value only when and if it fully comprehended the implications of competing via open standards.

21. Edward Smith, telephone interview with Charles Geschke, 7 April 1999.

22. Ibid.

23. David Liddle, telephone interview with author, 16 April 1999.

24. Edward Smith, telephone interview with John Warnock, 21 April 1999.

25. An entertaining example of the term *business model* in colloquial use comes from Michael Lewis's tongue-in-cheek analysis of the term: "'Business model' is one of those terms of art that were central to the Internet boom: it glorified all manner of half-baked plans. All it really meant was how you planned to make money." Michael Lewis, *The New New Thing* (New York: Penguin-Putnam, 2000), 256–257.

Chapter 5

1. The Sage system itself was the system responsible for providing early detection of a Soviet air attack and also served as the progenitor of the SABRE airline reservation system in the United States.

2. For an authoritative account of the System/360's development, see Emerson Pugh, Lyle Johnson, and Jack Palmer, *IBM's 360 and Early 370 Systems* (Cambridge, MA: MIT Press, 1991).

3. "Isabella's Legacy Is for All the World a Game," *Australian Financial Review*, 27 March 1987, 50.

4. This information comes from Henry Chesbrough, "Managing IBM Research in Internet Time," Case 9-601-058 (Boston: Harvard Business School, 2000). Another issue was how to evaluate the contributions of IBM's researchers as the firm became more concerned about the relevance of research as well as its academic quality. IBM decided to add a second evaluation approach to its traditional evaluation of a researcher's scientific output. Called the Research Contract, this new approach involved a set of measures that assessed the impact of research on IBM's other divisions on an annual basis. This assessment determined the size of the bonus pool for all research staff, from which the individual bonuses would be paid. Important items tracked in the Research Contract included technical leadership, the strategic vision contributed to the company, the number of patents that a researcher had received, whether the researcher stayed within budget, and the satisfaction level of other IBM units with the Research Division.

Once the pool was established, the researchers were evaluated individually. The very top researchers were given a rating of 1, which this was limited to the top 15 percent of researchers. Researchers from the broad middle tier were given a rating of 2. And the bottom-ranked researchers were given a rating of 3. This was a forced distribution, with only so many 1's, 2's, and 3's allowed. If departmental and corporate goals were met, bonuses were paid annually to the scientists out of a created pool.

5. James McGroddy, telephone interview with author, 23 July 1999.

6. Paul Horn, interview with author at IBM Research Center in Yorktown Heights, NY, 27 July 1999.

7. Ambuj Goyal, interview with author at IBM Research Center in Yorktown Heights, NY, 28 July 1999.

8. *Bloomberg Business News*, 26 January 1993.

9. Gerstner's remarks are from Steve Lohr, "Gerstner to Step Down as IBM Chief," *New York Times*, 30 January 2002, <http://www.nytimes.com/2002/01/30/technology/30BLUE.html> (accessed 27 September 2002).

10. McGroddy, telephone interview with author.

11. Goyal, interview with author.

12. Horn, interview with author.

13. Ibid.

14. The evolution of IBM to the Internet was no doubt due to many people, but one critical evangelist within the company was John Patrick. His *Net Attitude* (Cambridge,

MA: Perseus Publishing, 2001) provides an entertaining account of some of the struggles he encountered in nudging the company to adopt a proactive view of the Internet.

15. This section draws on the analysis of Henry Chesbrough and Clay Christensen, "Technology Markets, Technology Organization, and Appropriating the Returns to Research," working paper 99–115, Harvard Business School, Boston, 1999. In this paper, we present the underpinnings of technical modularity and the use of market modularity to partition a complex technology architecture into more horizontal layers. The paper also presents additional material on the development of MR heads and examines the impact of their introduction on the merchant head suppliers in the hard-disk-drive industry.

Chapter 6

1. See Robert Burgelman, "Fading Memories," *Administrative Science Quarterly* 39, no. 1 (1994): 24–56, for a scholarly account of Intel's decision to withdraw from DRAMs.

2. In addition to field interviews, this section also uses material from Gordon Moore, "Some Personal Perspectives on Research in the Semiconductor Industry," in *Engines of Innovation*, ed. Richard Rosenbloom and William Spencer (Boston: Harvard Business School Press, 1996).

3. Paolo Gargini, telephone interview with author, 9 February 1999.

4. Moore, "Some Personal Perspectives," 165.

5. Gargini, telephone interview with author, 9 February 1999, and published in "Intel Labs (A): Photolithography Strategy in Crisis," Case 9-600-032 (Boston: Harvard Business School, 1999).

6. Ibid.

7. Moore, "Some Personal Perspectives," 168.

8. Gargini, interview with author, Santa Clara, CA, 2 August 1999, and published in "Intel Labs (A): Photolithography Strategy in Crisis."

9. Ibid.

10. The role of the CRL in one technology area, photolithography, is illustrated further in "Intel Labs (B): A New Business Model for Photolithography," Case 9-600-033 (Boston: Harvard Business School, 1999).

11. Intel's Research Fellows are the most senior, most respected researchers at the company. These Fellows represent the top technical rank at Intel. There is a separate management track for those who elect to move out of research.

12. The Semiconductor Research Corporation was a nonprofit organization created by the Semiconductor Industry Association to direct research grants to U.S. universities toward research projects of potential use to the U.S. semiconductor industry. Sematech was an industry consortium organized by leading U.S. semiconductor organizations that also received matching federal moneys. Although the mission of Sematech evolved over the years, its primary contributions came from supporting semiconductor equipment companies and establishing technical standards and specifications for new-generation semiconductor equipment. See Rosemarie Ham et al., "The Evolving Role of Semiconductor Consortia in the U.S. and Japan," *California Management Review* 41 (1998): 137–163.

13. I was a recipient of a Robert Noyce Memorial Fellowship for two years, 1995 and 1996, during my Ph.D. program in business administration at the University of California–Berkeley.

14. Sun-Lin Chou, telephone interview with author, 19 August 1999.

15. This information comes from Intel's Intel Capital Web site, <http://www.intel.com/capital/news/earnings.htm> (accessed 8 October 2002).

16. Les Vadasz, interview with author, Santa Clara, CA, 2 April 2000. Jim Moore, *The Death of Competition* (New York: HarperBusiness, 1996), helped crystallize Intel's thinking about business ecosystems. Moore applied the principles of environmental ecosystems, and how different organisms in a food chain competed and collaborated in particular ecosystems, to the situation facing many companies operating in complex webs of economic interdependency.

17. Les Vadasz, interview with author, Santa Clara, CA, 2 April 2000, and published in "Intel Capital: The Berkeley Networks Investment," Case 9-600-069 (Boston: Harvard Business School, 2000).

18. Ibid.

19. Ibid.

20. Ibid.

21. Ibid.

22. Nachtsheim's quote is taken from "Intel Capital: The Berkeley Networks Investment."

23. This is a key point of departure from economic theorizing about corporate venture capital. In an interesting paper, Thomas Hellman, "A Theory of Corporate Venture Investing," working paper, Graduate School of Business, Stanford University, Stanford, CA, 1996, studies a model that compares the incentives of private venture capitalists to the incentives of corporate venture capitalists. He finds that these incentives differ systematically as a result of how much complementarity exists between the portfolio investment and the corporation's own business. Companies will pay more for investments that enhance the value of their own current business, relative to venture capitalists. Hellman's model assumes that the corporate investor knows the degree of complementarity, that is, the increase in one's own business that will occur after investing. In practice, I find that companies lack any way to quantitatively assess this complementarity. Instead, I argue that corporate venture capital should be primarily focused on advancing the strategy of the company, rather than on generating financial returns in the portfolio. See Henry Chesbrough, "Making Sense of Corporate Venture Capital," *Harvard Business Review*, March 2002, 90–99.

24. Sun-Lin Chou, telephone interview with author, 18 February 1999.

Chapter 7

1. See Henry Chesbrough and Stephen Socolof, "Creating New Ventures Out of Bell Labs Technology," *Research-Technology Management*, March 2000, 1–11, for a more complete description of Lucent's New Ventures Group. This section draws heavily from that paper. Socolof is one of the primary architects of the NVG model.

2. The history of corporate venture capital is ably summarized in Z. Block and I. Macmillan, *Corporate Venturing: Creating New Businesses Within the Firm* (Boston:

Harvard Business School Press, 1993), and updated in Chesbrough "Designing Corporate Ventures in the Shadow of Private Venture Capital," *California Management Review* 42, no. 3 (2000): 31–49, and chapter 7 of Paul Gompers and Josh Lerner, *The Money of Invention: How Venture Capital Creates New Wealth* (Boston: Harvard Business School Press, 2001). A poignant example of a failed attempt at corporate venturing is the experience of the Exxon Corporation, which is documented by one of its former managers, in H. Sykes, "The Anatomy of a Corporate Venturing Program: Factors Influencing Success," *Journal of Business Venturing* 1 (1986): 275–293.

3. This is the same David Liddle of Metaphor fame in chapter 4. Liddle made this observation both in direct interviews and in a 1998 *Red Herring* article: "In the United States, corporate research is done only by companies that have at least a 50 percent share in a multibillion-dollar market," says Liddle. "However, to be in that position, they have to have a business so good that it's usually a dumb idea for them to go into a new one. The good idea will be a distraction. This is the silicon paradox: the companies best qualified to do research are the least qualified to take advantage of it." David Liddle, quoted in Deborah Claymon, "David Liddle Forsakes Corporate Research for Independent Interval," *Red Herring*, August 1998, <http://www.redher ring.com/mag/issue57/profile.html> (accessed 27 September 2002). Of course, this paradox has nothing to do with silicon in particular; the label appears to reflect the prevalence of this problem in Silicon Valley.

4. Lucent Technologies, "Creating New Ventures at Lucent: An Overview," company document, August 1999, Lucent Technologies, quoted in Chesbrough and Socolof, "Commercializing New Ventures from Bell Labs Technology: The Design and Experience of Lucent's New Ventures Group," *Research-Technology Management* 43 (2000): 1–11.

5. Steve Socolof, interview with author, 7 December 2000, Murray Hill, NJ.

6. Here the NVG model has to be careful. If all its ventures end up getting reacquired by one of Lucent's own businesses, soon there won't be any outside bidders for the next ventures that come along. If outside firms don't make a competitive bid for the venture, then the NVG will not know how to value the venture. The NVG needs to preserve the option of an external acquisition of some of its ventures, and the only way to do that is to make sure that some ventures do get sold to outside firms.

7. Lucent Technologies, "New Ventures Group 2000 Results," internal company document, 12 October 2000.

8. Andrew Garman, interview with author, 8 December 2000, Murray Hill, NJ.

9. Ibid.

10. More specifically, the NVG compensation plan was based on a percentage of the equity gains in the portfolio, after the deduction of Lucent's investment to the portfolio and a cost-of-capital charge for Lucent's equity.

11. Proponents of the compensation structure pointed out that members of the NVG team and the ventures did not get a venture unit award payout unless they actually created value. The partner-level managers in the NVG and a few of its directors were compensated like venture capitalists. This compensation system was important to establish credibility in the outside world. This credibility was critical both in the eyes of managers and CEOs hired into the NVG ventures from outside Lucent and for negotiations with outside investors. As NVG principal Garman recalled, "When

we go out and raise money, if people do not know us already, they are suspicious. They see us as some big corporation that is going to move slowly on some weird strategic agenda that will stop the venture from selling out to a major competitor even if the price is right. We put that immediately to rest by saying, 'Time out. We are on a carried interest plan just like you; we really care about the appreciation of the stock price as much as you do'" (Andrew Garman, interview with author, 8 December 2000, Murray Hill, NJ), quoted in "Lucent Technologies: The Future of the New Ventures Group," Case 9-601-102 (Boston: Harvard Business School, 2001).

12. Lucent Technologies, "Results of Operations," in *2001 Financial Review: Management's Discussion and Analysis of Results of Operations and Financial Conditions*, <http://www.lucent.com/investor/annual/01/financial_review/02_result_ops_c.html> (accessed 27 September 2002).

13. Socolof, interview with author, 9 November 2000, Murray Hill, NJ.

14. Tony Massaro, interview with Edward Snyder, 2 March 2001, Palo Alto, CA.

15. This $100 million may seem inconsistent with the $200 million in value claimed by the NVG. But the $200 million included three ventures that Lucent had reacquired, as well as two others that had already been sold. These are excluded from the portfolio that Coller purchased. Valuations for telecom ventures in 2002 were very low, and Coller likely bought the remaining portfolio at a discount to Lucent's claimed value above as a result.

16. Andrew Garman, interview with author, 8 December 2000, Murray Hill, NJ.

17. This is intended to illustrate the need to convert uncertain technology ventures into activities able to be valued by external capital markets. Other, more sophisticated financial engineering mechanisms that might be employed to accomplish the same purpose include a tracking stock keyed to the portfolio of ventures out of Bell Labs and direct distribution of shares or cash (or both) to shareholders when portfolio ventures achieve a liquidity event (though taxes would play a role here as well). One useful feature of the innovation bond, though, is the shifting of risk from public capital markets to private capital markets, where the monitoring and governance of the ventures may be better suited to those who bear the risks.

Chapter 8

1. Kevin Rivette and David Kline, "Discovering New Value in Intellectual Property," *Harvard Business Review*, January–February 2000, 59.

2. The value need not come only from the company's own business model. There can be value in IP beyond a company's current business model if, for example, a patent happens to block a critical pathway in another company's business model. If the patent is critical to another company's model, then the owner of that patent may be able to extract a healthy portion of that value for herself or himself—thanks, of course, to the presence of the other's business model. Kevin Rivette and David Kline, *Rembrandts in the Attic: Unlocking the Hidden Value of Patents* (Boston: Harvard Business School Press, 1999), provide some useful concepts on how to map the usage of patents and potentially identify such blocking patents.

3. There are many useful references that inform the management of IP. Two highly readable sources are notes authored by my colleagues at Harvard Business

School: Myra Hart and Howard Zaharoff, "The Protection of Intellectual Property in the United States," note 9-897-046 (Boston: Harvard Business School, 1997), and Michael Roberts, "The Legal Protection of Intellectual Property," note 9-898-230 (Boston: Harvard Business School, 1998). An influential managerial book that called attention to the latent value hidden in intellectual property is Rivette and Kline, *Rembrandts in the Attic.*

4. See the U.S. Department of Commerce, Bureau of Economic Analysis Web site for the most recently available data on this topic, at <http://www.bea.doc.gov/bea /dn/nipaweb>.

5. National Science Foundation, National Science Board, "Science and Engineering Indicators: 1998," publication NSB 98-1 (Arlington, VA: National Science Foundation, 1998), 6–15.

6. Michael A. Mann and Laura L. Brokenbough, "Survey of Current Business: U.S. International Services," report prepared for U.S. Department of Commerce, Bureau of Economic Analysis, October 1999, 72–75.

7. Peter Grindley and David Teece, "Managing Intellectual Capital: Licensing and Cross-Licensing in Semiconductors and Electronics," *California Management Review* 39, no. 2 (1997): 8–41.

8. Business Planning & Research International, "Intellectual Property Rights Benchmark Study," report prepared for BTG International (London, June 1998). The authors surveyed 133 corporations and 20 universities in Europe, North America, and Japan. Interestingly, approximately 25 percent of respondents replied "Don't Know," to the query of how many nonperforming patents they held.

9. For an excellent analysis of the relationship between the product market structure (e.g., whether it is vertically integrated) and the impact on the licensing of technology, see Ashish Arora, Andrea Fosfuri, and Alfonso Bambardella, *Markets for Technology: The Economics of Innovation and Corporate Strategy* (Cambridge, MA: MIT Press, 2001).

10. Dow's experience is recounted by the executive then in charge of Dow's IP management activity, Gordon Petrash, and his coauthor, Wendy Bukowitz, in "Visualizing, Measuring, and Managing Knowledge," *Research Technology Management* 40 (July–August 1997): 67–74.

11. Josh Lerner, "Patenting in the Shadow of Competitors," *Journal of Law and Economics* 38 (October 1995): 466–473.

12. In 1990, Eastman Kodak paid $909 million in damages (including interest) to Polaroid for infringement of several of its instant-camera patents. The fine included treble damages for "willful" infringement. And the $909 million excludes the costs that Kodak incurred to withdraw its inventory from its distribution channels, the write-off of its work-in-process inventory, and rebates paid to consumers. Including all these costs, the total cost to Kodak greatly exceeded $1 billion.

13. Samuel Kortum and Josh Lerner, "What Is Behind the Recent Surge in Patenting?" *Research Policy* 28 (January 1999): 1–22.

14. Jeff George, "The Patent Pipeline," presentation to the Innovators' Breakfast Series, hosted by the *MIT Technology Review*, Cambridge, MA, 13 April 2000.

15. Sarah Milstein, "Protecting Intellectual Property," New York Times, 18 February 2002, <http://www.nytimes.com/2002/02/18/technology/ebusiness/18NECO.html>.

16. See F. Scherer and D. Harhoff, "Technology Policy for a World of Skew-Distributed Outcomes," *Research Policy* 29 (April 2000): table 1, p. 560, for these data, and for a general discussion of the highly skewed distribution of value from patents. They report that 84 percent of the royalties from Harvard University's patents came from the top 10 percent of its patents, and that 84 percent of the value of all German patents granted in 1977 (including industry as well as university patents) came from the top 10 percent of patents granted.

17. My survey is decidedly informal and not statistically representative of all companies, or even high-technology companies. I contacted most companies mentioned here between 1997 and 2000; some of their practices may have changed since I spoke with them. Despite the individual changes that may have occurred since I interviewed these companies, the incentives inventors receive from their employers likely remain very weak, and there is likely still to be no corresponding reward for identifying external technology.

18. Stanford's policy is contained on its Stanford University, Office of Technology, Web site, <http://otl.stanford.edu/inventors/policies.html#royalty> (accessed 14 February 2002).

19. This section draws heavily from Michael Watkins, "Strategic Deal-Making at Millennium Pharmaceuticals," Case 9-800-032 (Boston: Harvard Business School, 2000). Other helpful materials on Millennium can be found in Stefan Thomke, "Millennium Pharmaceuticals (A)," Case 9-600-038 (Boston: Harvard Business School, 1999), and in Mark Levin, "Mastering the Value Chain," *Harvard Business Review*, June 2001, 108–115.

20. This market value had risen to more than $13 billion by the end of 2001. In 2002, however, Millennium's valuation has retreated significantly, as have other valuations in the biotechnology market.

21. Millennium would be horrified to be called a CRO, and there are important differences between what it was doing and what CROs typically do. Millennium was involved in more open-ended research far further upstream than are most CROs, which are typically involved in discrete tasks working on other people's IP (e.g., performing toxicity studies). In these studies, the discoveries are relatively binary (e.g., it's toxic or it's not). By contrast, Millennium's work focused on areas in which discoveries were much more informative—areas involving genomics, informatics, robotics, and so on—each of which created a strong base IP portfolio for the company. CROs typically are not able to develop such a strong IP portfolio from the research they perform. I am indebted to Cameron Peters of Millennium for clarifying these differences.

22. Watkins, "Strategic Deal-Making," 9.

23. Millennium also inserted a clause that stipulated that the IP would revert to Millennium if the partner did not proceed with developing the molecule in the specified field of use within a certain number of years. This is another kind of forcing function, prompting a customer to "use it, or lose it." The clause was similar in its effect to the stipulation that Lucent's NVG group had on Lucent's business units (chapter 7), or Procter & Gamble's commitment to out-license any technology not being used after a three-year period (Introduction).

24. Watkins, "Strategic Deal-Making," 12.

25. Watkins, "Strategic Deal-Making," 10.

26. See Millennium Pharmaceuticals, 10-K form (7 March 2002), 17, which includes the following statement:

> We formed the Bayer alliance in September 1998. This alliance is for a five-year term and covers several disease areas, including cardiovascular disease, cancer, pain, blood diseases and viral infections. In September of 2001, we expanded this alliance to include the identification of important new drug targets relevant to thrombosis and urology. Under this alliance, we are eligible to receive up to $465 million from Bayer over the five-year term of the alliance. Bayer has already made a $96.6 million equity investment in us and paid substantial research and development funding to us. By the end of 2001, we had delivered to Bayer more than 180 disease-relevant qualified drug targets for assay configuration, of which 43 qualified drug targets had moved into high-throughput screening or lead identification. By the end of 2001, six projects had entered lead optimization with structurally attractive compounds, including four projects that have shown disease efficacy in animals. In January 2001, one of these projects moved forward to clinical development, and Bayer and we announced our discovery of the first genome-derived small-molecule drug candidate to emerge from our joint research alliance.

27. Levin's quote is taken from an interview by David Champion, "Mastering the Value Chain: An Interview with Mark Levin of Millennium Pharmaceuticals," *Harvard Business Review*, June 2001, 111.

28. All of this data comes from the IBM Web site, <http://www.ibm.com/annual report/2001/financial_reports/fr_md_ops_results.html> (accessed 9 October 2002).

29. Intel's actions against AMD and departing employees are documented in an entertaining book by Tim Jackson, *Inside Intel: Andy Grove and the Rise of the World's Most Powerful Chip Company* (New York: Dutton, 1997).

30. For a more elaborate treatment of these three means of valuation, see Gordon Smith and Russell Parr, *Valuation of Intellectual Property and Intangible Assets*, 2nd ed. (New York: John Wiley & Sons, 1994). No mention is made of a company's business model anywhere in the book.

31. See Christina Darwall and Henry Chesbrough, "PlaceWare: Issues in Structuring a Xerox Technology Spinout," Case 9-699-001 (Boston: Harvard Business School, 1999); as well as associated teaching note, 5-601-118 (Boston: Harvard Business School, 1999).

Chapter 9

1. If you find yourself saying, "But I don't know any venture capitalists!" then that is a huge warning sign. Unless your industry has been neglected by venture capitalists for a decade, your lack of VC contacts is a significant limitation on your ability to track important changes in your industry. If venture capitalists have been actively investing in your industry, then you must find ways to get to know some of them. See

if any of your colleagues or friends know someone who knows someone. This may seem strange to you, but venture capitalists take social networking very seriously and won't be at all troubled by your introduction via a friend of a friend.

2. Companies differ on whether their managers should take voting seats on start-ups' boards of directors. As a practical matter, you will not be offered a seat unless you are a major investor in the company. As a legal matter, there is a possible conflict of interest in your duty as a board member to the start-up's shareholders, and your duty as an employee to your employer. Intel manages this conflict by avoiding it: No Intel manager takes a voting seat on a company's board. Other companies, such as Lucent, choose to manage the conflict, to have more direct influence over the actions of the start-up firm.

3. This is a critical insight from the theoretical model put forward by Giovanni Gavetti and Dan Levinthal, "Looking Forward and Looking Backward: Cognitive and Experiential Search," *Administrative Science Quarterly* 45 (2000): 113–137. As business environments become more complex and more turbulent, it becomes increasingly important to be adaptive. Playing poker becomes more and more useful, whereas playing chess in such environments is less and less effective.

4. Robert Metcalfe, interview with author at his residence in Boston, MA, 1 July 1999.

Index

Adams, Robert, 84
Adobe Systems
  business model evolution, 83, 84–85
  dominant logic creation, 90
  product's place in value chain, 85
  start at PARC, 84
Ad*Star, IBM expected spin-off of, 101
Advanced Micro Devices (AMD), 114, 171
American Research and Development
  Corporation (ARD), 98
Apple Computer, 107
architecture and role of internal R&D
  modular mode advantages, 61–62
  need for internal R&D, 190
  strategy of controlling interconnec-
    tion problem, 58–59
  system interdependence considerations, 59–60
  value chain and ecosystem structure
    implications, 60–61
Arthur D. Little, report to IBM on
  xerography, 72, 73
AT&T, 29, 119

Basic research 95, 125 127 136 (handwritten annotation)

Bayer AG, 166, 168
Bayh-Dole Act (1980), 193
Bell, Gordon, 81
Bell Laboratories, xxi. See also Lucent
  Technologies
Berners-Lee, Tim, 103
Brown, John Seely, 14, 88

Bush, Vannevar, 26, 28
business model for Open Innovation
  basis of, xxiv
  competitive strategy and, 68
  cost structure considerations, 67
  definition and functions overview, 64–65
  dominant logic creation, 90–91
  dominant logic reliance trap, 70–71
  IBM's for PCs, 78, 79
  IBM's shift to Open Innovation, 106–107
  implications for Open Innovation, 88–89
  at Intel (*see* Intel)
  linking of technical and economic
    domains, 69
  market segment identification, 66
  methods of value creation/capture
    from new technology, 63–64
  PARC spin-offs (*see* Adobe Systems;
    Metaphor; 3Com)
  profit potential considerations, 67
  transition into Open Innovation and,
    187–188, 189
  value chain construction, 66–67
  value derived from, 174–176
  value network creation, 68
  value proposition definition, 65
  venture capital and, 89
  Xerox copier example, 72 (*see also*
    Model 914, Xerox)

Internal research 133, 136 (handwritten annotation)

217

Carlson, Chester, 71
Chandler, Alfred, 24
Chou, Sun-Lin, 123, 132–133
Cisco, xviii
Citicorp, 102
Closed Innovation
    achievements and limits example,
        14–17 (*see also* PARC)
    difficulty of transferring new research
        discoveries into production, 115
    erosion factors, 34–36
    evolution in industry, 23–24 (*see also*
        knowledge landscape, early twenti-
        eth century; knowledge landscape,
        mid-twentieth century)
    flowchart, figure, 30–31
    at IBM (*see* IBM, Closed Innovation)
    lack of benefits from breakthroughs,
        xxiv
    logic and rules for, xx–xxii
    patent management, 172
    principles of, xxvi
    R&D management, xx–xxii
    switch to Open Innovation (*see* transi-
        tion into Open Innovation)
Coller Capital, purchase of Lucent
    NVG, 151, 152
commercialization of new technology
    avoidance of false negatives at Lucent,
        144–146
    flexible approach need, 19
    guidelines, 13
    new technologies/new markets versus
        advancement of technologies/current
        markets, 13–14
    phases in NVG, 140
    scientists' dissatisfaction at PARC, 80
    successes at PARC, 77–78
    technical and market uncertainty,
        11–13
    venture capital process effectiveness,
        17–18
Components Research Lab (CRL),
    Intel, 120–121
contract research organization (CRO) in

biotechnology, 164
copier machine business model, 71–74.
    See also Model 914, Xerox
Copy Exactly methodology, 117–118
cost structure considerations in a busi-
    ness model, 67
customers
    First of a Kind (FOAK) program at
        IBM, 110–111
    market segment identification in busi-
        ness model, 66
    PARC's reliance on current, 15
    partnership in Open Innovation, 56
    value chain and, 66–67, 102–103

corporate venturing — see VC

Defense Advanced Research Projects
    Agency (DARPA), 124
Delphion, 169
Digital Equipment Corporation (DEC),
    81, 97–98
DIX (DEC, Intel, Xerox) alliance, 81
Doriot, Georges, 98

Eli Lilly, 167
erosion factors for Closed Innovation
    diffusion of knowledge throughout
        industry, 34–36, 37
    external options for shelved ideas,
        38–39
    external suppliers' increasing capabili-
        ties, 39–40
    influx of talented foreigners, 36
    logic challenge, xxii–xxiv
    from mobility of engineers and man-
        agers, 98
    results of, 40–41
    venture capital market, 37–38
Ethernet products, 8, 9, 78–80, 81, 82

Fairchild Camera and Instrument, 113,
    115
Federal Express, 105

Funding gap between R vs D 114, 138

Financial eng 212

First of a Kind (FOAK) program at
    IBM, 110–111

Gargini, Paolo, 115, 116, 117–118
Garman, Andrew, 148
George, Jeff, 159
Gerstner, Lou, 101
Geschke, Charles, 84–85, 87
GI Bill of Rights, 28
government
    intellectual property management
        and, 192–193
    patent process, 160
    role in knowledge landscape, 23,
        26–27, 191–193
Goyal, Ambuj, 100, 104
Grove, Andrew, 113
q ld balapton 128

Haloid Corporation, 71–74. *See also*
    Xerox
Holtzman, Steven, 165, 166, 167
Horn, Paul, 103, 105

IAL (Intel Architecture Lab), 120,
    121–122
IBM
    acceptance of third-party hardware
        for PCs, 80
    business model for PCs, 78, 79
    Closed Innovation at (1945–1980)
        business model success, 96–97
        early industry leadership, 94
        internal research capability start, 95
        research leadership, 96
        technical advances and contributions,
            94
        vertical integration for System 360
            development, 95–96
    Closed Innovation shifts (1980–1992)
        computer science field growth, 97
        decline in market and technical
            leadership, 100–101

        erosion from mobility of engineers
            and managers, 98
        Joint Programs initiation, 99–100
        new entrants in minicomputer
            market, 97–98
        revelation about contribution to
            customers' value chain, 102–103
        separation of research from devel-
            opment, 100
    commercial benefits from central
        research labs, 29
    diffusion of knowledge workers, 35
    IP strategies, 109–110, 169–170
    new focus on customer's value chain,
        104–105
    Open Innovation, 106–109
    R&D relationship with suppliers,
        118–119
    royalty payments received, 158
industrial innovation
    commercial benefits from central
        research labs, 29
    conflicting objectives between R&D,
        33
    development viewed as a profit center,
        32–33
    Open Innovation examples (*see* Intel;
        New Ventures Group (NVG);
        Open Innovation at IBM)
    paradoxes that confront companies, xix
    principles for innovation, xxvi
    R&D funding, 27
    relationship between universities and
        corporations, 25–26, 171
    research viewed as a cost center, 32
    scientific achievements from expan-
        sion of industrial labs, 28–29
    shelving/storing of new ideas, 33–34
innovation. *See also* Closed Innovation;
        innovation roadmap; Open
        Innovation
    approaches to R&D, xviii
    continuum of, xxvii–xxviii
    paradoxes that confront companies,
        xix

innovation (*continued*)
  principles for in companies, xxvi
innovation bond concept, 153–154
innovation roadmap
  finding blind spots in current business,
    181, 183
  funding start-ups, 184
  identifying gaps in current business,
    180, 183
  licensing external technology,
    182–183
  reviewing external technologies, 182
Intel
  background, 113–114
  business model considerations,
    172–173
  Capital group (*see* Intel Capital)
  connecting of internal with external
    knowledge, 130–131
  Copy Exactly methodology, 117–118
  corporate VC program, 125–126
  diligence in defending IP rights,
    170–171
  external innovation access mecha-
    nisms, 122–124
  faster use of IBM-funded equipment
    technology advances, 119–120
  focus on manufacturing, 115–117
    innovation management approach
      evaluation, 124–125
  limitations and risks to innovation
    approach, 132–133
  publish-versus-patent approach, 172
  research agreements with universities,
    171
  research laboratories, 120–122
  risks incurred by business model, 173
  strategies for accessing external
    knowledge, 50–51
Intel Architecture Lab (IAL), 120,
  121–122
Intel Capital
  corporate VC program, 125–126
  investment process, 128–130
  strategic role, 126–128

intellectual property (IP). *See also* patents
  business model's impact on value of,
    174–176
  in Closed versus Open Innovation, 155
  fallacy of assuming high potential
    value, 156
  at IBM, 109–110, 169–170
    market for, 156–158
  at Millennium Pharmaceuticals,
    165–167
  need for better government oversight,
    192–193
  Open Innovation and, 56–57
intellectual property management at
    Intel
  business model considerations,
    172–173
  diligence in defending IP rights,
    170–171
  publish-versus-patent approach, 172
  research agreements with universities,
    171
  risks incurred by business model, 173
Internet, 103–104
Internet Capital Group, 169
invention disclosure, 160. *See also*
  patents
investment project authorization (IPA),
  Intel, 128–129
IP. *See* intellectual property

knowledge landscape, early twentieth
    century
  companies' need to create internal
    R&D organization, 23–24
  government's limited role in support-
    ing the sciences, 23
  pure versus applied science, 22–23
  relationship between universities and
    corporations, 25–26, 171
knowledge landscape, late twentieth
    century
  distribution of R&D spending in
    United States, 48

end of need for do-it-all-yourself approach, 49
new logic of innovation, 51–52, 53
new role of research inside firms, 52–54
patents and, 45–48
rise in college and post-college graduates, 48–49
strategies for accessing external knowledge, 50
universities' role, 44–45
venture capital's contribution, 54–56
knowledge landscape, mid-twentieth century
adoption of using federal monies to stimulate R&D, 26–27
commercial benefits from central research labs, 29
expanded role of universities in U.S. innovation system, 28
flowchart of Closed Innovation, 30–31
recognition of U.S. need to capitalize on wartime advances, 26
scientific achievements from expansion of industrial labs, 28–29
tension between research and development in industry, 32–34
vertical integration necessity, 30
knowledge workers
diffusion of, 35, 45–49
impact of mobility of engineers and managers, 98
increase due to GI Bill, 34
influx of talented foreigners, 36

Lawrence, Victor, 144
LDV (Lucent Digital Video), 144–146
lead users, 56
Levin, Mark, 168
licensing
antitrust suit against Xerox and, 74
cross-licensing agreements with IBM, 109–110, 170
restrictions on profitability for universities, 193

strategy at Millennium, 167
for transitioning to Open Innovation, 182–183
Liddle, David, 86, 87, 137
Lucent Digital Video (LDV), 144–146
Lucent Technologies
approaches to R&D, xviii
avoidance of false negatives in commercialization process, 146–147
background, 136
NVG and Open Innovation, 136–137 (*see also* New Ventures Group (NVG))
royalty payments received, 158
venture capital use, 55–56
Ludwick, Andy, 8

market segment identification in a business model, 66
market uncertainty
challenge from, 12–13
commercialization of new technology and, 11–13
Massaro, Donald, 86
McColough, Peter, 2, 77
McGroddy, James, 13–14, 99, 102
Merck, 53–54
metal oxide semiconductor (MOS), 115
Metaphor
database query product, 86
lack of success, 87–88
use of Xerox's business model, 86–87, 90–91
Metcalfe, Robert, 81, 194
Microprocessor Research Lab (MRL), Intel, 120, 121
Microsoft, 103–104
Millennium Pharmaceuticals
business model, 164–166
decision to license key technologies, 167
leveraging of residual IP, 165, 166
measurements of success, 168
research partnerships, 166

hctbors 149

Model 914, Xerox
  ADL's view of no value proposition,
    72–73
  lease model, 73–74
  long-term effects of business model,
    74–75
  xerography invention, 71
Monsanto, 167, 168
Moore, Gordon, 113, 115, 116
Moore's Law, 114, 125, 173
Morrill Act, 25
MOS (metal oxide semiconductor), 115
MRL (Microprocessor Research Lab),
  Intel, 120, 121

Nachtsheim, Steven, 129
Netscape, 103
New Ventures Group (NVG)
  avoidance of false negatives in com-
    mercialization process, 146–147
  commercialization process phases,
    140
  difficulty in quantifying strategic
    benefits, 149
  innovation bond concept, 153–154
  innovation model, 138–139
  operating model, 137, 143–144
  payout to principals, 150
  political costs, 149–150
  portfolio, 141
  process example, 144–146
  purpose and mission, 136–137
  risk and reward model, 142–144
  staff's role, 139–140
  tensions with Lucent's businesses,
    151–152
  value to Lucent, 146, 147–148,
    152–153
  value to shareholders, 151, 153
New Venture Partners (NVP), 152
not-invented-here (NIH) virus, 30, 49,
    182
not-sold-here (NSH) virus, 186
Noyce, Robert, 113, 115, 116

Open Innovation
  approach to R&D, xxiv
  company examples (*see* Intel; New
    Ventures Group (NVG); Open
    Innovation at IBM)
  government's role in, 191–193
  internal competition's value, 58
  IP management and, 56–57
  monopolies not justified in,
    194–195
  partnership with customers, 56
  prevalence of, xxvi–xxviii
  principles of, xxvi
  public policy and, 191
  publish-versus-patent approach,
    172–173
  role of research, 52–54
  sources of ideas, xxiv–xxv
  value to shareholders considerations,
    151, 153
  venture capital's role in, 54–56
Open Innovation at IBM
  business model shift's impact,
    106–107
  change in insistence on internal inno-
    vation, 107–108
  First of a Kind (FOAK) program,
    110–111
  Internet challenge, 103–105
  leveraging of external technology,
    105–106
  licensing of intellectual property,
    109–110
  research staff duties, 111
  value chain unbundling, 108–109
Optical Networking Group, Lucent,
    145–146

Pake, George, 2
Papanicalou, Andreas, 145
PARC (Palo Alto Research Center)
  commercializing of new technologies,
    12, 77–78
  creation of, 2

inability to capture value from technology, 3–4
innovation process, 14–17
innovations from, 3
market value of successful spin-offs, 10–11
patent portfolio, 174
reliance on Closed Innovation, 4, 18
scientists' dissatisfaction with commercialization efforts, 80
spin-off companies' histories, 5–8
spin-offs' business models (*see* Adobe; Metaphor; 3Com)
SynOptics' leveraging of existing technologies, 8–9, 12
use of Xerox business model for new technologies, 78
venture capital support of spin-offs, 17
patents. *See also* intellectual property (IP)
Closed Innovation and, 172
companies' lack of connecting patents with their strategic value, 161–162, 163
distribution of knowledge and, 45–48
filing alternatives, 173–174
maintenance and enforcement costs, 159
management at IBM, 168–169
market for, 157–158
need for process improvement, 192
online searches, 168–169
process of obtaining, 160
shortfalls in companies' reward policies, 162, 163
value's dependency on the business model used, 162
worth of, 160–161
personal computers (PCs)
IBM's acceptance of third-party hardware for, 80
IBM's business model for, 78, 79
PARC and, 3
PlaceWare, 175–176

Porter, Michael, 67
PostScript, 84
Procter & Gamble, xxvii
profit potential considerations in a business model, 67

R&D management
Closed Innovation paradigm, xx–xxii
evolution in industry (*see* knowledge landscape, early twentieth century; knowledge landscape, mid-twentieth century)
IBM's relationship with suppliers, 118–119
Intel's Copy Exactly approach, 117–118
internal R&D's role in Open Innovation, 58–59 (*see also* architecture and role of internal R&D)
Open Innovation paradigm, xxiv
role of research inside firms, 52–53
trends in investment models, 152
university funding and, 27
vertical integration at IBM, 95–96
vertical integration at Xerox, 30
RCA, 2
Research Council, Intel, 122–124
research managers
need to consider Open Innovation role of research, 52–53
staff duties in Open Innovation, 111, 139–140
Roche, 165
Roosevelt, Franklin D., 26
Rosenbloom, Richard, 64, 72
Rowland, Henry, 22

Schmidt, Ronald, 8
Science: The Endless Frontier (Bush), 26
scientific advisory board (SAB), 182
Scientific Data Systems (SDS), 77
Sematech, 123
semiconductor industry, 115

Syndication of investment 140
143
147

Invested project authority 128

Semiconductor Research Corporation, 123
Shugart, Al, 35
Snyder, Edward, 151
Socolof, Steve, 144, 145, 150
Star workstation (Xerox), 78–80
SynOptics, 8–9, 12

technology commercialization. *See* commercialization of new technology
Tennenhouse, David, 124
Tensilica, 169, 170
Texas Instruments, 158
3Com
   DIX (DEC, Intel, Xerox) alliance, 81
   dominant logic creation, 90
   start at PARC, 81
   success due to business model, 82–83
   value proposition, 82
   VC support, 81–82
360 family of IBM computers, 95–96
transition into Open Innovation
   business model decision, 187–188, 189
   growing a new business, 184–185
   internal R&D need, 190
   path to market decision, 186–187, 188
   surveying internal and external activities, 178–180
   university research partnerships, 188–190

U.S. Patent and Trademark Office (USPTO), 168
Uhlman, Tom, 144, 147, 150
university system in United States
   R&D funding, 27
   relationship with industry, 25–26, 171, 180, 193–194
   restrictions on licensing, 193
   role in U.S. innovation system, 28, 44–45

Vadasz, Leslie L., 126, 127, 129
value chain
   Adobe's products' place in, 85
   in a business model, 66–67
   customers and, 102–104
   for Star workstation, 78–80
   system architecture and, 60–61
   unbundling of, at IBM, 108–109
value network creation in a business model, 68
value proposition definition, 65
venture capital (VC)
   backing of nascent computer companies, 98
   building a relationship with, 179
   corporate program at Intel, 125–126
   difficulty in quantifying strategic benefits of internal VC, 149
   as an erosion factor for Closed Innovation, 37–38
   first organization, 98
   Open Innovation business model and, 89
   process used, 17–19
   role in Open Innovation, 54–56
   support of 3Com, 81–82
von Hippel, Eric, 56

corporate venture

Warnock, John, 84, 87
Watson, Thomas Jr., 94
Wilford, Paul, 144
Wilson, Joe, 71

Xerox. *See also* PARC
   background as Haloid, 71–74
   business model creation, 74–75 (*see also* Model 914, Xerox)
   challenge from Japanese copier companies, 74, 75–76
   commercial benefits from central research labs, 29
   fundamental flaw in research process, 11

Univ + Intel p. 171, 122
Value fm 151, 153
+ shareholder value

versus IBM's business model, 78–80
IP management risks example,
    175–176
lessons learned from RCA, 2
limited success outside current mar-
    kets, 12
long-term business model, 74–75, 77
missed value proposition with copiers,
    65

Star workstation value chain, 78–80
success in developing new technolo-
    gies for current market, 12
vertical integration for R&D, 30

Zschau, Ed, 101

About the Author

HENRY CHESBROUGH is currently a professor at Harvard Business School with appointments in both the technology and entrepreneurship departments. He holds a B.A. from Yale University, an M.B.A. from Stanford University, and a Ph.D. from the University of California, Berkeley. Before joining academia, Chesbrough worked for more than a decade in the computer disk-drive industry, first as a senior executive at Quantum and later as an industry consultant. Previously, he worked at Bain & Company. His work combines academic theory with industry experience in the areas of technology management and innovation. He frequently presents to and advises innovative companies in the information technology, life science, and financial services industries. His research has been published widely in academic journals such as *Research Policy, Industrial and Corporate Change, Business History Review*, and the *Journal of Evolutionary Economics*. He has also published articles for managers in the *Harvard Business Review, California Management Review*, and *Sloan Management Review*. He is a founder of NeuroTherapy Ventures, an early-stage venture fund targeting epilepsy and related neurological disorders. He and his family divide their time between the San Francisco Bay Area and Boston. He can be reached at henry@chesbrough.com.